enVisionmath 2.0

SCOTT FORESMAN · ADDISON WESLEY

Volume 2 Topics 9–14

Authors

Randall I. Charles
Professor Emeritus
Department of Mathematics
San Jose State University
San Jose, California

Jennifer Bay-Williams
Professor of Mathematics Education
College of Education and Human
Development
University of Louisville
Louisville, Kentucky

Robert Q. Berry, III
Associate Professor of
Mathematics Education
Department of Curriculum,
Instruction and Special Education
University of Virginia
Charlottesville, Virginia

Janet H. Caldwell
Professor of Mathematics
Rowan University
Glassboro, New Jersey

Zachary Champagne
Assistant in Research
Florida Center for Research in Science,
Technology, Engineering, and
Mathematics (FCR-STEM)
Jacksonville, Florida

Juanita Copley
Professor Emerita, College of Education
University of Houston
Houston, Texas

Warren Crown
Professor Emeritus of Mathematics
Education
Graduate School of Education
Rutgers University
New Brunswick, New Jersey

Francis (Skip) Fennell
L. Stanley Bowlsbey Professor
of Education and Graduate and
Professional Studies
McDaniel College
Westminster, Maryland

Karen Karp
Professor of Mathematics Education
Department of Early Childhood and
Elementary Education
University of Louisville
Louisville, Kentucky

Stuart J. Murphy
Visual Learning Specialist
Boston, Massachusetts

Jane F. Schielack
Professor of Mathematics
Associate Dean for Assessment and
Pre K–12 Education, College of Science
Texas A&M University
College Station, Texas

Jennifer M. Suh
Associate Professor for
Mathematics Education
George Mason University
Fairfax, Virginia

Jonathan A. Wray
Mathematics Instructional Facilitator
Howard County Public Schools
Ellicott City, Maryland

PEARSON

Glenview, Illinois   Boston, Massachusetts   Chandler, Arizona   Hoboken, New Jersey

Mathematicians

Roger Howe
Professor of Mathematics
Yale University
New Haven, Connecticut

Gary Lippman
Professor of Mathematics and
Computer Science
California State University, East Bay
Hayward, California

ELL Consultants

Janice R. Corona
Independent Education Consultant
Dallas, Texas

Jim Cummins
Professor
The University of Toronto
Toronto, Canada

Common Core State Standards Reviewers

Debbie Crisco
Math Coach
Beebe Public Schools
Beebe, Arkansas

Kathleen A. Cuff
Teacher
Kings Park Central School District
Kings Park, New York

Erika Doyle
Math and Science Coordinator
Richland School District
Richland, Washington

Susan Jarvis
Math and Science Curriculum Coordinator
Ocean Springs Schools
Ocean Springs, Mississippi

Velvet M. Simington
K–12 Mathematics Director
Winston-Salem/Forsyth County Schools
Winston-Salem, North Carolina

ISBN-13: 978-0-328-82735-0
ISBN-10: 0-328-82735-5

13   18

You'll be using these digital resources throughout the year!

Digital Resources

Go to PearsonRealize.com

MP
Math Practices Animations to play anytime

Glossary
Animated Glossary in English and Spanish

Help
Another Look Homework Video for extra help

ACTIVe-book
Student Edition online for showing your work

Solve
Solve & Share problems plus math tools

Tools
Math Tools to help you understand

Games
Math Games to help you learn

Learn
Visual Learning Animation Plus with animation, interaction, and math tools

Assessment
Quick Check for each lesson

eText
Student Edition online

PEARSON realize™ Everything you need for math anytime, anywhere

Hi, we're here to help you.
Let's have a great year!
I'm Jada.
I'm Emily.
I'm Marta.
I'm Carlos.
I'm Daniel.
I'm Alex.
I'm Jackson.

Contents

KEY

 Major Cluster

Supporting Cluster

Additional Cluster

The content is organized to focus on Common Core clusters.

For a list of clusters, see Volume I pages F15–F17.

Digital Resources at PearsonRealize.com

And remember your eText is available at PearsonRealize.com!

TOPICS

PearsonRealize.com

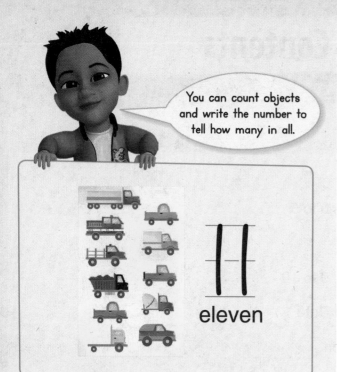

You can count objects and write the number to tell how many in all.

11
eleven

TOPIC 9
Count Numbers to 20

The equation tells how many cubes in all.

$$10 + 2 = 12$$

TOPIC 10
Compose and Decompose Numbers 11 to 19

PearsonRealize.com

You can use part of a hundred chart to count and find patterns.

1	2	3	4	5	6	7	8	9	10
11	12	13	14	15	16	17	18	19	20
21	22	23	24	25	26	27	28	29	30

TOPIC 11
Count Numbers to 100

There are flat and solid objects in our environment. The notebook paper and envelope are flat. The cup and tissue box are solid.

TOPIC 12
Identify and Describe Shapes

PearsonRealize.com

The side of this cube is a square.

TOPIC 13
Analyze, Compare, and Create Shapes

You can compare the sizes of different objects.

Shorter

TOPIC 14
Describe and Compare Measurable Attributes

STEP UP to Grade 1

These lessons help prepare you for Grade 1.

Math Practices

MP.1	Make sense of problems and persevere in solving them.
MP.2	Reason abstractly and quantitatively.
MP.3	Construct viable arguments and critique the reasoning of others.
MP.4	Model with mathematics.
MP.5	Use appropriate tools strategically.
MP.6	Attend to precision.
MP.7	Look for and make use of structure.
MP.8	Look for and express regularity in repeated reasoning.

There are good Thinking Habits for each of these math practices.

Make sense of problems and persevere in solving them.

My plan was to count the bees. The last number I counted was the total number of bees.

Good math thinkers know what the problem is about. They have a plan to solve it. They keep trying if they get stuck.

How many bees are there in all? How do you know?

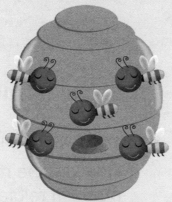

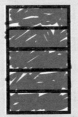

Thinking Habits

What do I need to find?

What do I know?

What's my plan for solving the problem?

What else can I try if I get stuck?

How can I check that my solution make sense?

This problem is about the number 4. I can show 4 in a different way to solve the problem.

Good math thinkers know how to think about words and numbers to solve problems.

Daniel sees 4 frogs. He wants to draw 4 dragonflies in a different arrangement. What other way can he show the number 4?

4

4

Thinking Habits

What do the numbers stand for?

How are the numbers in the problem related?

How can I show a word problem using pictures or numbers?

How can I use a word problem to show what an equation means?

Math Practices and Problem Solving Handbook

MP.3 Construct viable arguments and critique the reasoning of others.

Good math thinkers use math to explain why they are right. They talk about math that others do, too.

I used a picture and words to explain my thinking.

How is the second box like the first box?
Explain your answer.

Thinking Habits

How can I use math to explain my work?

Am I using numbers and symbols correctly?

Is my explanation clear?

What questions can I ask to understand other people's thinking?

Are there mistakes in other people's thinking?

Can I improve other people's thinking?

I counted the stars. I counted the counters. Both boxes have 3 things.

MP.4 Model with mathematics.

Good math thinkers use math they know to show and solve problems.

I used the colored boxes to show the correct answer.

Place 2 counters in the nest. Peeps found these worms for her babies. How can you use the model below the nest to show how many worms Peeps found?

Thinking Habits

How can I use the math I know to help solve this problem?

Can I use a drawing, diagram, table, or objects to show the problem?

Can I write an equation to show the problem?

Math Practices and Problem Solving Handbook

MP.5 Use appropriate tools strategically.

Good math thinkers know how to pick the right tools to solve math problems.

I chose counters to solve the problem.

How many leaves are there in all? Use counters, connecting cubes, or other objects to show how many, and then write the number to tell how many.

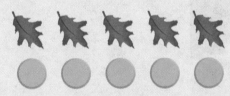

5

Thinking Habits

Which tools can I use?

Is there a different tool I could use?

Am I using the tool correctly?

MP.6 Attend to precision.

Good math thinkers are careful about what they write and say, so their ideas about math are clear.

I was careful when I counted and colored.

Each bird found some worms for her babies. Did they find the same number or different numbers of worms? Color the boxes to show how you know.

Thinking Habits

Am I using numbers, units, and symbols correctly?

Am I using the correct definitions?

Is my answer clear?

Math Practices and Problem Solving Handbook

MP.7 Look for and make use of structure.

Good math thinkers look for patterns in math to help solve problems.

I found a pattern.

How can you tell how many objects you see without counting first?
Explain how you know you are right.

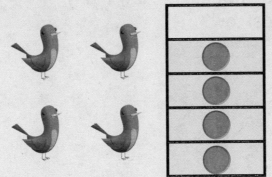

Thinking Habits

Is there a pattern?

How can I describe the pattern?

Can I break the problem into simpler parts?

Look for and express regularity in repeated reasoning.

I know that the 1 more repeats. That helped me solve the problem.

Good math thinkers look for things that repeat in a problem. They use what they learn from one problem to help them solve other problems.

The first row has 1 counter colored. Each row has 1 more counter than the row before. How many counters will be in the last row?

Thinking Habits

Does something repeat in the problem?

How can the solution help me solve another problem?

Math Practices and Problem Solving Handbook

Math Practices and Problem Solving Handbook

Problem Solving Guide

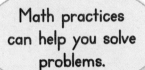

Math practices can help you solve problems.

Make Sense of the Problem

Reason
- What do I need to find?
- What given information can I use?
- How are the quantities related?

Think About Similar Problems
- Have I solved problems like this before?

Persevere in Solving the Problem

Model with Math
- How can I use the math I know?
- How can I show the problem?
- Is there a pattern I can use?

Use Appropriate Tools
- What math tools could I use?
- How can I use those tools?

Check the Answer

Make Sense of the Answer
- Is my answer reasonable?

Check for Precision
- Did I check my work?
- Is my answer clear?
- Is my explanation clear?

Some Ways to Show Problems
- Draw a Picture
- Write an Equation

Some Math Tools
- Objects
- Technology
- Paper and Pencil

This sheet helps you organize your work.

Name **Gretchen**

Teaching Tool
1

Problem Solving Recording Sheet

Problem:
5 birds are on a fence.
2 birds fly away.
How many birds are left?

MAKE SENSE OF THE PROBLEM

Need to Find	Given
I need to find how many birds are left.	5 birds are on a fence. 2 birds fly away.

PERSEVERE IN SOLVING THE PROBLEM

Some Ways to Represent Problems
☑ Draw a Picture
☑ Write an Equation

Some Math Tools
☐ Objects
☐ Technology
☑ Paper and Pencil

Solution and Answer

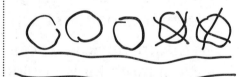

3 birds
5 − 2 = 3

CHECK THE ANSWER

I listened to the problem again. I checked my picture and counted the birds that were left, 3 birds. My answer is correct.

 TT1

Math Practices and Problem Solving Handbook

TOPIC 9 Count Numbers to 20

Essential Question: How can numbers to 20 be counted, read, written, and pictured to tell how many?

Some plants make fruit to protect their seeds.

Oranges

Math and Science Project: What Can We Get From Plants?

Directions Read the character speech bubbles to students. **Find Out!** Have students find out ways plants impact and change their environment. Say: *Talk to friends and relatives about what plants do for the environment. Ask them how humans and animals use things in the environment, such as plants, to meet their needs.* **Journal: Make a Poster** Have students make a poster. Ask them to draw some ways that plants can provide food and shelter for animals and humans. Finally, have students draw an orange tree with 15 oranges.

Name _____

 1

$$5 + 4 = 9$$

$$5 - 4 = 1$$

2

$$6 - 3 = 3$$

3

$$7 - 4 = 3$$

4

5   15   10

5

_____   _____   _____

_ _ _ _ _ _   **+**   _ _ _ _ _ _   **=**   _ _ _ _ _ _

_____   _____   _____

Directions Have students: **1** draw a circle around the equation that shows addition; **2** draw a circle around the minus sign; **3** draw a circle around the difference; **4** draw a circle around the correct number of counters shown; **5** count the red counters, count the yellow counters, and then write the equation to find the sum.

My Word Cards

Directions Have students cut out the vocabulary cards. Read the front of the card, and then ask them to explain what the word or phrase means.

A-Z
Glossary

eleven

twelve

thirteen

fourteen

fifteen

sixteen

Directions Review the definitions and have students study the cards. Extend learning by having students draw pictures for each word on a separate piece of paper.

13

Point to the apples.
Say: *There are 13 apples.*

12

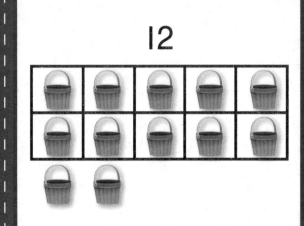

Point to the pails.
Say: *There are 12 pails.*

11

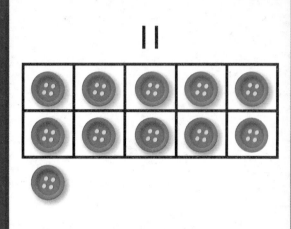

Point to the buttons.
Say: *There are 11 buttons.*

16

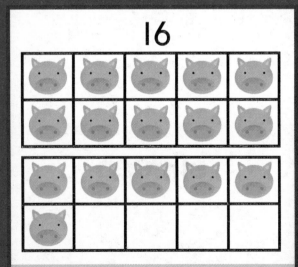

Point to the pigs.
Say: *There are 16 pigs.*

15

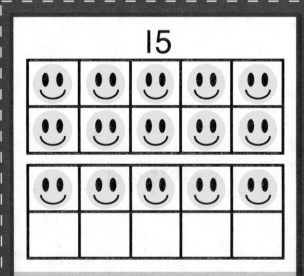

Point to the smiley faces.
Say: *There are 15 smiley faces.*

14

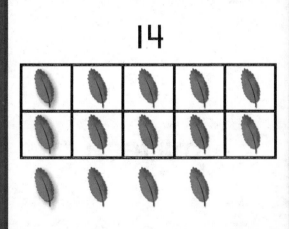

Point to the leaves.
Say: *There are 14 leaves.*

A-Z Glossary

My Word Cards

Directions Have students cut out the vocabulary cards. Read the front of the card, and then ask them to explain what the word or phrase means.

seventeen	eighteen	nineteen
twenty	row	

My Word Cards

19

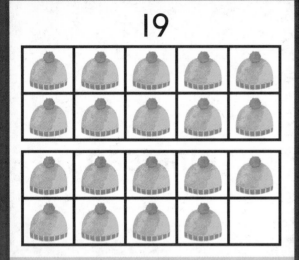

Point to the hats.
Say: *There are 19 hats.*

18

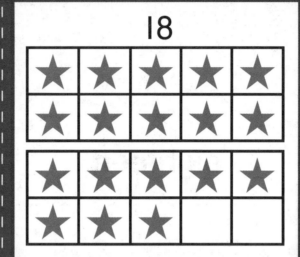

Point to the stars.
Say: *There are 18 stars.*

17

Point to the moons.
Say: *There are 17 moons.*

1	2	3	4	5
11	12	13	14	15
21	22	23	24	25
31	32	33	34	35

Point to the circled row.
Say: *This is a **row**. Rows go side to side.*

20

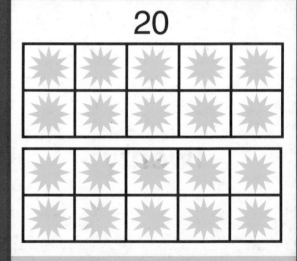

Point to the suns.
Say: *There are 20 suns.*

© Pearson Education, Inc. K

Solve & Share

I can ...
count and write the numbers
11 and 12.

Directions Say: *Carlos has a collection of toy cars. How can Carlos show the number of cars he has? Use counters, and then draw them to show one way.*

© **Content Standards**
K.CC.A.3, K.CC.B.5
Mathematical Practices
MP.2, MP.3, MP.4, MP.6

eleven

☆ Guided Practice

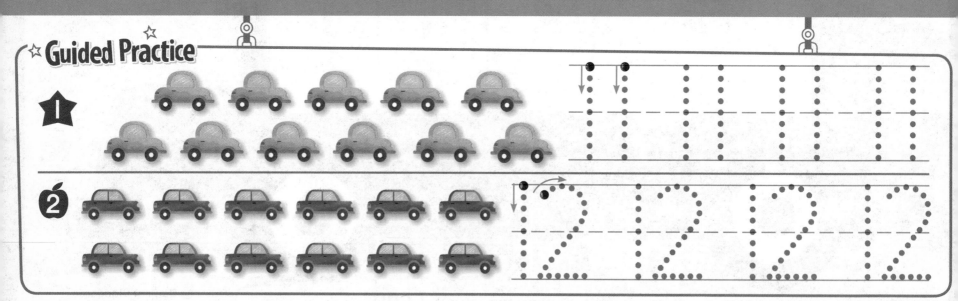

1 11 11 11 11 11 11 11 11

2 12 12 12 12

Directions ☝ and ✌ Have students count the cars in each group, and then practice writing the number that tells how many.

 Learn A-Z Glossary

514 five hundred fourteen

© Pearson Education, Inc. K

Topic 9 | Lesson 1

3

4

5

6

Directions **3–5** Have students count the toys in each group, and then practice writing the number that tells how many. **6** **Number Sense** Have students count the train cars, write the number to tell how many, and then write the number that comes after it.

Independent Practice

7

_____

- - - - - - - - - - - - - -

8

_____

- - - - - - - - - - - - - -

_____

9

_____

- - - - - - - - - - - - - -

_____

10

_____

- - - - - - - - - - - - - -

_____

_____

Directions **7**–**9** Have students count the toys in each group, and then practice writing the number that tells how many. **10 Higher Order Thinking** Have students draw 11 toys, and then practice writing the number that tells how many.

© Pearson Education, Inc. K **Topic 9 | Lesson 1**

Name _____

Another Look!

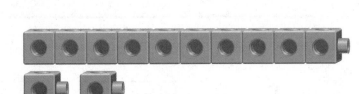

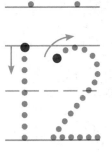

HOME ACTIVITY Draw groups of 11 and 12 circles, each on a separate index card. Have your child write the correct number on the back of each card. Then use the cards to practice counting and writing the numbers 11 and 12.

_____
- - - - - - -
_____

_____

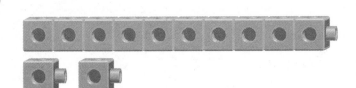

_____
- - - - - - -
_____

Directions Say: *Count the connecting cubes, and then write the number to tell how many.* and Have students count the connecting cubes, and then write the number to tell how many.

3

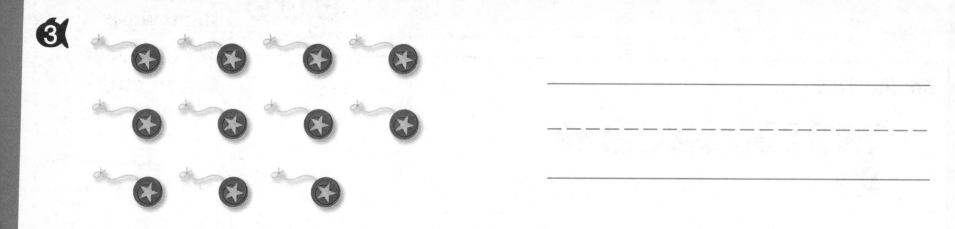

_____

- - - - - - - - - - - - -

_____

4

_____

- - - - - - - - - - - - -

_____

5

_____

- - - - - - - - - - - - -

_____

Directions ❸ Have students count the yo-yos, and then practice writing the number that tells how many. ❹ **Higher Order Thinking** Have students draw 12 toys, and then practice writing the number that tells how many. ❺ **Higher Order Thinking** Have students count each group of cars, and then write the numbers to tell how many.

© Pearson Education, Inc. K

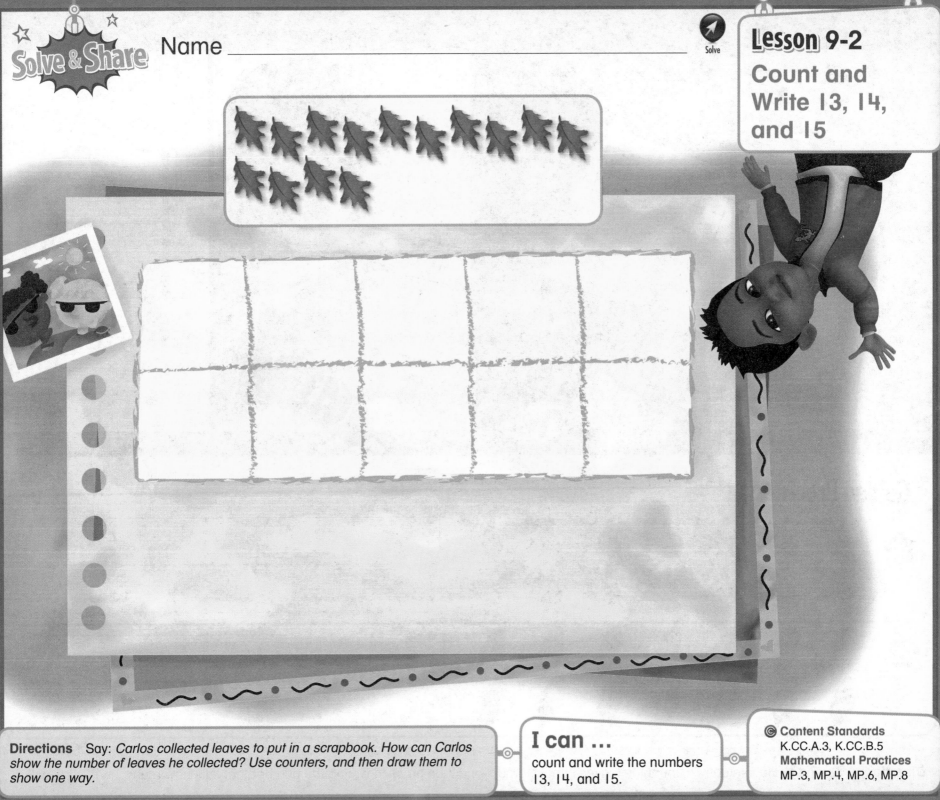
Solve & Share

Name _____

Solve

I can ...
count and write the numbers
13, 14, and 15.

Directions Say: *Carlos collected leaves to put in a scrapbook. How can Carlos show the number of leaves he collected? Use counters, and then draw them to show one way.*

© **Content Standards**
K.CC.A.3, K.CC.B.5
Mathematical Practices
MP.3, MP.4, MP.6, MP.8

13

thirteen

☆ Guided Practice

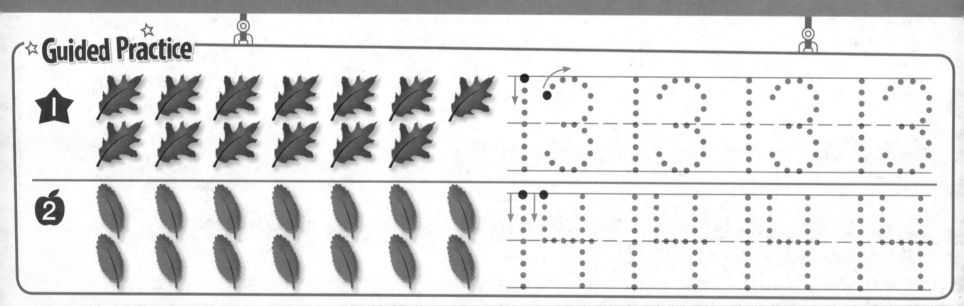

1

2

Directions ⭐ and ✌ Have students count the leaves in each group, and then practice writing the number that tells how many.

© Pearson Education, Inc. K

Topic 9 | Lesson 2

Name _____

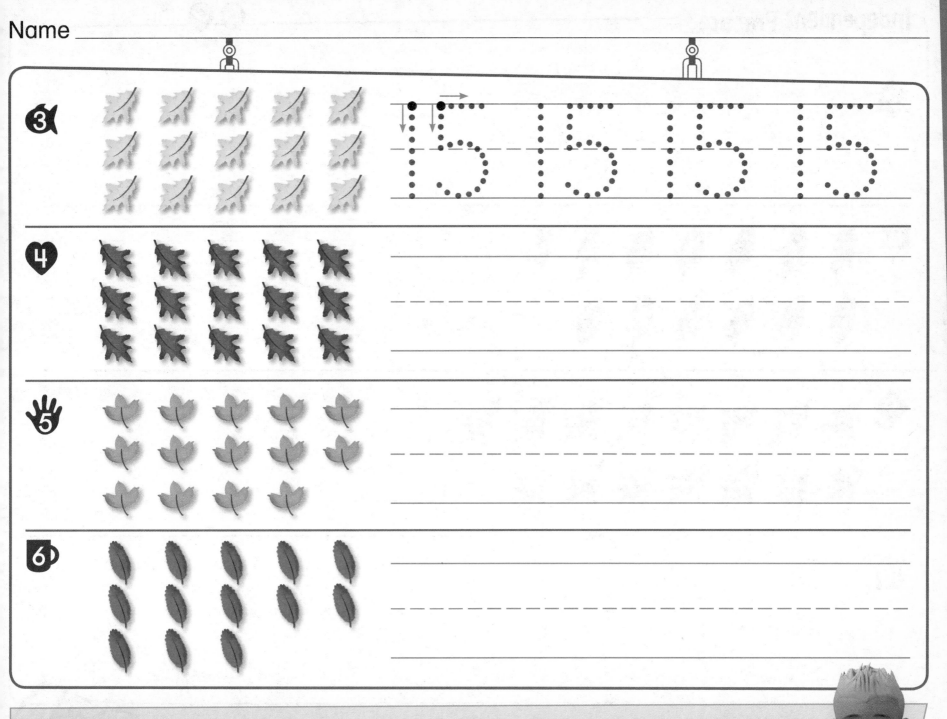

3 15 15 15 15 15

4

5

6

Directions **3**–**5** Have students count the leaves in each group, and then practice writing the number that tells how many.
6 **Math and Science** Say: *Trees use their leaves to turn sunlight into food.* Have students count the green leaves, and then practice writing the number that tells how many.

Topic 9 | Lesson 2

five hundred twenty-one **521**

7

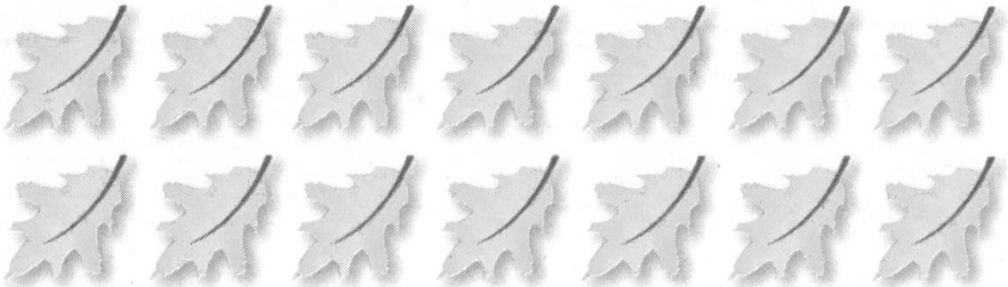

8

9

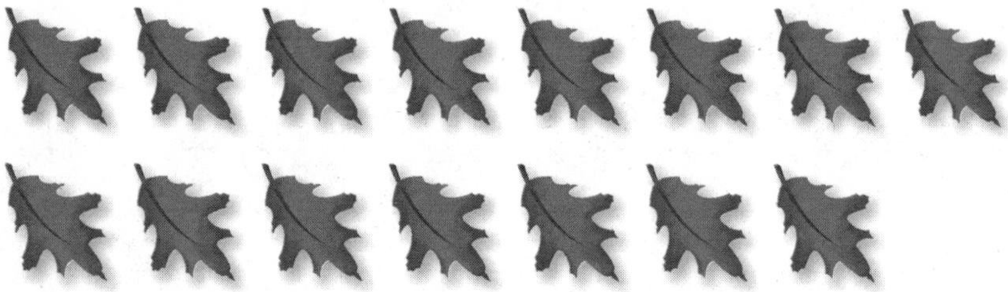

10

Directions **7—9** Have students count the leaves in each group, and then practice writing the number that tells how many. **10 Higher Order Thinking** Have students draw 14 leaves, and then practice writing the number that tells how many.

522 five hundred twenty-two   © Pearson Education, Inc. K   **Topic 9** | Lesson 2

Name _____

 **Another Look!**

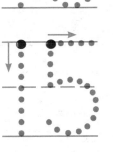

HOME ACTIVITY Have your child write the numbers 13, 14, and 15 on 3 index cards. Show your child groups of 13, 14, and 15 objects. Have her or him count the objects in each group, say the numbers, and match the number cards to the groups.

 1

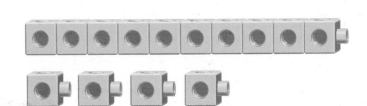

_ _ _ _ _ _

 2

_ _ _ _ _ _

Directions Say: *Count the connecting cubes, and then write the number to tell how many.* **1** and **2** Have students count the connecting cubes, and then write the number to tell how many.

3

_____

- - - - - - - - - - - - - - - -

_____

4

_____

- - - - - - - - - - - - - - - -

_____

5

_____   _____

- - - - - -   - - - - - -

_____   _____

Topic 9 | Lesson 2

Solve & Share

Name _____

Solve

Directions Say: *Jada has a collection of piggy banks. How can Carlos show the number of piggy banks Jada has? Use counters, and then draw them to show one way.*

I can ...
count and write the numbers
16 and 17.

© **Content Standards**
K.CC.A.3, K.CC.B.5
Mathematical Practices
MP.2, MP.4, MP.6, MP.7

Digital Resources at PearsonRealize.com

five hundred twenty-five **525**

17

seventeen

☆ Guided Practice

1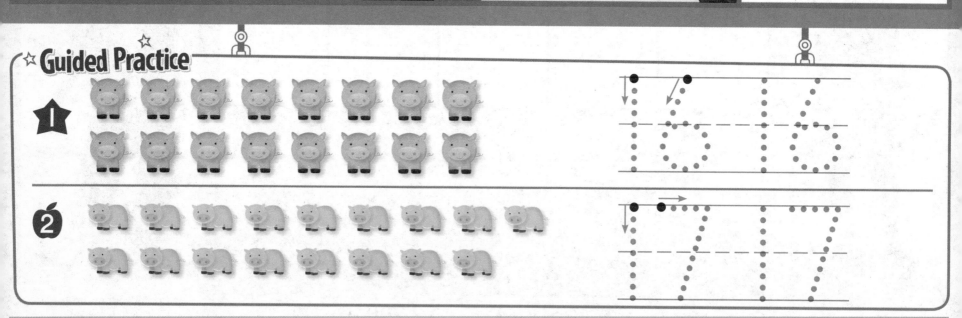

2

Directions **1** and **2** Have students count the piggy banks in each group, and then practice writing the number that tells how many.

© Pearson Education, Inc. K

Name _____

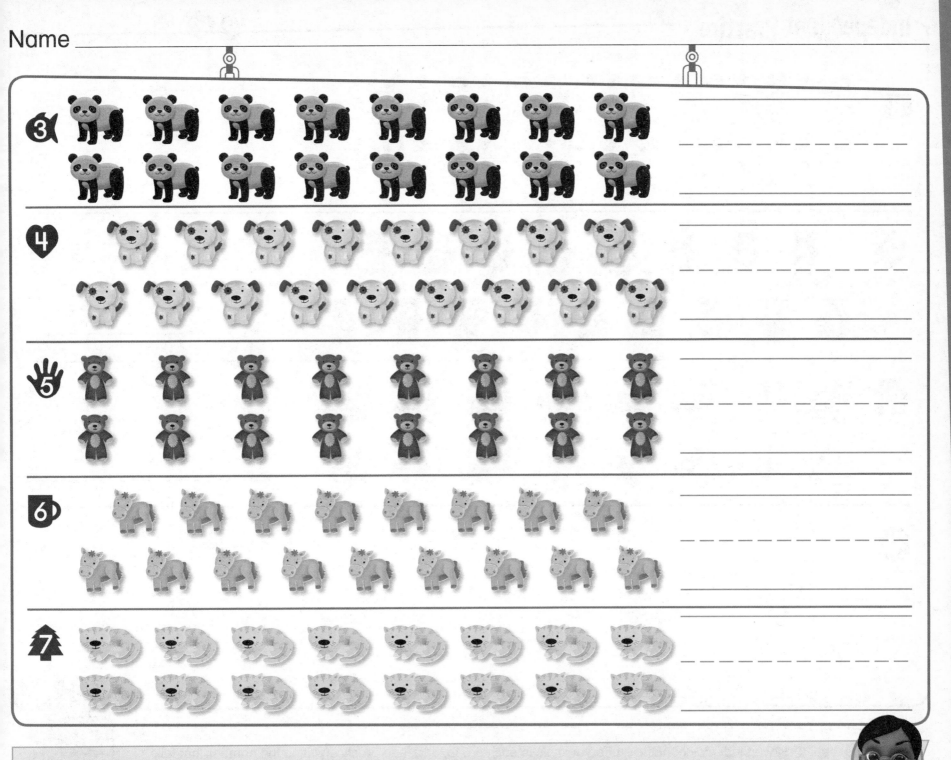

Directions ❸–❼ Have students count the stuffed animals in each group, and then practice writing the number that tells how many.

Topic 9 | Lesson 3

five hundred twenty-seven **527**

Independent Practice

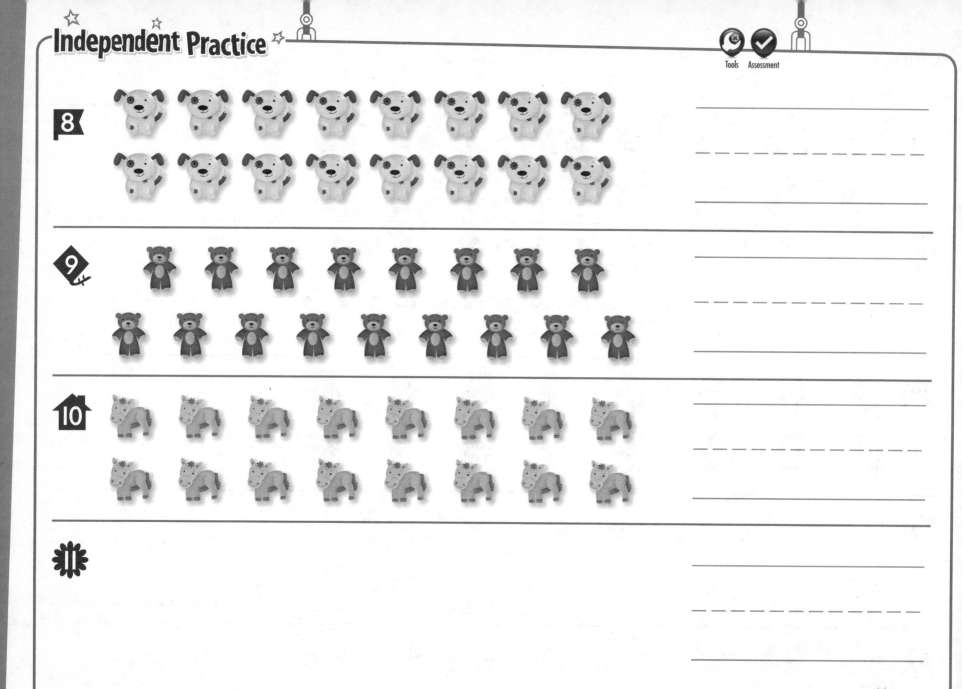

8 _____

9 _____

10 _____

※ _____

Directions **8–10** Have students count the stuffed animals in each group, and then practice writing the number that tells how many. **※ Higher Order Thinking** Have students draw 17 balls, and then practice writing the number that tells how many.

Topic 9 | Lesson 3

Name _____

Another Look!

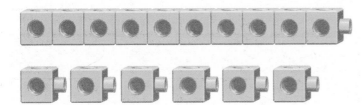

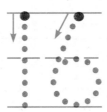

HOME ACTIVITY Have your child write the numbers 16 and 17 on 2 index cards. Show your child groups of 16 and 17 objects. Have him or her count the objects, say the numbers, and match the number cards to the groups.

 1

_____

- - - - - - -

_____

 2

_____

- - - - - - -

_____

Directions Say: *Count the connecting cubes, and then write the number to tell how many.* ⭐ and **2** Have students count the connecting cubes, and then write the number to tell how many.

3

_____

- - - - - - - - - - - - - - -

_____

4

_____

- - - - - - - - - - - - - - -

_____

5

_____   _____

- - - - - - - -   - - - - - - - -

_____   _____

Directions 3 Have students count the stuffed animals, and then practice writing the number that tells how many.
4 **Higher Order Thinking** Have students draw 16 balls, and then practice writing the number that tells how many.
5 **Higher Order Thinking** Have students count each group of piggy banks, and then write the numbers to tell how many.

© Pearson Education, Inc. K

Solve

Lesson 9-4
Count and Write
18, 19, and 20

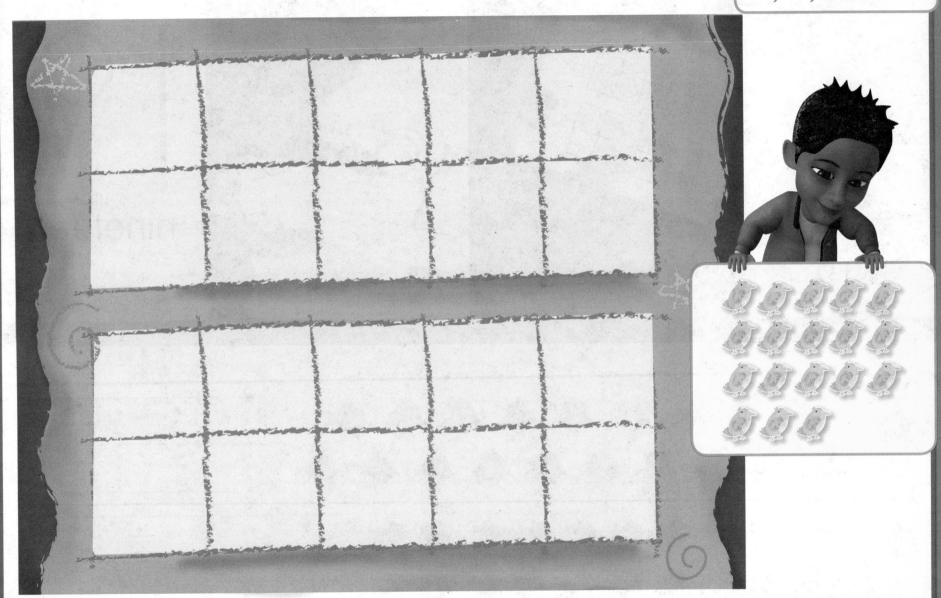

Directions Say: *Carlos has a collection of bird stickers in his sticker album. How can Carlos show the number of bird stickers he has? Use counters, and then draw them to show one way.*

I can ...
count and write the numbers 18, 19, and 20.

© **Content Standards**
K.CC.A.3, K.CC.B.5
Mathematical Practices
MP.1, MP.5, MP.7, MP.8

Digital Resources at PearsonRealize.com

19

nineteen

Guided Practice

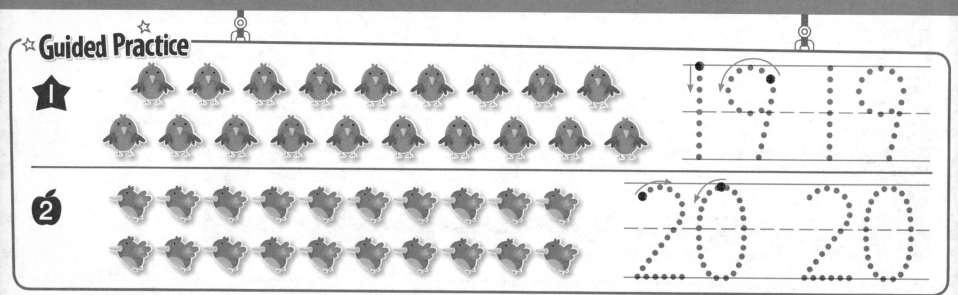

1

2

Directions **1** and **2** Have students count the bird stickers in each group, and then practice writing the number that tells how many.

© Pearson Education, Inc. K

Name _____

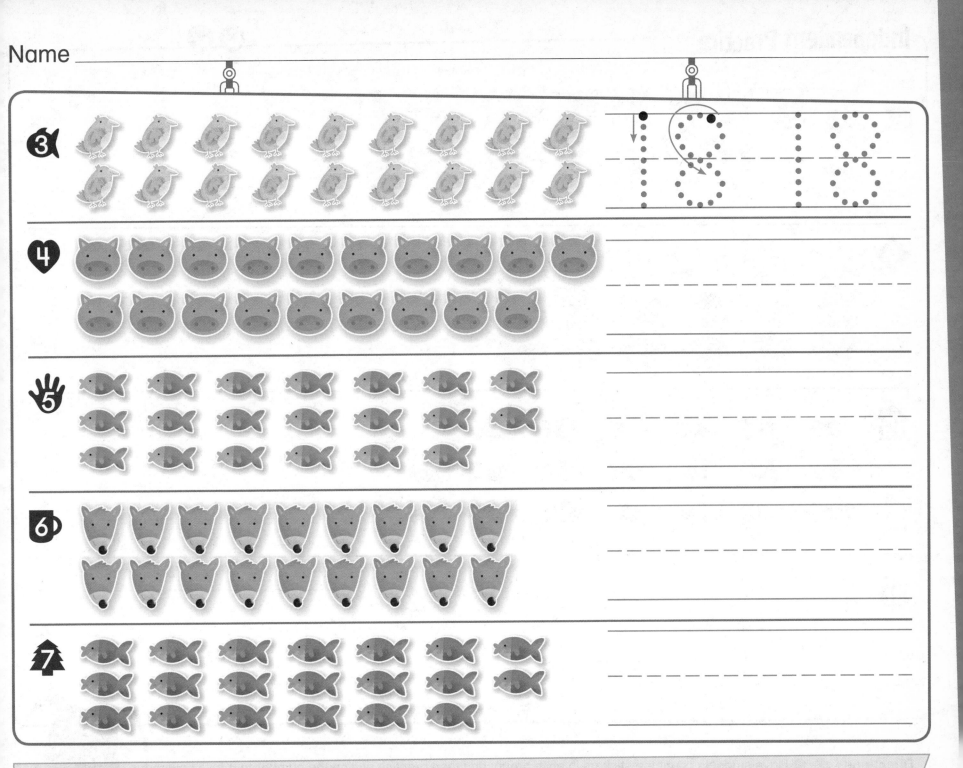

Directions ❸–❼ Have students count the stickers in each group, and then practice writing the number that tells how many.

Topic 9 | **Lesson 4**   five hundred thirty-three   **533**

Independent Practice

8 _____

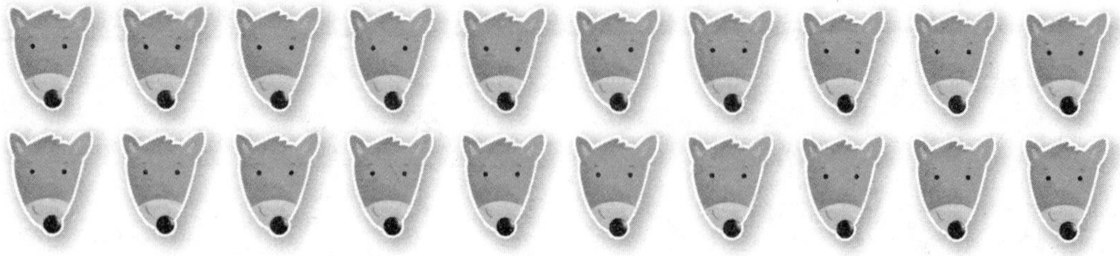

9 _____

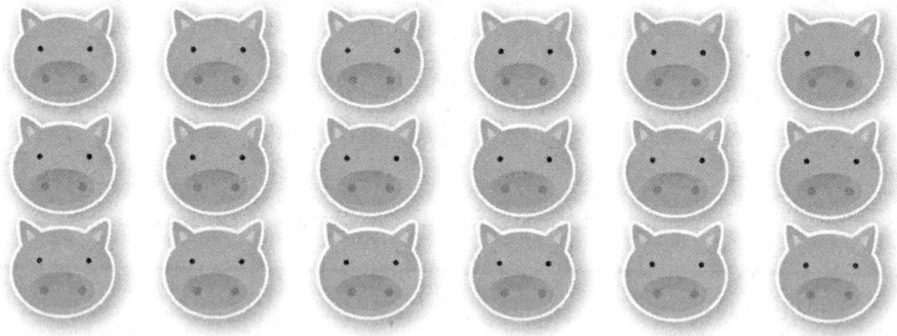

10 _____

✳ _____

Directions **8**–**10** Have students count the stickers in each group, and then practice writing the number that tells how many.
✳ Higher Order Thinking Have students draw 20 bug stickers, and then practice writing the number that tells how many.

© Pearson Education, Inc. K

Name _____

 Help   Tools   Games

Another Look!

HOME ACTIVITY Have your child draw 18 objects, and then write the number 18 below the group of objects. Repeat for the numbers 19 and 20.

 1

_____

- - - - - - - - -

_____

 2

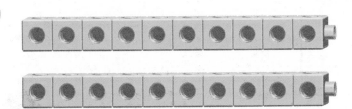

_____

- - - - - - - - -

_____

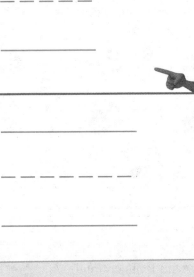

Directions Say: *Count the connecting cubes, and then write the number to tell how many.* **1** and **2** Have students count the connecting cubes, and then write the number to tell how many.

3

_____

- - - - - - - - - - - - - - - - - - -

_____

4

_____

- - - - - - - - - - - - - - - - - - -

_____

5

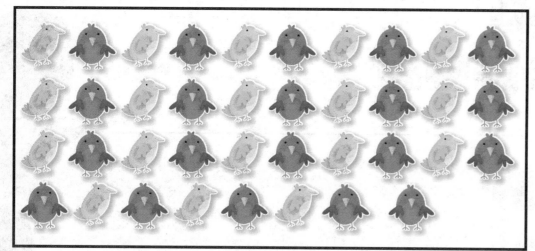

_____   _____

- - - - - - - - - - - - - - - - - - -

_____   _____

Directions ✸ Have students count the stickers, and then practice writing the number that tells how many.
♥ **Vocabulary** Have students draw **nineteen** worm stickers, and then practice writing the number that tells how many.
✋ **Higher Order Thinking** Have students count each group of stickers, and then write the numbers to tell how many.

536 five hundred thirty-six

© Pearson Education, Inc. K

Topic 9 | Lesson 4

Solve & Share

Start

2

End

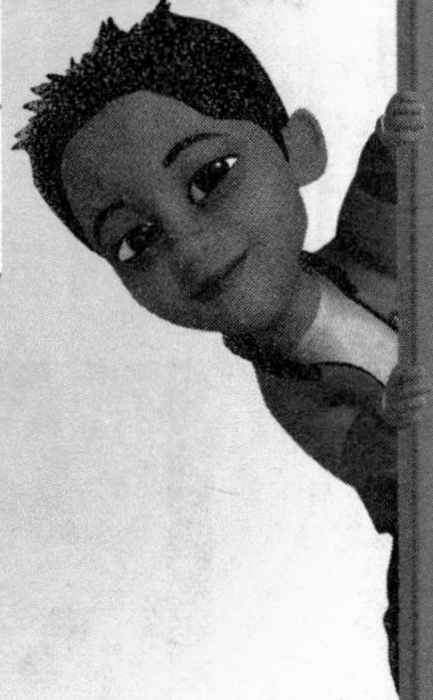

Directions Say: *Put 12 counters on the double ten-frame. Write the number to tell how many. Put 1 more counter on the double ten-frame, and then write the number. Repeat using 1 more counter. What do you notice about the numbers? Do they get larger or smaller as you count?*

I can ...
count forward from any number to a number within 20.

© **Content Standards**
K.CC.A.2, K.CC.B.4c
Mathematical Practices
MP.2, MP.4, MP.6, MP.7

| 1 | 2 | 3 | 4 | 5 | 6 | 7 | 8 | 9 | 10 |
| 11 | 12 | 13 | 14 | 15 | 16 | 17 | 18 | 19 | 20 |

Count forward.

8 9 10 11 12 13

☆ Guided Practice

| 1 | 2 | 3 | 4 | 5 | 6 | 7 | 8 | 9 | 10 |
| 11 | 12 | 13 | 14 | 15 | 16 | 17 | 18 | 19 | 20 |

15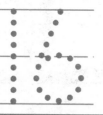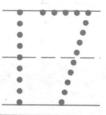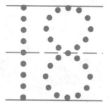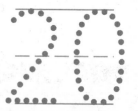

Directions ☆ Have students find the blue number on the number chart, count forward until they reach the stop sign, and then write each number they counted.

© Pearson Education, Inc. K

Topic 9 | Lesson 5

Name

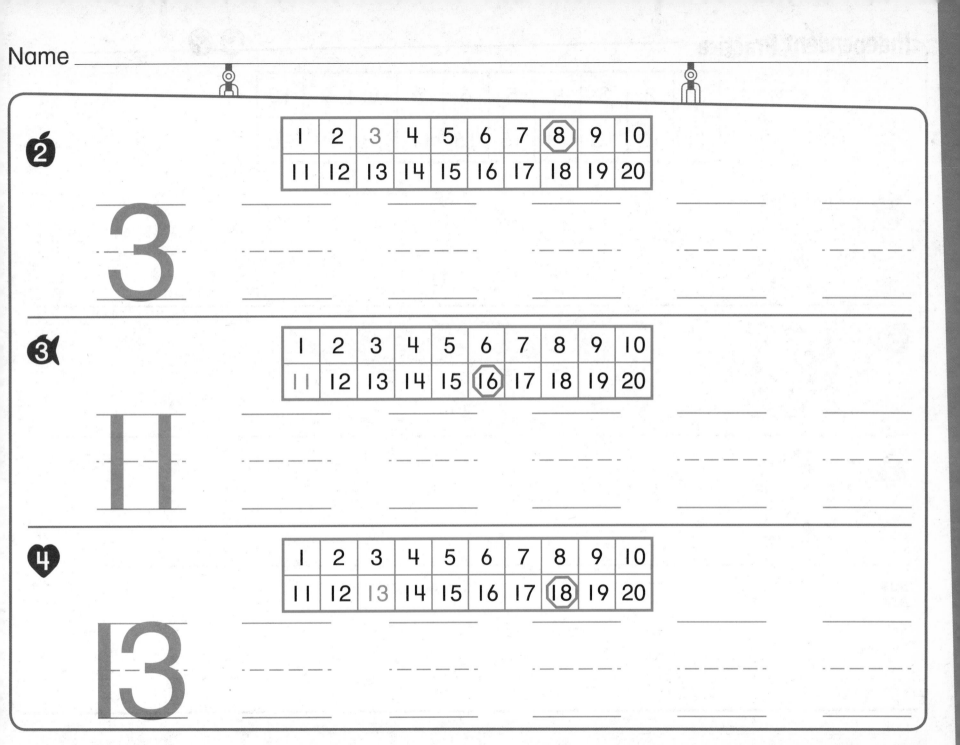

2

1	2	3	4	5	6	7	(8)	9	10
11	12	13	14	15	16	17	18	19	20

3

3

1	2	3	4	5	6	7	8	9	10
11	12	13	14	15	(16)	17	18	19	20

11

4

1	2	3	4	5	6	7	8	9	10
11	12	13	14	15	16	17	(18)	19	20

13

Directions **2**–**4** Have students find the blue number on the number chart, count forward until they reach the stop sign, and then write each number they counted.

1	2	3	4	5	6	7	8	9	10
11	12	13	14	15	16	17	18	19	20

✋ 5   7 — — — — — — — — — — — — — — — —
— — — — — — — — — — — — — — — —

☕ 6   10 — — — — — — — — — — — — — —
— — — — — — — — — — — — — — — —

🌲 7   12 — — — — — — — — — — — — — —
— — — — — — — — — — — — — — — —

🚩 8   — — — — — — — — — — — — — — — —
— — — — — — — — — — — — — — — —

Directions ✋–🌲 Have students start at the blue number and count forward, and then write each number they counted. Have students use the number chart at the top of the page, if needed. 🚩 **Higher Order Thinking** Have students pick a number between 1 and 15, and write it on the first line. Have them count forward, and then write each number they counted.

Name _____

Another Look!

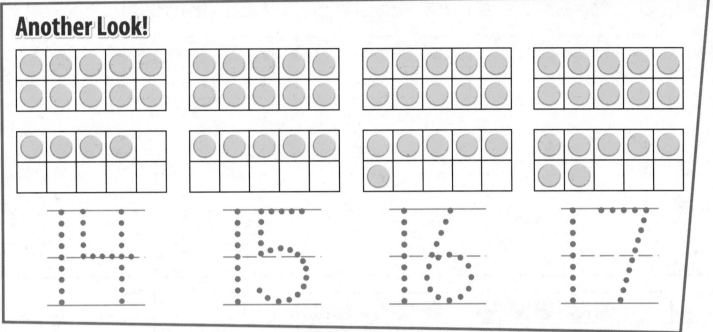

HOME ACTIVITY Pick a start number between 1 and 15. Have your child write the next four numbers. Repeat using different numbers.

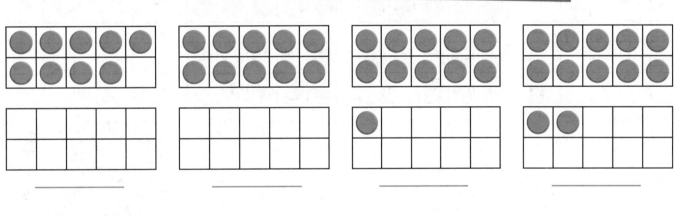

_____   _____   _____   _____

- - - - - -   - - - - - -   - - - - - -   - - - - - -

- - - - - -   - - - - - -   - - - - - -   - - - - - -

Directions Say: *The first double ten-frame shows 14 counters. The second double ten-frame shows 1 more counter. Count the counters in each double ten-frame, and then write the numbers to tell how many. Count forward to say each number you wrote.* ⭐ Have students count the counters in each double ten-frame, and then write the numbers to tell how many. Then have them count forward to say each number they wrote.

2

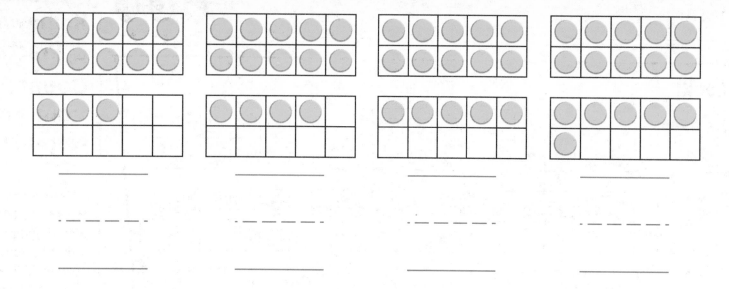

3

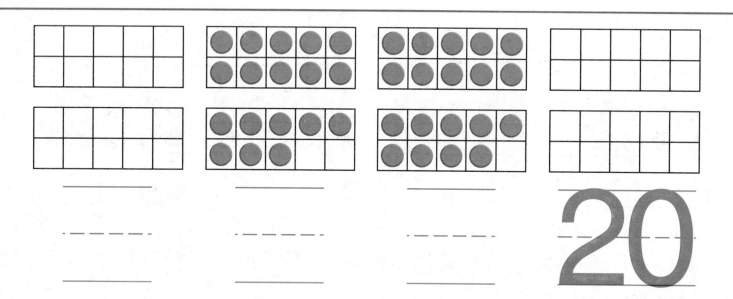

20

Directions ❷ Have students count the counters in each double ten-frame, and then write the numbers to tell how many. Then have them count forward to say each number they wrote. ❸ **Higher Order Thinking** Have students look at the counters and the number given and find the pattern. Then have them draw the missing counters in each double ten-frame, and then write the numbers to tell how many. Have students count forward to say each number they wrote.

Directions Say: *Daniel has 13 cherries on a tray. Jada has 11 cherries on a tray. How can you show this? Use counters to show the cherries on the trays, and then draw the pictures. How can you tell that your drawings are correct?*

I can ...
count to find how many are in a group.

© **Content Standards**
K.CC.B.5
Mathematical Practices
MP.1, MP.5, MP.7, MP.8

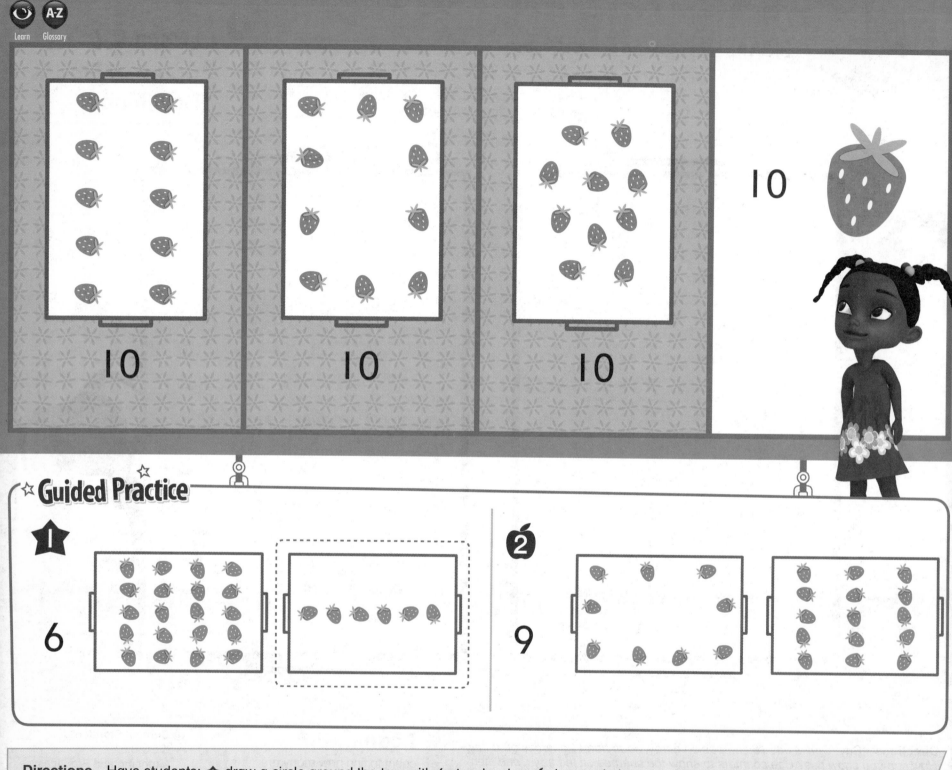

10

10

10

10

☆ Guided Practice

1

6

2

9

Directions Have students: 1 draw a circle around the tray with 6 strawberries; 2 draw a circle around the tray with 9 strawberries.

Name _____

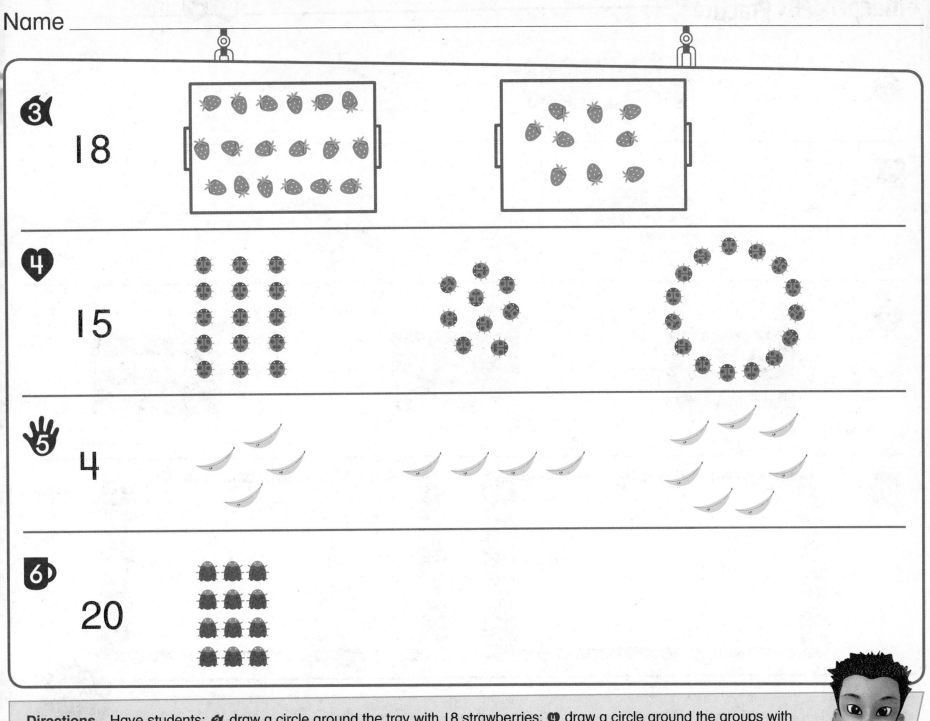

3

18

4

15

5

4

6

20

Directions Have students: **3** draw a circle around the tray with 18 strawberries; **4** draw a circle around the groups with 15 bugs; **5** draw a circle around the groups with 4 bananas. **6 Algebra** Have students count the bugs in the group, and then draw another group of bugs so that there are 20 bugs in all.

Topic 9 | Lesson 6

five hundred forty-five **545**

Independent Practice

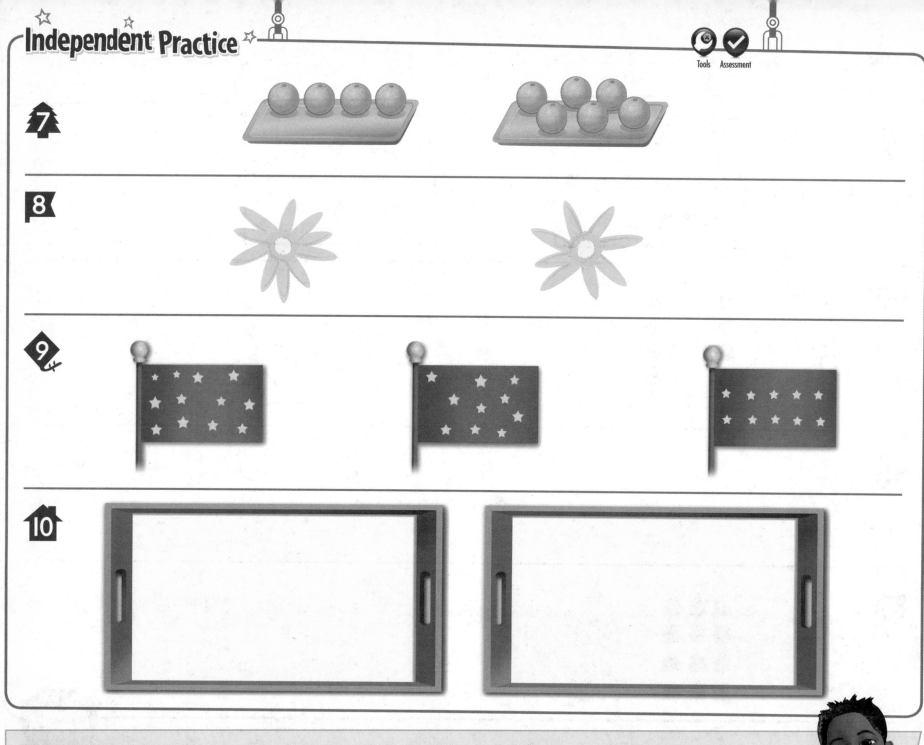

7

8

9

10

Directions Have students: **7** draw a circle around the tray with 6 oranges; **8** draw a circle around the flower with 8 petals; **9** draw a circle around the flags with 10 stars. **10** **Higher Order Thinking** Have students draw 19 strawberries in two different ways.

© Pearson Education, Inc. K

Name _____

Another Look!

HOME ACTIVITY Give your child a handful of small items such as pennies, buttons, or dry beans. Have him or her count how many of each item there are. Count together to check your child's answers. Then line up the same number of objects in another arrangement. Have him or her count to see that the number is the same.

 1

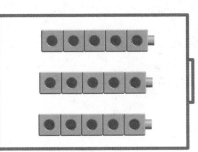 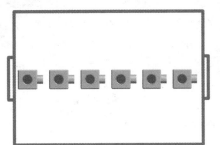 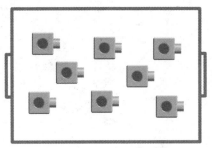

 2

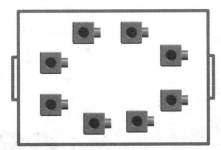 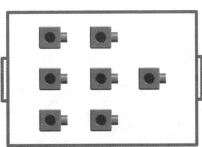 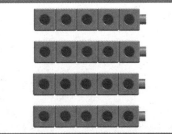

Directions Say: *Which trays have 20 connecting cubes on them? Draw a circle around the trays. How did you find how many?*
Have students: 1 *draw a circle around the tray with 8 cubes;* 2 *draw a circle around the tray with 7 cubes.*

3

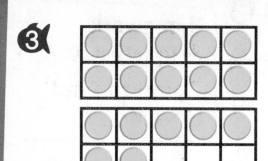

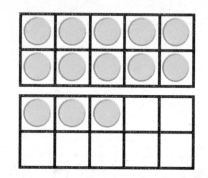

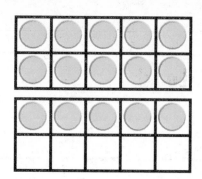

4

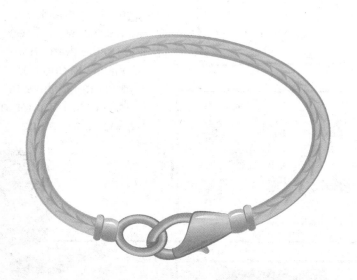

5

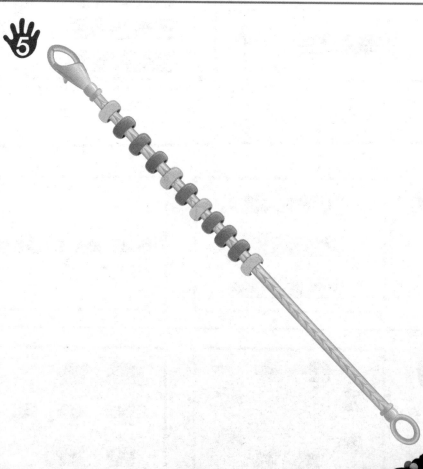

Directions ❸ Have students draw a circle around the double ten-frame with 17 counters. ❹ **Higher Order Thinking** Have students draw 11 beads on the bracelet. ✋ **Higher Order Thinking** Have students draw more beads to show 20 beads on the bracelet.

Solve & Share

10   11   12   13   14

Directions Say: *Carlos wants to put some or all of the eggs in the carton. Draw a circle around all the numbers that tell how many eggs he could put in the carton. Explain why there could be more than one answer.*

I can ...
use reasoning to count and write numbers to the number 20.

© **Mathematical Practices**
MP.2 Also MP.1, MP.3, MP.4
Content Standards
K.CC.A.2, K.CC.B.5

Digital Resources at PearsonRealize.com

Think. 10, 11, 12, 13, or 14?

I see 12.

3 possible answers

I̶0̶ I̶I̶ (12) (13) (14)

☆ Guided Practice

1

8   9   (10)   (11)   (12)

Directions ⭐ Say: *There are more than 8 cows on a farm. Some cows are outside the barn. 1 or more cows are inside the barn. Count the cows that are outside of the barn, and then draw a circle around the numbers that tell how many cows there could be in all.*

© Pearson Education, Inc. K

Independent Practice

2

12   13   14   15   16

3

16   17   18   19   20

4

3   4   5   6   7

Directions   Say: **2** *There are more than 12 horses on the farm. Some horses are outside the stable. 0, 1, or 2 horses are inside the stable. Count the horses outside the stable, and then draw a circle around the numbers that tell how many horses there could be in all.* **3** *Some dogs are playing in the park. 1 or 2 dogs are resting in a doghouse. Count the dogs playing in the park, and then draw a circle around the numbers that tell how many dogs there could be in all.* **4** *The fish tank can hold up to 15 fish. Count the fish in the tank, and then draw a circle around the numbers that tell how many more fish could fit in the tank.*

10 11 12 13 14

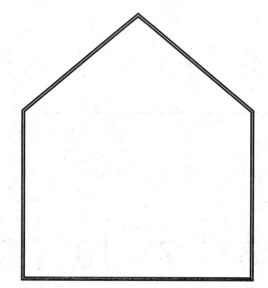

Directions Read the problem to students. Then have them use multiple math practices to solve the problem. Say: *Alex lives on a farm with so many cats that they are hard to count. Sometimes the cats are outside and sometimes they hide in the shed. Alex knows that the number of cats is greater than 11. There are less than 15 cats on the farm. How can Alex find out the number of cats that could be on his farm?* ✋ **MP.2 Reasoning** *What numbers do you know from the problem? Mark an X on the numbers that do NOT fit the clues. Draw a circle around the numbers that tell the number of cats that could be on the farm.* ☕ **MP.4 Model** *How can you show a word problem using pictures? Draw a picture of the cats on Alex's farm. Remember that some may hide inside the shed.* 🌲 **MP.3 Explain** *Is your drawing complete? Tell a friend how your drawing shows the number of cats on Alex's farm.*

Name _____

Another Look!

13 14 15 16 (17) (18)

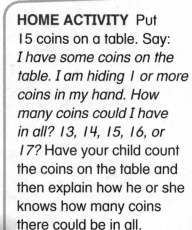

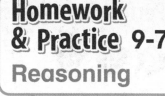

HOME ACTIVITY Put 15 coins on a table. Say: *I have some coins on the table. I am hiding 1 or more coins in my hand. How many coins could I have in all? 13, 14, 15, 16, or 17?* Have your child count the coins on the table and then explain how he or she knows how many coins there could be in all.

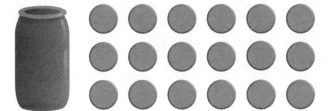

16 17 18 19 20

10 11 12 13 14

Directions Say: *There are 1 or more counters inside the jar. Count the yellow counters, and then draw a circle around the numbers that tell how many counters there could be in all.* ⭐ and 🍎 Say: *There are 1 or more counters inside the jar. Count the counters, and then draw a circle around the numbers that tell how many counters there could be in all.*

Directions Read the problem to students. Then have them use multiple math practices to solve the problem. Say: *Jada knows that there are 17 bunnies at the animal sanctuary. Some are sitting in the grass. Some are hiding behind a bush. What clues can she write to have her friends guess the number of bunnies in all?* **③ MP.1 Make Sense** *What do you know about the problem? How many bunnies are there in all?* **④ MP.2 Reasoning** *Tell your friend the clues. How many bunnies can he or she see?* **⑤ MP.3 Explain** *If your friend says there are 14 bunnies in all, what mistake did he or she probably make?*

⭐1

2 + 3	5 − 1	2 + 2	1 + 3	4 − 0
5 − 2	0 + 4	0 + 3	2 + 1	1 + 4
2 − 1	3 + 1	5 − 1	4 + 0	1 + 3
3 + 0	2 + 2	5 − 3	5 − 4	2 + 0
1 − 1	4 − 0	2 − 0	3 + 2	1 + 0

②2

I can ...
add and subtract fluently to 5.

Directions Have students: ⭐ color each box that has a sum or difference that is equal to 4; ② write the that letter they see.

© **Content Standard** K.OA.A.5

A-Z Glossary

13   16   18 | **2** 12   15   17 | **3**

_____
- - - - - -
_____

4

5

6

_____
- - - - - -
_____

Directions   **Understand Vocabulary** Have students: ☝ draw a circle around the number **sixteen**; **2** draw a circle around the number **twelve**; **3** write the number **eighteen**; **4** draw **eleven** counters in the box, and then write the number; ✋ draw a circle around **fourteen** cubes; **6** write the number **twenty**.

Name _____

Set A _____

19

⭐1 ★ ★ ★ ★ ★ ★

★ ★ ★ ★ ★ ★

★ ★ ★ ★ ★

🍎2

_____

_____

_____

Set B _____

1	2	3	4	5	6	7	8	9	10
11	12	13	14	15	⑯	17	18	19	20

🐟3

1	2	3	4	5	6	7	8	9	10
⑪	12	13	14	15	16	17	18	19	20

14 15 16

9 _ _ _ _ _ _ _ _

Directions Have students: ⭐ and 🍎 count the objects in each group, and then write the number to tell how many; 🐟 find the blue number on the number chart, count forward until they reach the stop sign, and then write each number they counted.

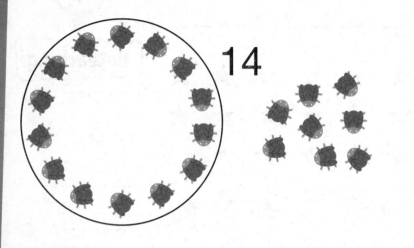 14

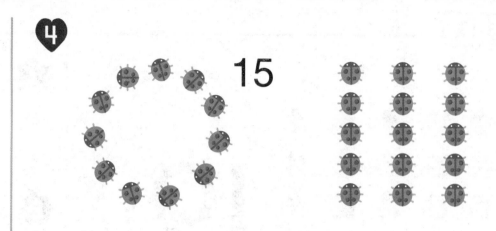

♥ 15

2 3 ④ ⑤

9 10 11 12 13

Directions Have students: ♥ draw a circle around the group with 15 bugs; ✋ listen to the story and use reasoning to find the answer. *Some bunnies are resting in the grass. 2 or 3 bunnies are playing behind the bush. Count the bunnies in the grass, and then draw a circle around the numbers that show how many bunnies there could be in all.*

© Pearson Education, Inc. K   **Topic 9** | Reteaching

Name _____

 1

(A) 13

(B) 14

(C) 15

(D) 16

 2

(A)

(B)

(C)

(D)

3

14   15   16   17

☐   ☐   ☐   ☐

Directions Have students mark the best answer. **1** Which number tells how many? **2** Which shows 11? **3** Have students listen to the story, and then mark all the possible answers. *There are some bees outside of the beehive. 1 or more bees are inside the beehive. Count the bees outside of the beehive, and then mark all the numbers that tell how many bees there could be in all.*

4 ♥

5 ✋

6 (mug icon)

7 🌲

1	2	3	4	5	6	7	8	9	10
11	12	13	14	15	16	17	18	19	20

16 _ _ _ _ _ _ _ _

Directions Have students: **4** count the leaves, and then write the number to tell how many; **5** draw a circle around the group that shows 15 ladybugs; **6** draw eighteen marbles, and then write the number to tell how many; **7** find the blue number on the number chart, count forward until they reach the stop sign, and then write each number they counted.

Name _____

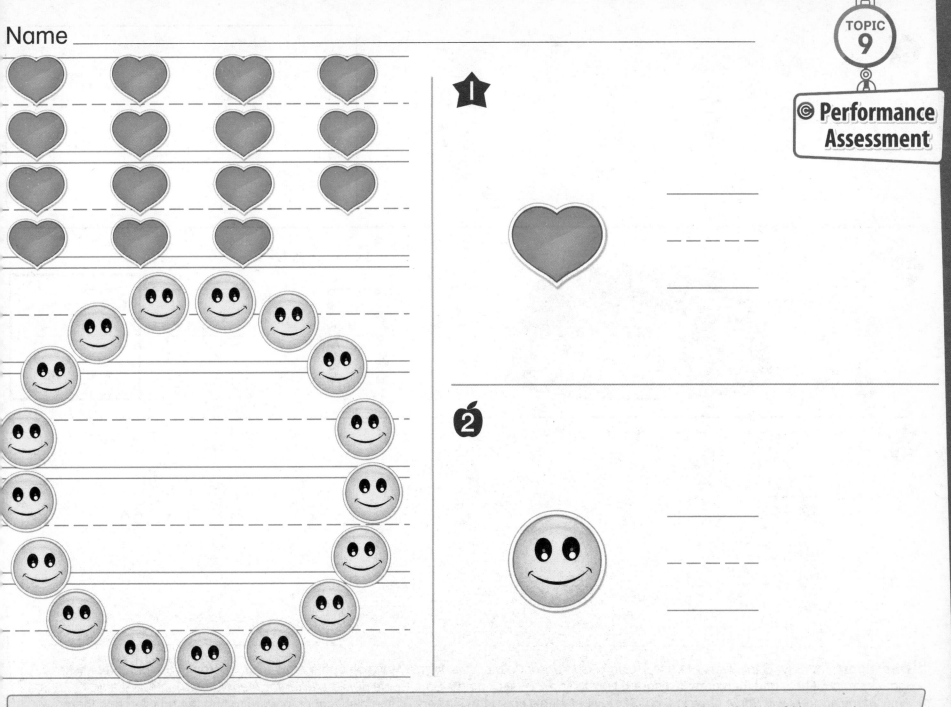

⭐ 1

_____
- - - - - - - -
_____

🍎 2

_____
- - - - - - - -
_____

Directions **Sadie's Stickers** Say: *Sadie puts many stickers in her notebook. How many of each type of sticker is there?* Have students: ⭐ count the number of heart stickers, and then write the number to tell how many; 2 count the number of smiley face stickers, and then write the number to tell how many.

3

4

5

16   17   18   19   20

Directions ❸ Say: *Sadie wants to use 14 stickers to decorate a picture frame.* Have students draw a circle around the group of stickers that she should use, and then draw a different way to show 14 stickers. ❹ Say: *Sadie gets a sticker for feeding her dog every day. How many stickers will Sadie have in 2 days?* Have students count the stickers on the dish, count forward to find the answer, and then write each number they counted. ✋ Say: *Sadie puts some stickers on the front of a card. She puts 1 or more stickers on the back of a card.* Have students count the stickers she put on the front of the card, and then draw a circle around the numbers that show how many stickers there could be in all. Have students explain their answer.

© Pearson Education, Inc. K   **Topic 9** | Performance Assessment

Compose and Decompose Numbers 11 to 19

Essential Question: How can composing and decomposing numbers from 11 to 19 into ten ones and some further ones help you understand place value?

Digital Resources

Solve Learn Glossary

Tools Assessment Help Games

A desert

Sunlight causes water to evaporate faster.

Math and Science Project: Sunlight and Earth's Surface

Directions Read the character speech bubbles to students. **Find Out!** Have students find out how sunlight affects Earth's surface. Say: *Talk to friends and relatives about sunlight and how it affects Earth.* **Journal: Make a Poster** Have students make a poster that shows 3 things sunlight does for Earth. Have them draw a sun with 16 rays. Then have them write an equation for parts of 16.

Name _____

⭐ Review What You Know

1

2

3

4

_____

- - - - - - -

_____

5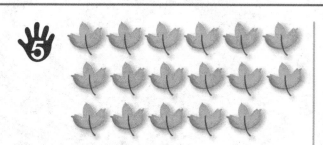

_____

- - - - - - -

6

_____

- - - - - - -

Directions Have students: **1** draw a circle around the group with 16; **2** draw a circle around the group with 20; **3** draw a circle around the group that is less than the other group; **4**–**6** count the leaves, and then write the number to tell how many.

© Pearson Education, Inc. K   **Topic 10**

My Word Cards

Directions Have students cut out the vocabulary cards. Read the front of the card, and then ask them to explain what the word or phrase means.

A-Z
Glossary

How many more?

Directions Review the definitions and have students study the cards. Extend learning by having students draw pictures for each word on a separate piece of paper.

13

Point to the 3 counters below the ten-frame.
Say: *13 is 10 and* **how many more**? *3 more.*

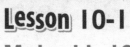
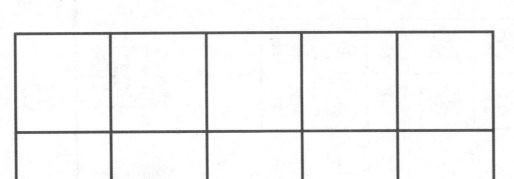

$$10 + \underline{\hspace{2cm}} = \underline{\hspace{2cm}}$$

I can ...
use drawings and equations to make the numbers 11, 12, and 13.

© Content Standards
K.NBT.A.1
Mathematical Practices
MP.2, MP.4, MP.5, MP.7

Directions Say: *Use counters to fill the ten-frame. Put 1, 2, or 3 counters outside of the ten-frame. Draw all of the counters. What equation can you write to tell how many counters there are in all?*

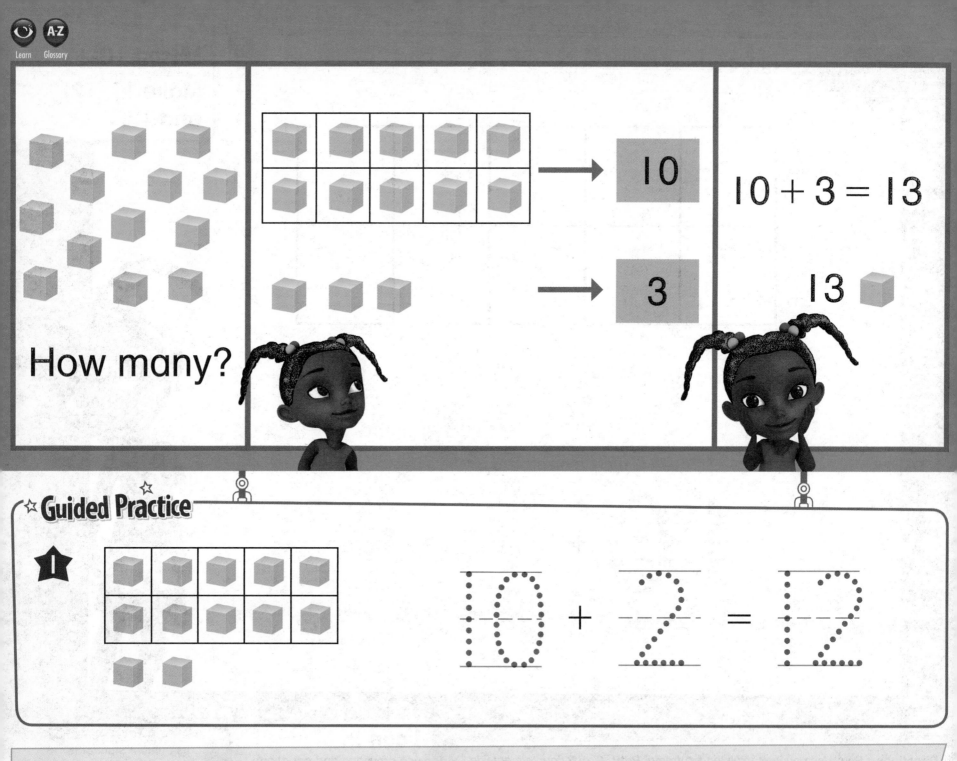

How many?

$$10 + 3 = 13$$

☆ Guided Practice

★ 1

$$10 + 2 = 12$$

Directions ★ Have students write an equation to match the number of blocks shown. Then have them tell how the picture and equation show 10 ones and some more ones.

© Pearson Education, Inc. K

Name _____

2

_____ _____

– – – – – + – – – – = – – – – –

_____ _____

3

_____ _____

– – – – – + – – – – = – – – – –

_____ _____

4

5

10 + 2 = 12   10 + 3 = 13

Directions Have students: **2** and **3** write an equation to match the number of blocks shown. Then have them tell how the picture and equation show 10 ones and some more ones; **4** and **5** draw blocks to match the equation. Then have them tell how the picture and equation show 10 ones and some more ones.

Tools   Assessment

_____ _____

- - - - - $+$ - - - - - $=$ - - - - -

_____ _____

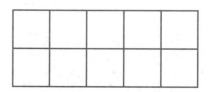

_____ _____

- - - - - $+$ - - - - - $=$ - - - - -

_____ _____

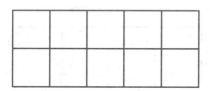

$10 + $ - - - - - $ = 12$

$13 = 10 + $ - - - - -

© Pearson Education, Inc. K

Name _____

Another Look!

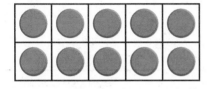

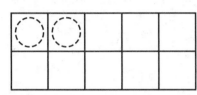

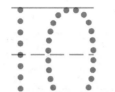  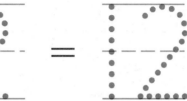

$$10 + 2 = 12$$

HOME ACTIVITY Have your child use pennies to model and explain how to make 11, 12, and 13 with 10 ones and some more ones.

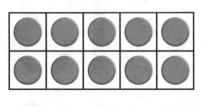

_____ + _____ = _____

Directions Say: *You can use counters and a double ten-frame to show 12 as 10 ones and some more ones. Fill the first ten-frame with 10 counters. Then draw more counters to make 12, and write an equation to match the picture.* ★ *Have students draw counters to make 13 and write an equation to match the picture. Then have them tell how the picture and equation show 10 ones and some more ones.*

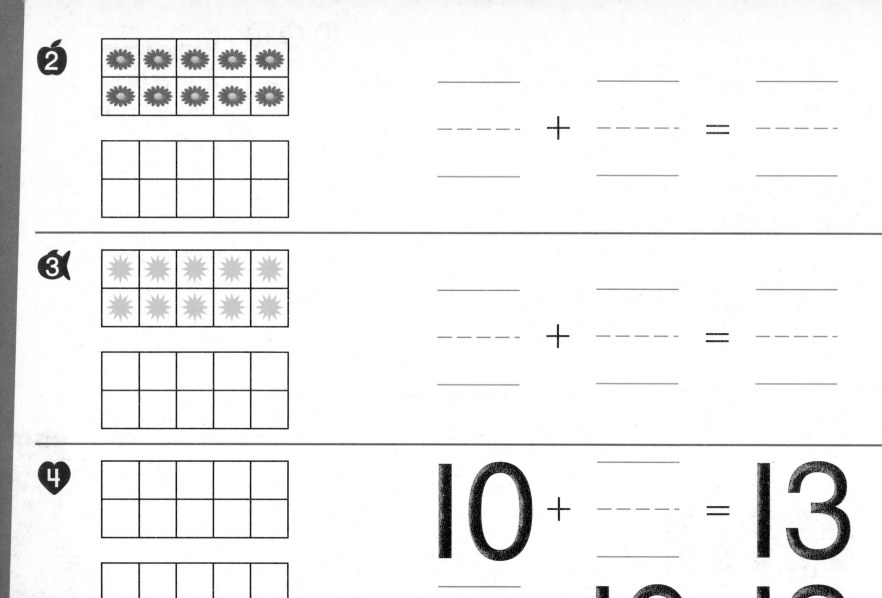

2

_____ + _____ = _____

_____ _____ _____

3

_____ + _____ = _____

_____ _____ _____

4

$10 + \text{\_\_\_\_} = 13$

$\text{\_\_\_\_} + 10 = 13$

© Pearson Education, Inc. K

$$\_\_\_ + \_\_\_ = 15$$

I can ...
make the numbers 14, 15, and 16.

© Content Standards
K.NBT.A.1
Mathematical Practices
MP.2, MP.3, MP.4, MP.7

Directions Say: *Put 15 counters in the double ten-frame to show 10 ones and some more ones. Then complete the equation to match the counters.*

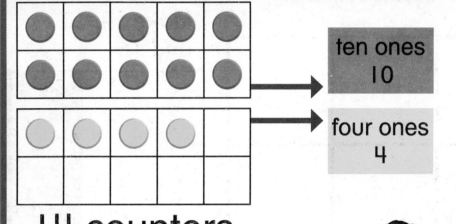

ten ones
10

four ones
4

14 counters

10 + 4 = 14

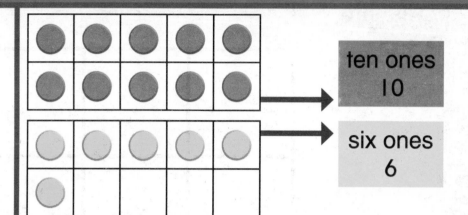

ten ones
10

six ones
6

16 counters

10 + 6 = 16

☆ Guided Practice

⭐ **1**

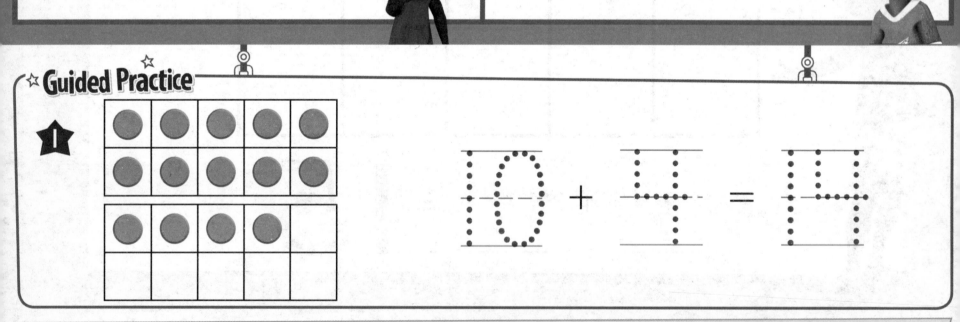

$$10 + 4 = 14$$

Directions ⭐ Have students write an equation to match the counters. Then have them tell how the picture and equation show 10 ones and some more ones.

574 five hundred seventy-four © Pearson Education, Inc. K **Topic 10 | Lesson 2**

2

_____   _____   _____

- - - - - **+** - - - - - **=** - - - - -

_____   _____   _____

3

_____   _____   _____

- - - - - **+** - - - - - **=** - - - - -

_____   _____   _____

4

10 + 4 = 14

5

10 + 5 = 15

Directions Have students: **2**–**3** write an equation to match the counters. Then have them tell how the picture and equation show 10 ones and some more ones; **4**–**5** draw counters to match the equation. Then have them tell how the picture and equation show 10 ones and some more ones.

6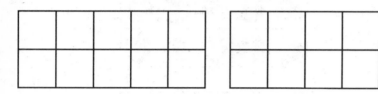

___ ___

- - - + - - - = - - -

___

7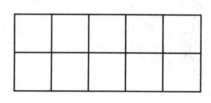

___ ___

- - - + - - - = - - -

___

8

___ ___

- - - + - - - = - - -

___

9

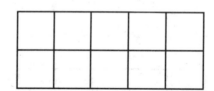

16 = 10 + - - -

___

Directions Have students: **6** draw counters and write an equation to show how to make 16. Then have them tell how the picture and equation show 10 ones and some more ones; **7** draw counters and write an equation to show how to make 14. Then have them tell how the picture and equation show 10 ones and some more ones. **8 Number Sense** Have students write an equation to show 15 as 10 ones and some more ones. **9 Higher Order Thinking** Have students draw counters to find the missing number in the equation. Then have them tell how the picture and equation show 10 ones and some more ones.

Name _____

Another Look!

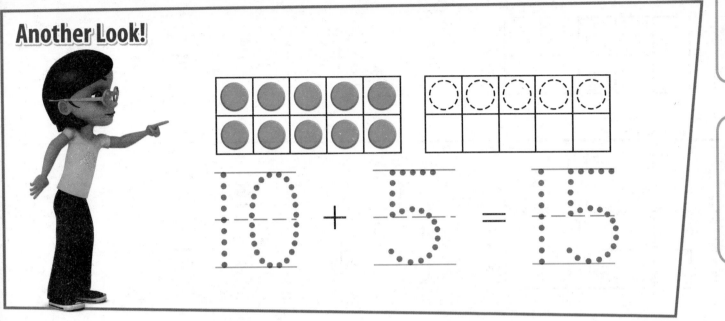

$$10 + 5 = 15$$

HOME ACTIVITY Have your child model the number 14 by drawing a big circle with 10 Xs inside the circle and 4 Xs outside the circle. Repeat with the numbers 15 and 16.

1 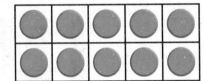 $\_\_\_ + \_\_\_ = \_\_\_$

2 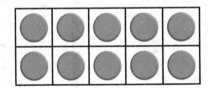 $\_\_\_ + \_\_\_ = \_\_\_$

Directions Say: *Finish drawing counters in the ten-frame to make 15. Then write an equation to match the picture. The picture and equation show one way to make 15 with 10 ones and some more ones.* Have students: **1** draw counters to make 14, and write an equation to match the picture. Then have them tell how the picture and equation show 10 ones and some more ones; **2** draw counters to make 16 and write an equation to match the picture. Then have them tell how the picture and equation show 10 ones and some more ones.

Topic 10 | Lesson 2   Digital Resources at PearsonRealize.com   five hundred seventy-seven **577**

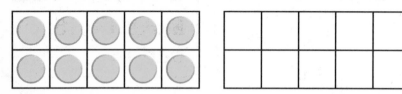

$$\_\ \_\ \_ \ + \ \_\ \_\ \_ \ = \ \_\ \_\ \_$$

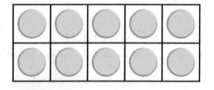

$$\_\ \_\ \_ \ + \ \_\ \_\ \_ \ = \ \_\ \_\ \_$$

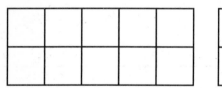

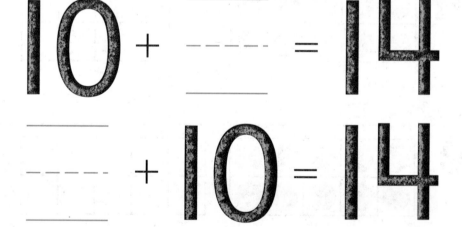

$$10 + \_\ \_\ \_ = 14$$

$$\_\ \_\ \_ + 10 = 14$$

Name _____

$\underline{\hspace{3cm}}$

$\underline{\hspace{2cm}} + \underline{\hspace{2cm}} = \underline{\hspace{2cm}}$

Directions Say: *Jada made 10 prizes for the school carnival. She makes 8 more. Use counters to show how many prizes Jada made in all. Then write an equation to match the counters, and tell how the counters and equation show 10 ones and some more ones.*

I can ...
make the numbers 17, 18, and 19.

© **Content Standards**
K.NBT.A.1
Mathematical Practices
MP.1, MP.2, MP.4, MP.7

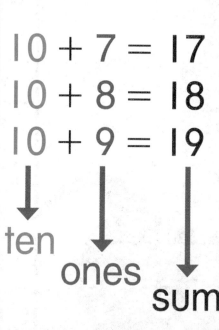

$$10 + 7 = 17$$
$$10 + 8 = 18$$
$$10 + 9 = 19$$

ten ones sum

$$10 + 7 = 17$$

$$10 + 8 = 18$$

$$10 + 9 = 19$$

☆ Guided Practice

 1

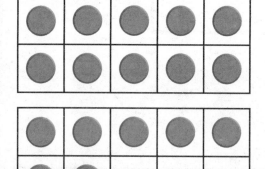

$$10 + 7 = 17$$

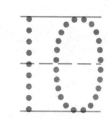

Directions ⬆ Have students complete the equation to match the counters. Then have them tell how the picture and equation show 10 ones and some more ones.

© Pearson Education, Inc. K

Topic 10 | Lesson 3

Name _____

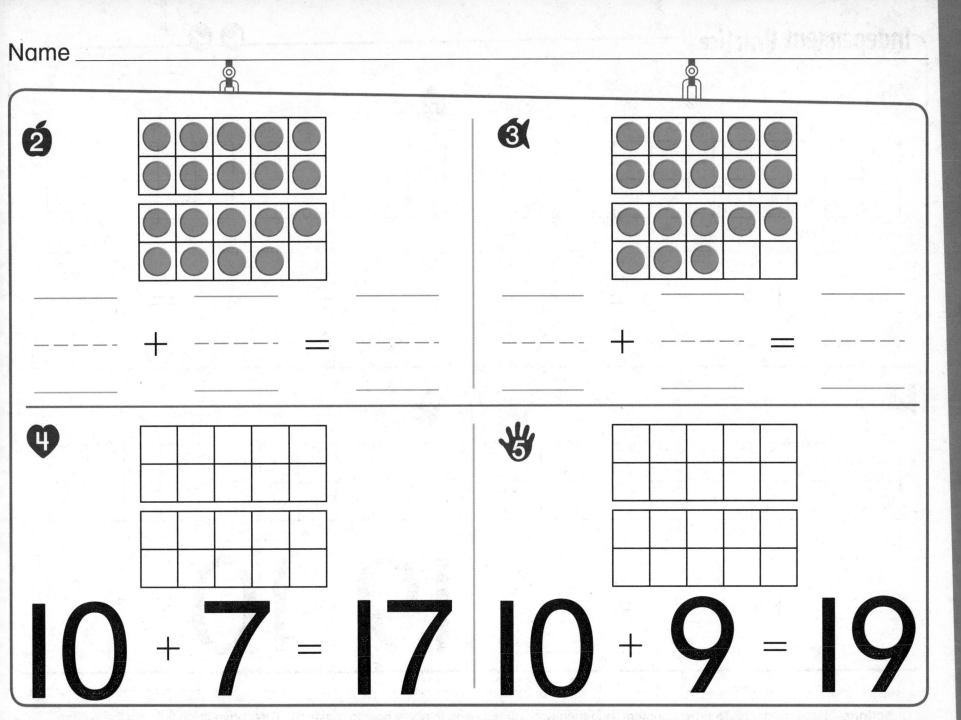

2 _____ _____ _____
     _ _ _ _   +   _ _ _ _   =   _ _ _ _
     _____   _____

3 _____ _____ _____
     _ _ _ _   +   _ _ _ _   =   _ _ _ _
     _____   _____

4 10 + 7 = 17

5 10 + 9 = 19

Directions Have students: **2** and **3** write an equation to match the counters. Then have them tell how the picture and equation show 10 ones and some more ones; **4** and **5** draw counters to match the equation. Then have them tell how the picture and equation show 10 ones and some more ones.

Topic 10 | Lesson 3   five hundred eighty-one   **581**

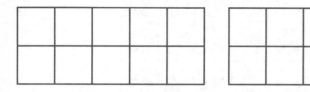

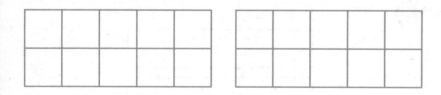

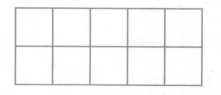

6

_____   _____

_ _ _ _ _ _ + _ _ _ _ _ _ = _ _ _ _ _ _

_____

7

_____   _____

_ _ _ _ _ _ + _ _ _ _ _ _ = _ _ _ _ _ _

_____

8

_____   _____

_____ + _____ = _____

_____

9

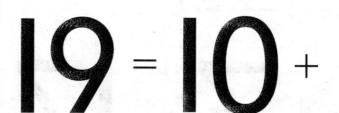

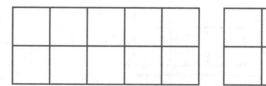

19 = 10 + _____

Directions Have students: 6 draw counters, and then write an equation to show how to make 18. Then have them tell how the picture and equation show 10 ones and some more ones; 7 draw counters, and then write an equation to show how to make 19. Then have them tell how the picture and equation show 10 ones and some more ones; 8 draw counters, and then write an equation to show how to make 17. Then have them tell how the picture and equation show 10 ones and some more ones. 9 **Higher Order Thinking** Have students draw counters to find the missing number in the equation. Then have them tell how the picture and equation show 10 ones and some more ones.

Topic 10 | Lesson 3

Name _____

 Help Tools Games

Another Look!

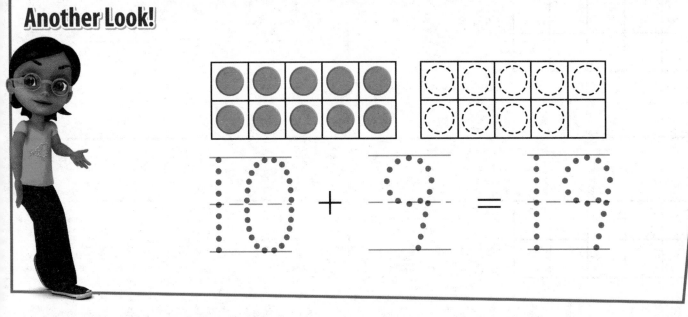

HOME ACTIVITY Place 10 marbles or other small objects in a bowl. In a second bowl, have your child count on from 10 while adding objects until there are 17 objects in all. Repeat with 19 and then 18 objects in all.

 1

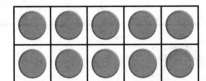 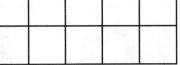 

 2

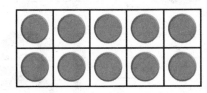 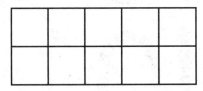    

Directions Say: *Finish drawing counters in the ten-frame to show how to make 19. Then write an equation to match the picture. The picture and equation show how to make 19 with 10 ones and some more ones.* Have students: **1** draw counters, and then write the equation to show how to make 17. Then have them tell how the picture and equation show 10 ones and some more ones; **2** draw counters to show how to make 18, and then write an equation to match the picture. Then have them tell how the picture and equation show 10 ones and some more ones.

3

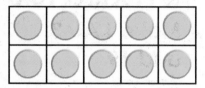 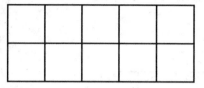

_____ + _____ = ____

4

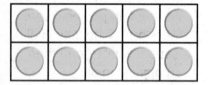 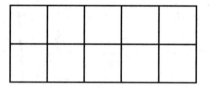

_____ + _____ = ____

5

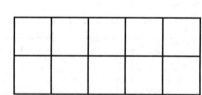

$18 = 10 + \underline{\quad\quad}$

$10 + \underline{\quad\quad} = 18$

© Pearson Education, Inc. K

Solve & Share

Name _____

Solve

Lesson 10-4
**Find Parts of
11, 12, and 13**

$$13 = \underline{} + \underline{}$$

Directions Say: *13 students wait for the train. There are only 10 seats in each train car. How many students will have to ride in a second car? Use counters to show your work. Then tell how the counters and equation show 10 ones and some more ones.*

I can ...
find parts of the numbers 11, 12, and 13.

© **Content Standards**
K.NBT.A.1
Mathematical Practices
MP.4, MP.6, MP.7, MP.8

Learn Glossary

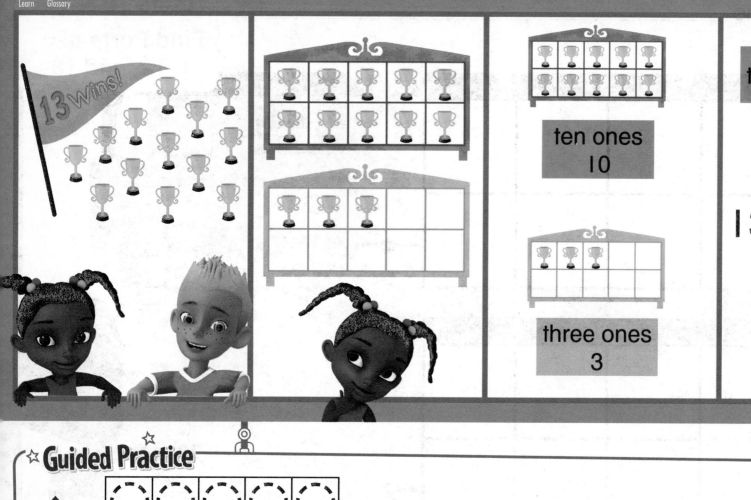

13 wins!

ten ones
10

three ones
3

ten ones   three ones

$13 = 10 + 3$

☆ Guided Practice

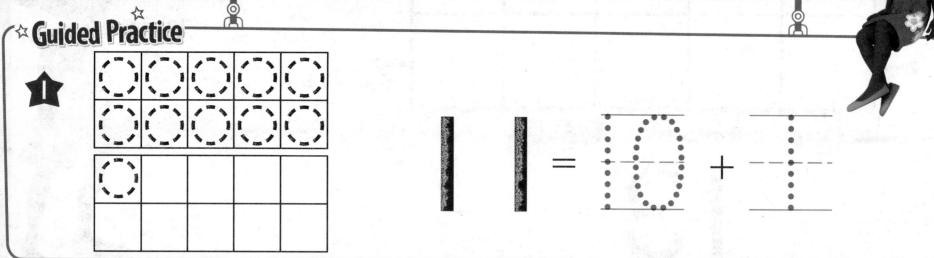

1

$11 = 10 + 1$

Directions ☆ Have students use counters to show 11, draw them in the double ten-frame, and complete the equation to match the picture. Then have them tell how the picture and equation show 10 ones and some more ones.

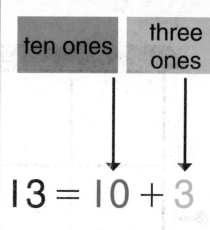

586 five hundred eighty-six   © Pearson Education, Inc. K   **Topic 10** | Lesson 4

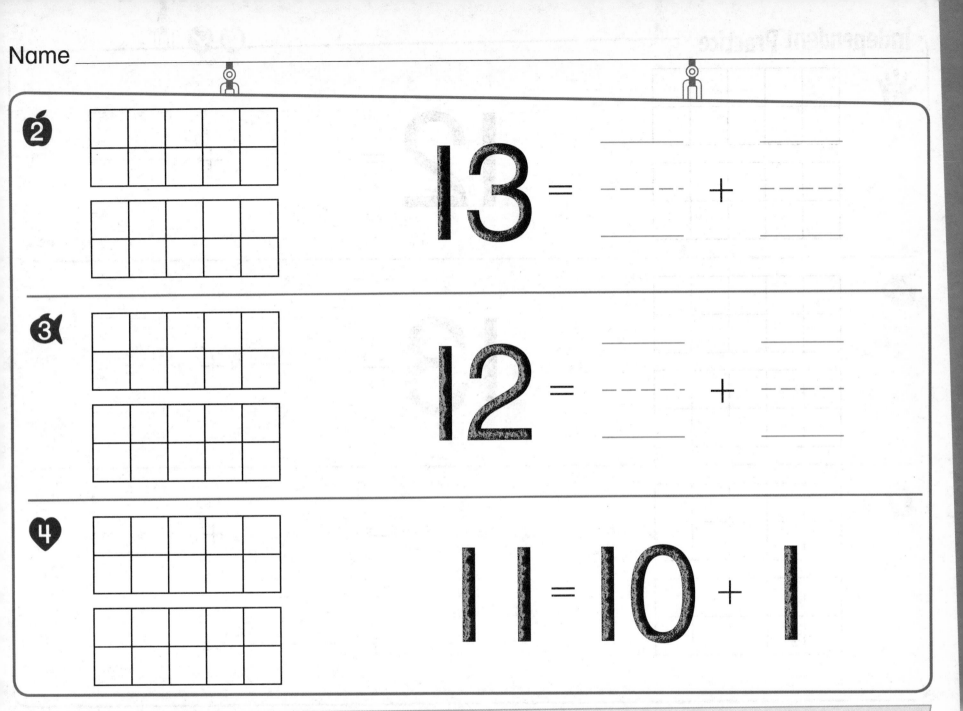

2 $13 = \underline{\hspace{2cm}} + \underline{\hspace{2cm}}$

3 $12 = \underline{\hspace{2cm}} + \underline{\hspace{2cm}}$

4 $11 = 10 + 1$

Directions Have students: **2** use counters to show 13, draw them in the double ten-frame, and complete the equation to match the picture. Then have them tell how the picture and equation show 10 ones and some more ones; **3** use counters to show 12, draw them in the double ten-frame, and complete the equation to match the picture. Then have them tell how the picture and equation show 10 ones and some more ones; **4** draw counters to match the equation. Then have them tell how the picture and equation show 10 ones and some more ones.

Independent Practice

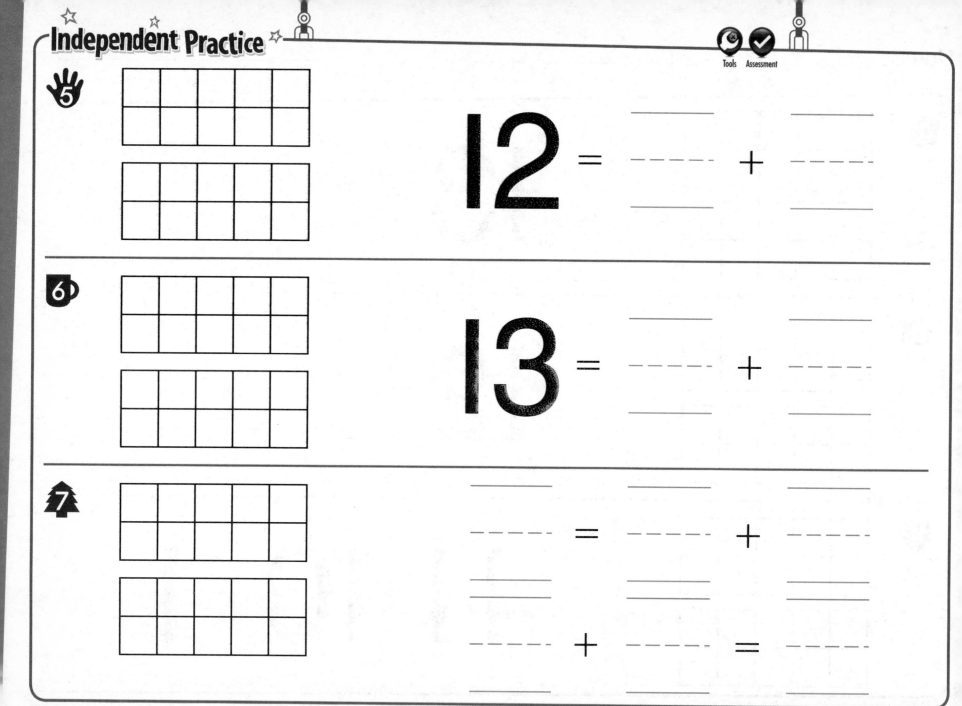

5

$$12 = \underline{\hspace{2cm}} + \underline{\hspace{2cm}}$$

6

$$13 = \underline{\hspace{2cm}} + \underline{\hspace{2cm}}$$

7

$$\underline{\hspace{2cm}} = \underline{\hspace{2cm}} + \underline{\hspace{2cm}}$$

$$\underline{\hspace{2cm}} + \underline{\hspace{2cm}} = \underline{\hspace{2cm}}$$

Directions Have students: **5** draw counters to make 12, and complete the equation to match the picture. Then have them tell how the picture and equation show 10 ones and some more ones; **6** draw counters to make 13, and complete the equation to match the picture. Then have them tell how the picture and equation show 10 ones and some more ones. **7 Higher Order Thinking** Have students draw counters to show 11 and write two equations to match the picture. Then have them tell how the picture and equations show 10 ones and some more ones.

Name _____

Another Look!

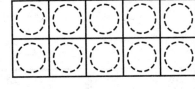
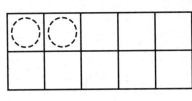

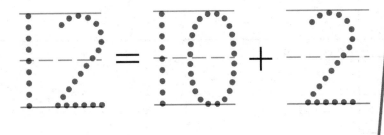

$$12 = 10 + 2$$

HOME ACTIVITY Have your child sort a group of 12 pencils into one group of 10 pencils and one group of 2 pencils. Discuss how many pencils are in each group and how many pencils there are in all. Repeat with 13 pencils and 11 pencils.

 1

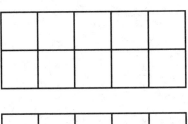

_____ = _____ + _____

Directions Say: *Draw counters in the double ten-frame to show 12 and write an equation to match the picture. The picture and equation show 10 ones and some more ones.* ⭐ Have students draw counters to show 11 and write an equation to match the picture. Then have them tell how the picture and equation show 10 ones and some more ones.

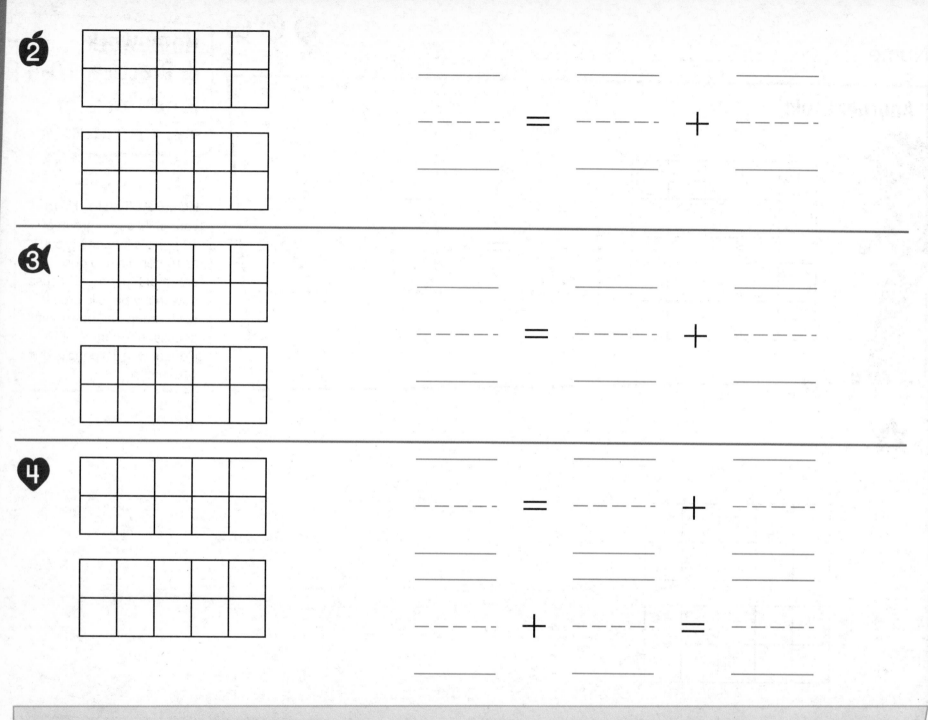

2 _____ = _____ + _____

_____

3 _____ = _____ + _____

_____

4 _____ = _____ + _____

_____ + _____ = _____

Solve & Share

Name _____

Solve

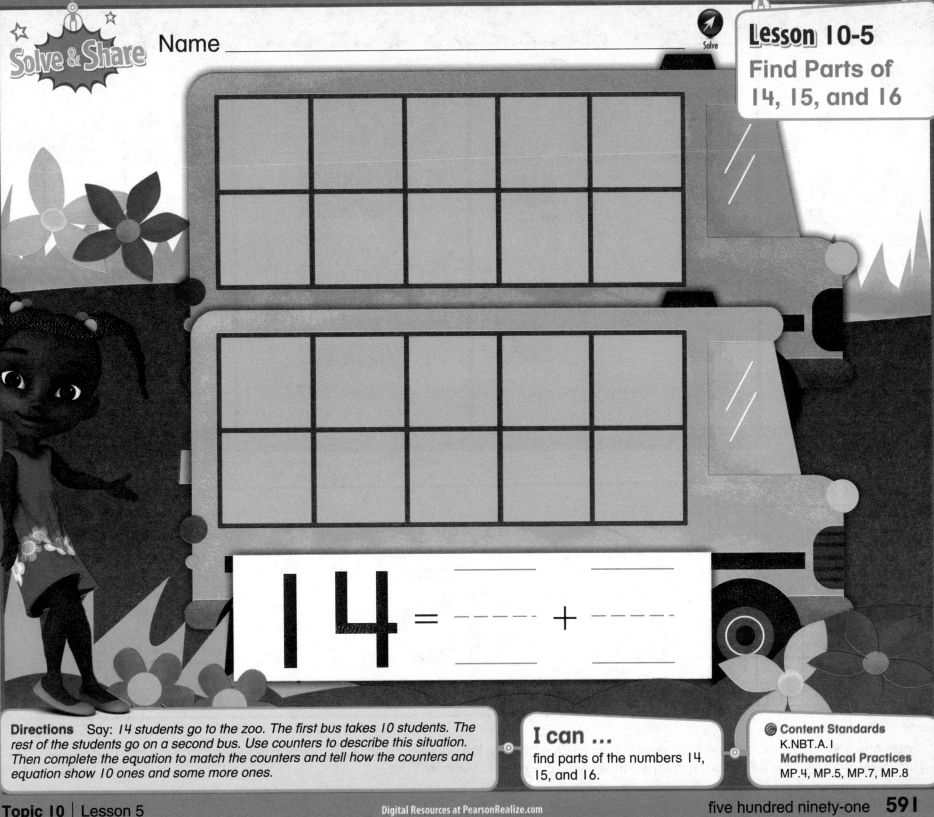

$$14 = \underline{\hspace{2cm}} + \underline{\hspace{2cm}}$$

Directions Say: *14 students go to the zoo. The first bus takes 10 students. The rest of the students go on a second bus. Use counters to describe this situation. Then complete the equation to match the counters and tell how the counters and equation show 10 ones and some more ones.*

I can ...
find parts of the numbers 14, 15, and 16.

© **Content Standards**
K.NBT.A.1
Mathematical Practices
MP.4, MP.5, MP.7, MP.8

Topic 10 | Lesson 5

Digital Resources at PearsonRealize.com

five hundred ninety-one **591**

16

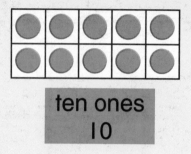

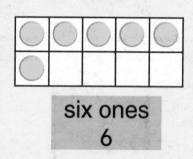

ten ones
10

six ones
6

ten ones   six ones

$16 = 10 + 6$

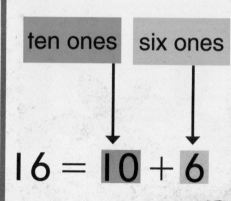

☆ Guided Practice

1

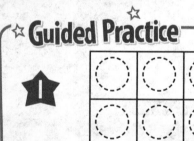

$$15 = 10 + 5$$

Directions 🟊 Have students use counters to show 15, draw them in the double ten-frame, and complete the equation to match the picture. Then have them tell how the picture and equation show 10 ones and some more ones.

592 five hundred ninety-two

Topic 10 | Lesson 5

2

14 = _ _ _ _ + _ _ _ _

3

16 = _ _ _ _ + _ _ _ _

4

15 = 10 + 5

Directions Have students: **2** use counters to show 14, draw them in the double ten-frame, and complete the equation to match the picture. Then have them tell how the picture and equation show 10 ones and some more ones; **3** use counters to show 16, draw them in the double ten-frame, and complete the equation to match the picture. Then have them tell how the picture and equation show 10 ones and some more ones; **4** draw counters to match the equation. Then have them tell how the picture and equation show 10 ones and some more ones.

Tools Assessment

5

$$16 = 10 + 6$$

6

$$14 = 10 + 4$$

7

_____ = _ _ _ _ + _____

_ _ _ _ = _ _ _ _ + _ _ _ _

_____ _____

_ _ _ _ + _ _ _ _ = _ _ _ _

Directions ✋ and ☕ Have students draw counters to match the equation. Then have them tell how the picture and equation show 10 ones and some more ones. 🌲 **Higher Order Thinking** Have students use counters to show 16, draw them in the double ten-frame, and complete two equations to match the picture. Then have them tell how the picture and equations show 10 ones and some more ones.

Name _____

Another Look!

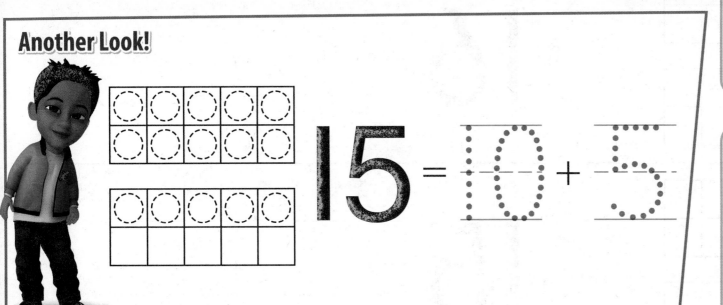

$$15 = 10 + 5$$

HOME ACTIVITY Draw 14 boxes, and then shade 10 of them. Have your child tell how many boxes there are in all. Then have your child tell how many boxes are shaded and how many boxes are NOT shaded. Repeat with 16 boxes and 15 boxes.

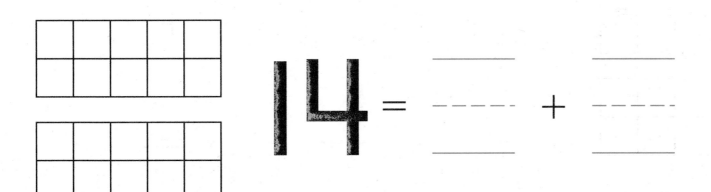

$$14 = \underline{\quad} + \underline{\quad}$$

Directions Say: *Draw counters in the double ten-frame to show 15 and complete the equation to match the picture. The picture and equation show 10 ones and some more ones.* ⭐ Have students draw counters to show 14 and complete the equation to match the picture. Then have them tell how the picture and equation show 10 ones and some more ones.

Topic 10 | Lesson 5   Digital Resources at PearsonRealize.com   five hundred ninety-five **595**

2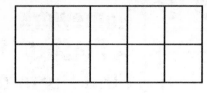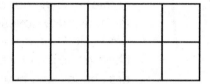

$16 = \underline{\hspace{2cm}} + \underline{\hspace{2cm}}$

3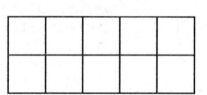

$15 = \underline{\hspace{2cm}} + \underline{\hspace{2cm}}$

4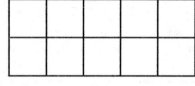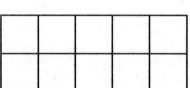

$\underline{\hspace{2cm}} = \underline{\hspace{2cm}} + \underline{\hspace{2cm}}$

$\underline{\hspace{2cm}} + \underline{\hspace{2cm}} = \underline{\hspace{2cm}}$

Directions Have students: **2** draw counters to show 16 and complete the equation to match the picture. Then have them tell how the picture and equation show 10 ones and some more ones; **3** draw counters to show 15 and complete the equation to match the picture. Then have them tell how the picture and equation show 10 ones and some more ones. **4 Higher Order Thinking** Have students draw counters to show 14 and write two equations to match the picture. Then have them tell how the picture and equations show 10 ones and some more ones.

© Pearson Education, Inc. K

Name _____

Directions Say: *How can these 18 boxes be split into ten ones and some more ones? Use 2 different color crayons to color the boxes to show your work. Then write an equation to match the picture.*

I can ...
Find parts of the numbers 17, 18, and 19.

© **Content Standards**
K.NBT.A.1
Mathematical Practices
MP.1, MP.4, MP.6, MP.8

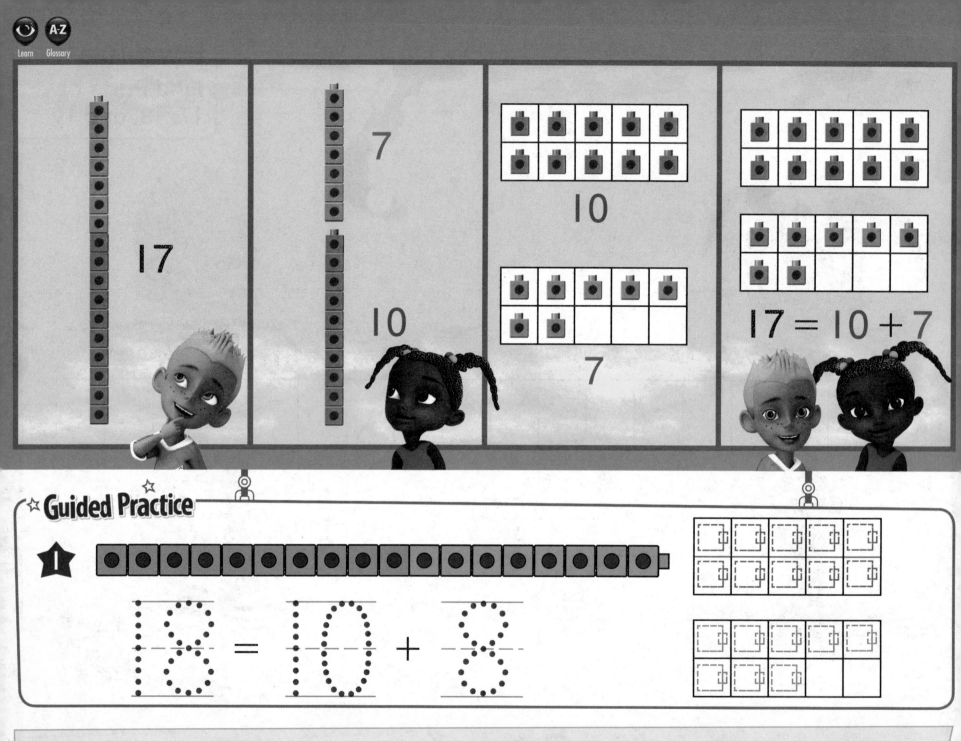

17

7

10

10

7

$17 = 10 + 7$

☆ Guided Practice

⭐ 1

$18 = 10 + 8$

Directions ⭐ Have students color 10 cubes blue to show 10 ones, and then draw 10 blue cubes in the top ten-frame. Have them color the remaining cubes in the train red to show more ones, count them, and then draw red cubes in the bottom ten-frame. Then have them write an equation to match the pictures.

598   five hundred ninety-eight   © Pearson Education, Inc. K   **Topic 10** | Lesson 6

Name

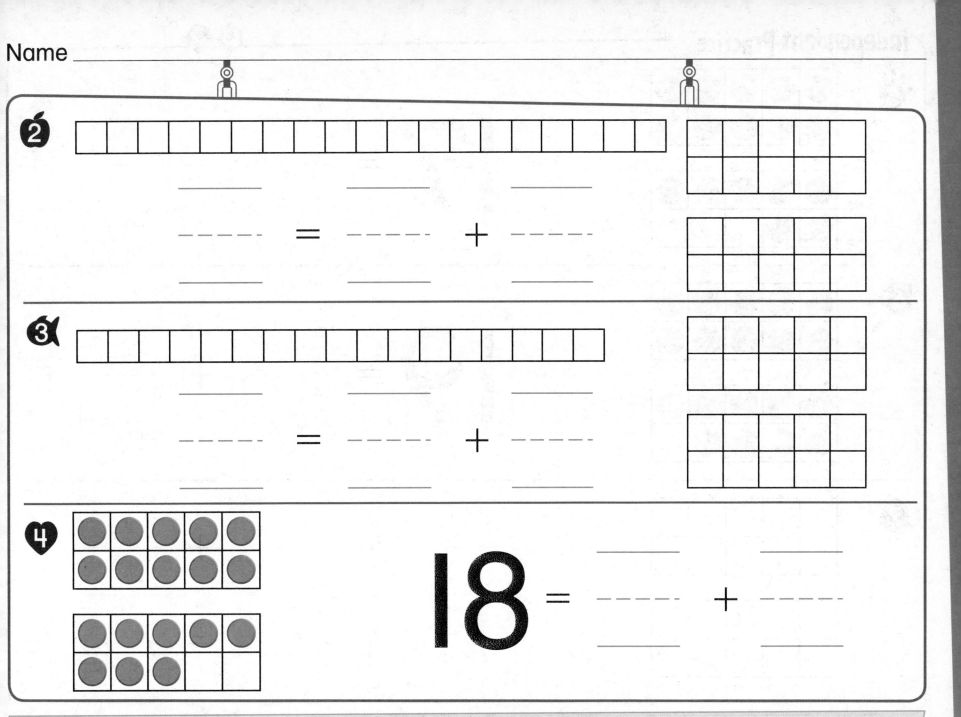

2

_____ = _____ + _____

3

_____ = _____ + _____

4

18 = _____ + _____

Directions Have students: **2** and **3** color 10 squares blue to show 10 ones, and then draw 10 blue squares in the top ten-frame. Have them color the remaining cubes in the train red to show more ones, count them, and then draw red squares in the bottom ten-frame. Then have them write an equation to match the pictures; **4** complete the equation to match the counters. Then have them tell how the picture and equation show 10 ones and some more ones.

Independent Practice

5

$17 =$ _____ $+$ _____

6

$19 =$ _____ $+$ _____

7

_____ $=$ _____ $+$ _____

_____ $+$ _____ $=$ _____

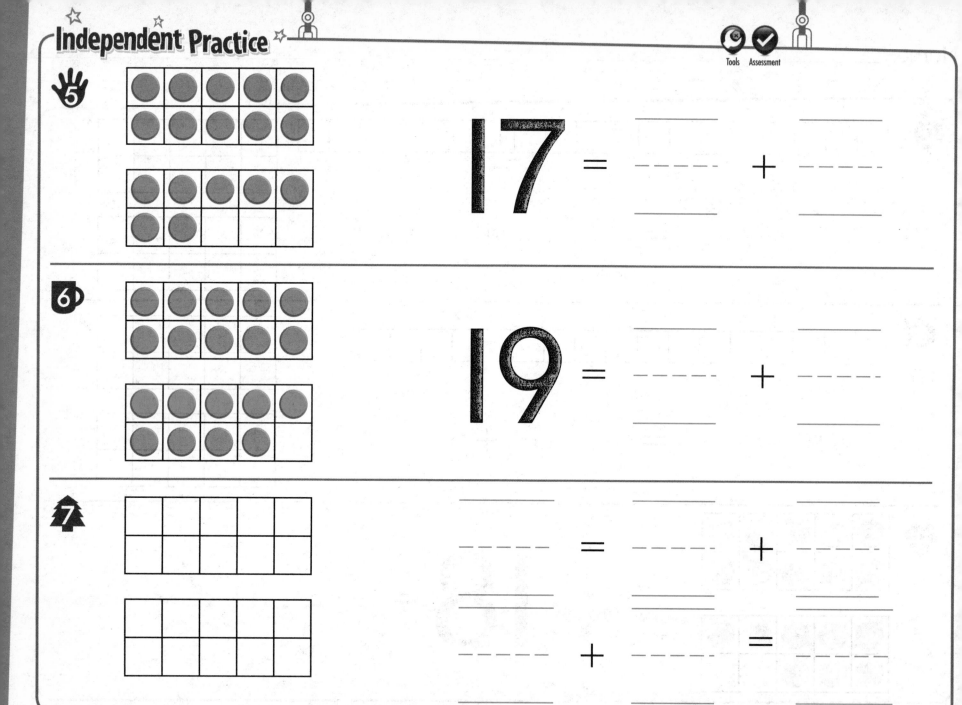

Directions ✋ and **6** Have students complete the equation to match the counters. Then have them tell how the picture and equation show 10 ones and some more ones. **7 Higher Order Thinking** Have students use counters to show 18, draw them in the double ten-frame, and write two equations to match the picture. Then have them tell how the picture and equations show 10 ones and some more ones.

     Topic 10 | Lesson 6

Name _____

Another Look!

$$18 = 10 + 8$$

HOME ACTIVITY Have your child sort a group of 18 objects into a group of 10 and a group of 8. Discuss how many objects there are in each group and how many there are in all. Repeat with 17 objects and 19 objects.

 1

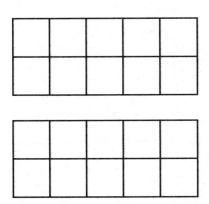

$$17 = \underline{} + \underline{}$$

Directions Say: *Draw counters to show 18, and then complete the equation to match. How does the picture and equation show 10 ones and some more ones?* ⭐ Have students draw counters to show 17, and then complete the equation to match the picture. Then have them tell how the picture and equation show 10 ones and some more ones.

2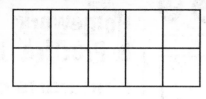

$$19 = \underline{\hspace{2cm}} + \underline{\hspace{2cm}}$$

3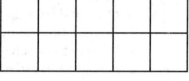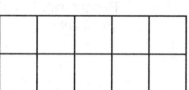

$$18 = \underline{\hspace{2cm}} + \underline{\hspace{2cm}}$$

4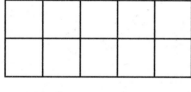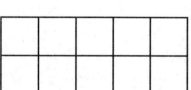

$$\underline{\hspace{2cm}} = \underline{\hspace{2cm}} + \underline{\hspace{2cm}}$$

$$\underline{\hspace{2cm}} + \underline{\hspace{2cm}} = \underline{\hspace{2cm}}$$

Directions Have students: **2** draw counters to show 19, and then complete the equation to match the picture. Then have them tell how the picture and equation show 10 ones and some more ones; **3** draw counters to show 18, and then complete the equation to match the picture. Then have them tell how the picture and equation show 10 ones and some more ones. **4 Higher Order Thinking** draw counters to show 17, and then write two equations to match the picture. Then have them tell how the picture and equations show 10 ones and some more ones.

Solve & Share

Directions Say: *Put some counters in the red five-frame. Use a red crayon and write the number that tells how many counters are in the red frame. Put the same number of counters in the blue five-frame. Use a blue crayon and write the number that tells how many counters are in the blue frames. Show the numbers to a partner. What patterns do you see?*

I can ...
use patterns to make and find the parts of numbers to 19.

© **Mathematical Practices**
MP.7 Also MP.3, MP.4, MP.5, MP.8
Content Standards
K.NBT.A.1

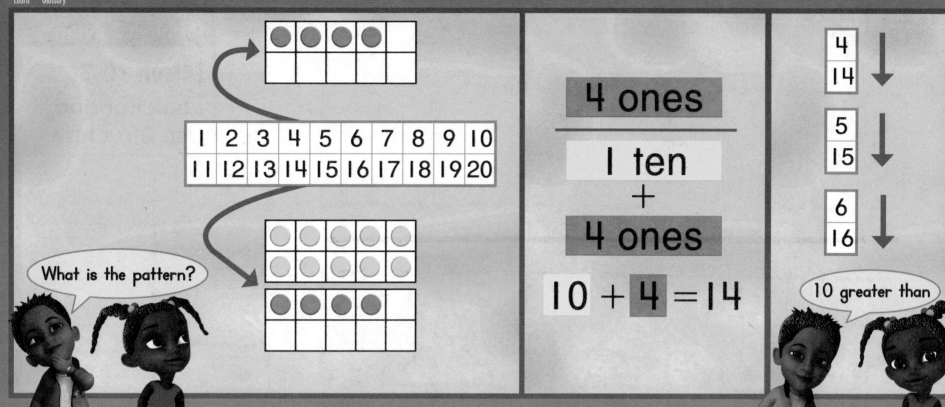

What is the pattern?

4 ones
_____
1 ten
+
4 ones

$10 + 4 = 14$

10 greater than

☆ Guided Practice

1

1	2	3	4	5	6	7	8	9	10
11	12	13	14	15	16	17	18	19	20

$$10 + 3 = 13$$

Directions ★ Have students find the number with the blue box around it, and then color the number that is 10 greater than the number in the blue box. Have them write an equation to match, and then tell how the equation shows 10 ones and some more ones. Then have students explain the pattern they made.

© Pearson Education, Inc. K

★ Independent Practice ★

 2

1	2	3	4	5	6	7	8	9	10
11	12	13	14	15	16	17	18	19	20

_____ + _____ = _____

 3

1	2	3	4	5	6	7	8	9	10
11	12	13	14	15	16	17	18	19	20

_____ + _____ = _____

 4

1	2	3	4	5	6	7	8	9	10
11	12	13	14	15	16	17	18	19	20

_____ + _____ = _____

 5

$10 + 1 = 11$ $10 + 2 = 12$

_____ + _____ = **13**

Directions Have students: **2**–**4** find the number with the blue box around it, and color the number that is 10 greater than the number in the blue box. Then have them write an equation to match, and then tell how the equation shows 10 ones and some more ones; **5** complete the equation to continue the pattern, and then explain the pattern they made.

Math Practices and Problem Solving

Performance Assessment

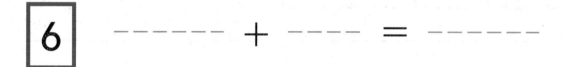

1	2	3	4	5	6	7	8	9	10
11	12	13	14	15	16	17	18	19	20

$$6 \quad \text{-----} + \text{-----} = \text{-----}$$

$$7 \quad \text{-----} + \text{-----} = \text{-----}$$

Directions Read the problem to students. Then have them use multiple math practices to solve the problem. Say: *Mr. Shepard's class will exchange cards at a holiday party. There are 16 students in the class. The store sells cards in packs of 10. Alex already has 6 cards. Marta already has 7 cards. How many cards will Alex and Marta have after they each buy one pack of cards?* ⑥ **MP.7 Use Structure** *How can the number chart help you solve the problem? Write the equations for the number of cards Alex and Marta will have.* ⑦ **MP.8 Generalize** *After you find the number of cards Alex will have, is it easier to find the number of cards Marta will have?* ⑧ **MP.3 Explain** *Tell a friend why your answers are correct. Then tell the friend about the patterns you see in the number chart and how the equations show 10 ones and some more ones.*

Name _____

Another Look!

9

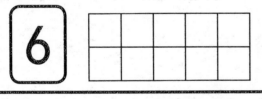

19

$10 + 9 = 19$

HOME ACTIVITY Take 11 pennies or other small household objects and arrange them in the following manner: two rows of 5 pennies, and a single penny underneath. Have your child write the equation that describes the number of pennies ($10 + 1 = 11$). Repeat for quantities of 12 pennies, 13 pennies, and so on, up to 19 pennies. Have your child explain the pattern in the equations that he or she has written.

6

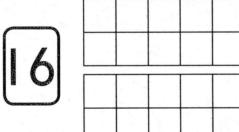

16

_____ + _____ = _____

Directions Say: *Read the numbers on the cards, and then draw counters in the top ten-frame to show 9 and in the bottom ten-frames to show 19. Write an equation to match the drawings in the ten-frames. Tell how the picture and the equation show 10 ones and some more ones.* ⭐ Have students read the numbers on the cards, and then draw counters in both the top and bottom ten-frames to show how many. Then have them write an equation to match the drawings in the ten-frames. Have students tell how the picture and the equation show 10 ones and some more ones.

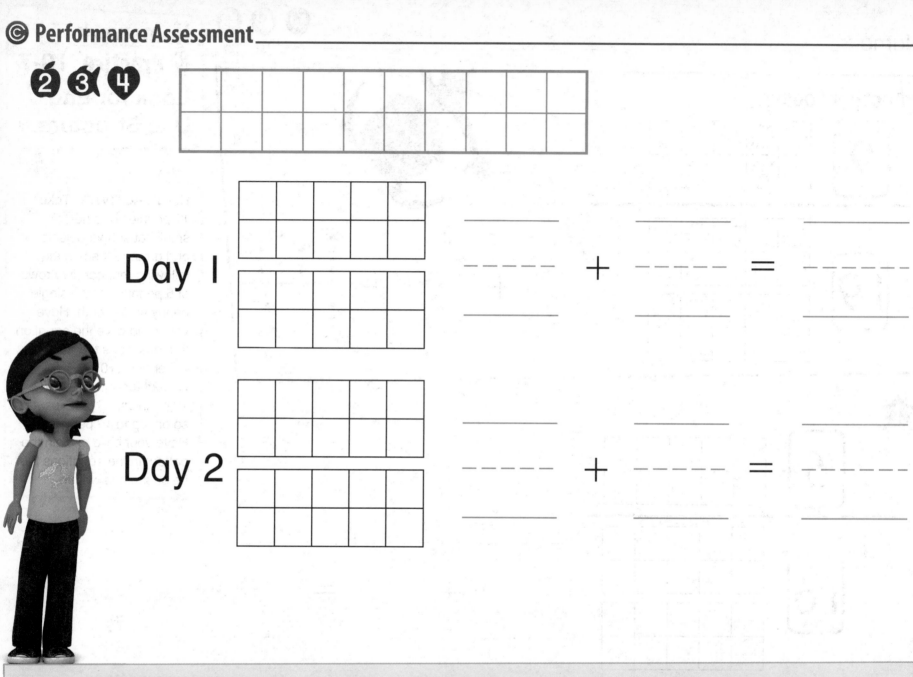

Day 1

Day 2

_____ + _____ = _____

_____ + _____ = _____

Directions Read the problem to students. Then have them use multiple math practices to solve the problem. Say: *Alex got a new tablet computer. It came loaded with 10 apps. Every day, Alex is allowed to upload 1 more app. How many apps will Alex have in two days?* ❷ **MP.4 Model** *Can a model help you solve the problem? Write the numbers in the number chart. Which numbers will help solve this problem?* ❸ **MP.5 Use Tools** *How can you use the ten-frames to help? Draw counters to show how many apps there will be on Alex's tablet for each day. Then write equations to help you see the pattern.* ❹ **MP.7 Use Structure** *How many apps will Alex have in three days? How did seeing a pattern help you solve the problem? Explain your answer.*

Find a Match   Name _____

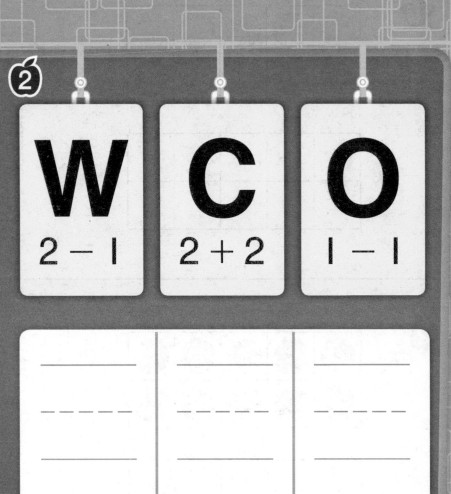

⭐1

O	G	D
2 + 3	4 − 2	5 − 2

②

W	C	O
2 − 1	2 + 2	1 − 1

4 − 1	4 + 1	1 + 1

1 + 3	0 + 0	5 − 4

Directions ⭐ and ② Have students find a partner. Have them point to a clue in the top row, and then solve the addition or subtraction problem. Then have them look at the clues in the bottom row to find a match, and then write the clue letter above the match. Have students find a match for every clue.

I can ...
add and subtract fluently within 5.

© Content Standard K.OA.A.5

1

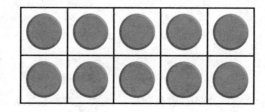

$$10 + \underline{\hspace{2cm}} = 15$$

2

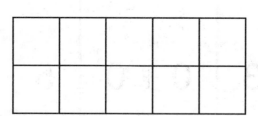

$$19 = 10 + \underline{\hspace{2cm}}$$

Directions **Understand Vocabulary** Have students: **1** complete the drawing and the equation to show **how many more** counters are needed to make 15; **2** complete the drawing and the equation to show **how many more** counters are needed to make 19.

610 six hundred ten

© Pearson Education, Inc. K

Topic 10 | Vocabulary Review

Set A _____

⭐ 1

$$10 + 1 = 11$$

_____   _____   _____

_ _ _ _ _ + _ _ _ _ _ = _ _ _ _ _ _

_____   _____

Set B _____

🍎 2

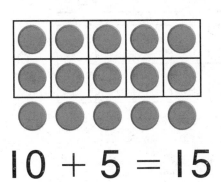

$$10 + 5 = 15$$

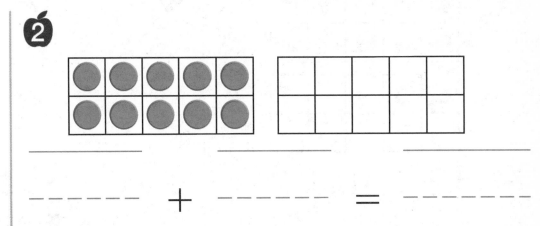

_____   _____   _____

_ _ _ _ _ + _ _ _ _ _ = _ _ _ _ _ _

_____   _____

Directions Have students: ⭐ write an equation to match the blocks. Then have them tell how the picture and equation show 10 ones and some more ones; 🍎 draw counters to show 16, and then write an equation to match the picture. Then tell how the picture and equation show 10 ones and some more ones.

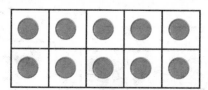

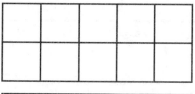

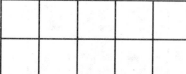

$$10 + 8 = 18$$

③

$$10 + 7 = 17$$

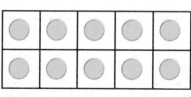

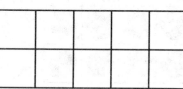

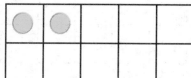

$$12 = 10 + 2$$

④

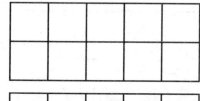

$$11 = \underline{\hspace{2cm}} + \underline{\hspace{2cm}}$$

Directions Have students: ③ draw counters to match the equation. Then have them tell how the picture and equation show 10 ones and some more ones; ④ draw counters to make 11, and then complete the equation to match the picture. Then have them tell how the picture and equation show 10 ones and some more ones.

Set E

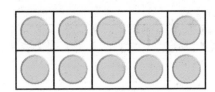

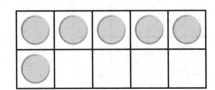

$$16 = 10 + 6$$

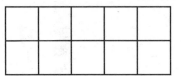

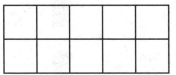

| 4 = - - - - - - + - - - - - - -

_____

Set F

1	2	3	4	5	6	7	8	9	10
11	12	13	14	15	16	17	18	19	20

6

1	2	3	4	5	6	7	8	9	10
11	12	13	14	15	16	17	18	19	20

- - - - - - - - - - - - - - - -

- - - - - - - + - - - - = - - - - - -

- - - - - - - - - - - - - - -

$$19 = 10 + 9$$

Directions Have students: ✋ use counters to show 14, draw them in the double ten-frame, and complete the equation to match the picture. Then have them tell how the picture and equation show 10 ones and some more ones; ☕ find the number with the blue box around it, and color the number that is 10 greater than the number in the blue box. Then have them write an equation to match, and then tell how the equation shows 10 ones and some more ones.

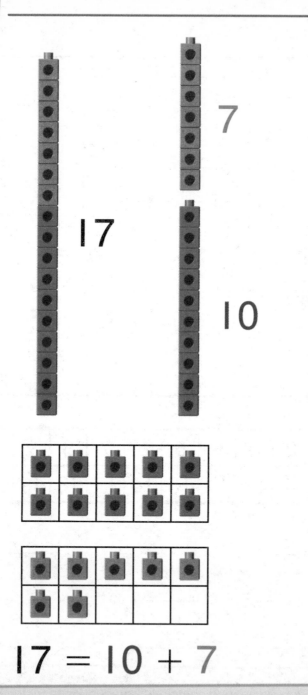

17

7

10

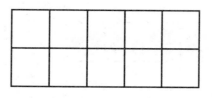

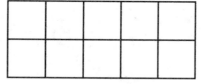

17 = 10 + 7

$$\_\_\_\_\_ = \_\_\_\_\_ + \_\_\_\_\_$$

Directions Have students: color 10 cubes blue in the train to show 10 ones, and then draw 10 blue cubes in the top ten-frame. Have them color the remaining cubes in the train red to show more ones, count them, and then draw the same number of red cubes in the bottom ten-frame. Then have them write an equation to match the pictures.

         Topic 10 | Reteaching

Name _____

1

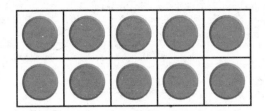

Ⓐ $16 = 10 + 6$

Ⓑ $15 = 10 + 5$

Ⓒ $14 = 10 + 4$

Ⓓ $13 = 10 + 3$

2

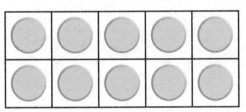

Ⓐ 10 and 6

Ⓑ 10 and 7

Ⓒ 10 and 8

Ⓓ 10 and 9

_____ + _____ = 18

3

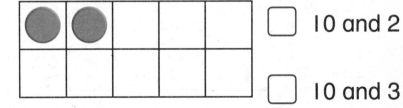

☐ 10 and 0

☐ 10 and 1

☐ 10 and 2

☐ 10 and 3

$12 =$ _____ + _____

Directions Have students mark the best answer. ⭐ Which equation matches the counters in the double ten-frame? ❷ Which numbers complete the equation and match the counters in the double ten-frame? ❸ Mark all the ways that could complete the equation.

1	2	3	4	5	6	7	8	9	10
11	12	13	14	15	16	17	18	19	20

_____   _____   _____

_ _ _ _ _ + _ _ _ _ _ = _ _ _ _ _

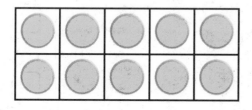
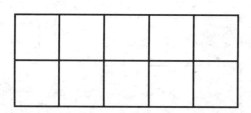

13 = _ _ _ _ _ + _ _ _ _ _

Directions Have students: ♥ find the number with the blue box around it, and then color the number that is 10 greater than the number in the blue box. Then have them write an equation to match; ✋ draw counters to make 13, and then complete the equation to match the picture.

© Pearson Education, Inc. K

Name _____

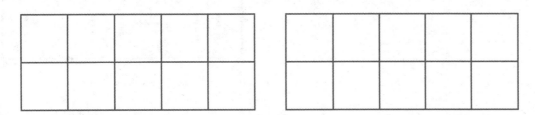

$$10 + 6 = 16$$

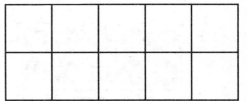

_____ _____ _____

_____ = _____ + _____

Directions Have students: 🍵 draw counters to match the equation; 🌲 color 10 cubes blue to show 10 ones, and then draw 10 blue cubes in the top ten-frame. Have them color the remaining cubes in the train red to show more ones, count them, and then draw the same number of red cubes in the bottom ten-frame. Then have them write an equation to match the pictures.

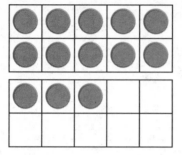

$$11 = 10 + 1$$

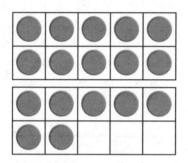

$$14 = 10 + 4$$

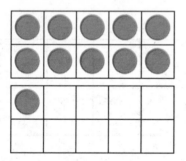

$$13 = 10 + 3$$

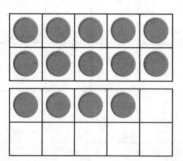

$$17 = 10 + 7$$

Directions 8 Have students draw a line from each double ten-frame to the equation that matches.

© Pearson Education, Inc. K **Topic 10** | Assessment

Name _____

⭐ 1

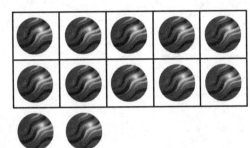

_ _ _ _ _ _ _ _ _ + _ _ _ _ _ _ _ _ = _ _ _ _ _ _ _ _ _

🍎 2

18 = _ _ _ _ _ + _ _ _ _ _

🐟 3

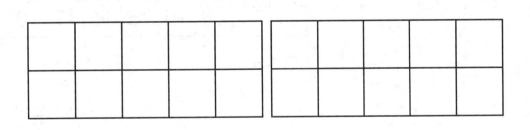

_ _ _ _ _ _ = _ _ _ _ _ + _ _ _ _ _ _ _ _ _ + _ _ _ _ _ = _ _ _ _ _

Directions Mason's Marbles Say: *Mason collects many different kinds of marbles. He uses ten-frames to help count his marbles.* Have students: ⭐ write the equation to show how many purple marbles Mason has; 🍎 draw red marbles in the second ten-frame to show 18 red marbles in all, and then complete the equation. Have them tell how the picture and equation show 10 ones and some more ones; 🐟 draw 17 yellow marbles in the double ten-frame, and then write two equations to match their drawing.

4

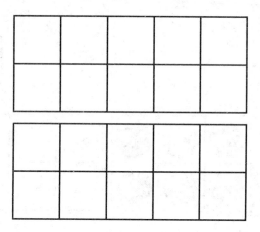

$$10 + 3 = 13$$

5

1	2	3	4	5	6	7	8	9	10
11	12	13	14	15	16	17	18	19	20

_____

- - - - -

_____   +   - - - - -   =   - - - - -

- - - - -

Directions ♥ Have students look at the equation Mason wrote to show how many green marbles he has, and then draw the marbles in the double ten-frame to show the number. Have them tell how the picture shows 10 ones and some more ones. ✋ Say: _Mason put his striped marbles in a five-frame. Then he buys 10 more striped marbles._ Have students write the number to tell how many striped marbles Mason had at first, and then color the part of the number chart to show how many striped marbles he has now. Then have them write an equation to tell how many striped marbles he has in all. Ask them to explain how the picture and equation show 10 ones and some more ones.

Topic 10 | Performance Assessment

TOPIC 11
Count Numbers to 100

Essential Question: How can numbers to 100 be counted using a hundred chart?

Ants

Ants live in colonies.

Math and Science Project: Ant Colonies

Directions Read the character speech bubbles to students. **Find Out!** Have students find out how ants live and work together in colonies. Say: *Talk to friends and relatives about ant colonies. Ask about the different jobs ants in a colony might have that help them survive.* **Journal: Make a Poster** Have students make a poster. Have them draw an ant colony with 5 groups of ants. There should be 10 ants in each group. Then have them count by tens to find how many ants there are in all. Have students use a hundred chart to practice counting by tens to 50.

Name _____

 1

11 17 19

2

10 + 6

3 + 10

3

10 + 4

8 + 10

4

_ _ _ _ _ _ _ _ _ _ _ _

_ _ _ _ _ _ _ _ _ _ _ _

5

_ _ _ _ _ _ _ _ _ _ _ _

_ _ _ _ _ _ _ _ _ _ _ _

6

_ _ _ _ _ _ _ _ _ _ _ _

_ _ _ _ _ _ _ _ _ _ _ _

Directions Have students: **1** draw a circle around the number *nineteen*; **2** draw a circle around the addition expression that makes 16; **3** draw a circle around the addition expression that makes 18; **4**–**6** count each set of objects, write the numbers to tell how many, and then draw a circle around the number that is greater than the other number.

My Word Cards

Directions Have students cut out the vocabulary cards. Read the front of the card, and then ask them to explain what the word or phrase means.

pattern	ones	tens
column	hundred chart	decade

My Word Cards

Directions Review the definitions and have students study the cards. Extend learning by having students draw pictures for each word on a separate piece of paper.

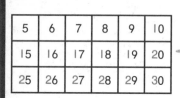

5	6	7	8	9	10
15	16	17	18	19	20
25	26	27	28	29	30

Point to the colored numbers.
Say: *The number to the left of the ones are the **tens**. We count up by 10 when we count by **tens**. 9...19...29...*

5	6	7	8	9	10
15	16	17	18	19	20
25	26	27	28	29	30

Point to the colored numbers.
Say: *When we count 5...6...7...8...9 we are counting by **ones**.*

10 20 30 40 50

Point to the numbers.
Say: *When you count by tens you are using a number **pattern**.*

1	2	3	4	5	6	7	8	9	10
11	12	13	14	15	16	17	18	19	20
21	22	23	24	25	26	27	28	29	30
31	32	33	34	35	36	37	38	39	40
41	42	43	44	45	46	47	48	49	50
51	52	53	54	55	56	57	58	59	60
61	62	63	64	65	66	67	68	69	70
71	72	73	74	75	76	77	78	79	80
81	82	83	84	85	86	87	88	89	90
91	92	93	94	95	96	97	98	99	100

Point to the shaded column.
Say: *The **decade** numbers are the numbers counted when counting by tens to 100.*

column →

row →

1	2	3	4	5	6	7	8	9	10
11	12	13	14	15	16	17	18	19	20
21	22	23	24	25	26	27	28	29	30
31	32	33	34	35	36	37	38	39	40
41	42	43	44	45	46	47	48	49	50
51	52	53	54	55	56	57	58	59	60
61	62	63	64	65	66	67	68	69	70
71	72	73	74	75	76	77	78	79	80
81	82	83	84	85	86	87	88	89	90
91	92	93	94	95	96	97	98	99	100

Point to the hundred chart.
Say: *A **hundred chart** helps us count larger numbers and find number patterns.*

1	2	3	4	5
11	12	13	14	15
21	22	23	24	25
31	32	33	34	35

Point to the circled column.
Say: *This is a **column**. Columns go up and down.*

Name _____

1	2	3	4	5	6	7	8	9	10
11	12	13	14	15	16	17	18	19	20
21	22	23	24	25	26	27	28	29	30

Directions Say: *Count aloud to 30 while you point to each number. What patterns do you see or hear when you count to 30 using the numbers on the chart? Color the boxes that show a pattern you find.*

I can ...
use patterns to count to 30.

© **Content Standards**
K.CC.A.1, K.CC.A.2
Mathematical Practices
MP.1, MP.2, MP.6, MP.7

☆ Guided Practice

1 | 1 | 2 | 3 | 4 | 5 | 6 | 7 | 8 | 9 | 10 |
| 11 | 12 | 13 | 14 | 15 | 16 | 17 | 18 | 19 | 20 |

2 | 21 | 22 | 23 | 24 | 25 | 26 | 27 | 28 | 29 | 30 |

Directions Have students: **1** count aloud all the numbers in the top row. Have them listen to the following numbers in the bottom row, and then draw a circle around the number in the top row and the part of the number in the bottom row that sound alike: *twenty-ONE, twenty-TWO, twenty-THREE, twenty-FOUR, twenty-FIVE, twenty-SIX.* **2** listen to the following numbers, and then complete the numbers in the chart: *twenty-seven, twenty-eight, twenty-nine.*

3

					6	7	8	9	10
11	12	13	14	15	16	17	18	19	20

4

21	22	23	24	2_	2_	2_	2_	2_	30

5

1	2	3		5	6	7	8	9	10
11	12	13		15	16				

6

21	22	23	2_	25	26	27	28	29	30

Directions **3 Number Sense** Have students write the missing numbers, and then explain how they know the numbers are correct. Have students: **4** count the numbers in the bottom row aloud, and then write the missing numbers as they say them; **5** write the missing numbers in the column, say them aloud, and then explain how the numbers in that column are alike; **6** use the chart to find the missing numbers in the middle row, and then explain how they used the chart.

Tools Assessment

1	2	3	4	5	6		8	9	10
11	12	13	14	15	16		18	19	20
21	2__	2__	2__	2__	26	2__	28	29	30

1	2	3	4	5	6	7	8	9	10
11	12							19	20
21	22	23	24	25	26	27	28	29	30

Directions Have students: ✿ write the missing numbers in the column, say them aloud, and then explain how the numbers in that column are alike; ⚑ count the numbers in the bottom row aloud, and then write the missing numbers as they say them aloud. ◆ **Higher Order Thinking** Have students write the missing numbers on the chart, count them aloud, and then explain the pattern they hear. Then have them draw a circle around the other number that fits the pattern.

© Pearson Education, Inc. K
Topic 11 | Lesson 1

Name _____

Another Look!

1	2	3	4	5	6	7	8	9	10
11	12	13	14	15	16	17	18	19	20
21	22	23	24	25	26	27	28	29	30

HOME ACTIVITY Tell your child a number between 1 and 10. Ask him or her to count up to 30 from that number.

⭐1

1	2	3	4	5	6	7	8	9	10
11	12	13	14	15	16	17	18	19	20
21	22	23	24	25	26	27	28	29	30

2️⃣

Directions Say: *Listen to these numbers, and then draw a circle around the numbers in the chart that you hear:* nine, nineteen, twenty-nine. *What number do you see in each box of the column? What number do you hear in each number?* Have students listen to the numbers, and then draw a circle around the numbers in the chart that they hear: ⭐ *four, fourteen, twenty-four;* 2️⃣ *sixteen, seventeen, eighteen, nineteen.*

3

	2	3	4	5	6	7	8	9	10
	12	13	14	15	16	17	18	19	20
2_	22	23	24	25	26	27	28	29	30

4

5

1	2	3	4	5	6	7	8	9	10
11	12	13	14	15	16	17	18	19	20
21	22	23	24	25	26	27	28	29	30

6

Name _____

1	2	3	4	5	6	7	8	9	10
11	12	13	14	15	16	17	18	19	20
21	22						28	29	30
31	32	33	34	35	36	37	38	39	40
41	42	43	44	45	46	47	48	49	50

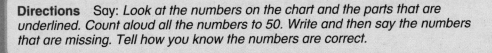

Directions Say: *Look at the numbers on the chart and the parts that are underlined. Count aloud all the numbers to 50. Write and then say the numbers that are missing. Tell how you know the numbers are correct.*

I can ...
use patterns to count to 50.

© **Content Standards**
K.CC.A.1, K.CC.A.2
Mathematical Practices
MP.1, MP.6, MP.7, MP.8

Topic 11 | Lesson 2

Digital Resources at PearsonRealize.com

six hundred thirty-one **631**

1	2	3	4	5	6	7	8	9	●
11	12	13	14	15	16	17	18	19	●
21	22	23	24	25	26	27	28	29	●
31	32	33	34	35	36	37	38	39	●
41	42	43	44	45	46	47	48	49	●

1	2	3	4	5	6	7	8	9	10
11	12	13	14	15	16	17	18	19	20
21	22	23	24	25	26	27	28	29	30
31	32	33	○	○	○	○	○	39	40
41	42	43	44	45	46	47	48	49	50

9 → **10** → 11
19 → **20** → 21
29 → **30** → 31
39 → **40** → 41
49 → **50** → 51

33 → 34 → 35 → 36 → 37 → 38 → 39

☆ Guided Practice

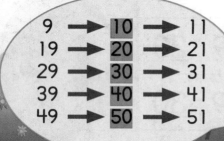

21	22	23	24	25	26	27	28	29	30
31	32	33	34	35	36	37	38	39	40
41	42	43	4	5	6	7	8	9	50

1 (first row below 21–30)

2 (bottom row with 41, 42, 43...)

Directions Have students: ★ count aloud the numbers in the top row. Then have them count all the numbers in the middle row aloud, and draw a circle around the part of the number that sounds the same; ② complete the numbers in the bottom row as they count the numbers aloud, and then explain how they knew which number to write in the tens place.

© Pearson Education, Inc. K **Topic 11** | Lesson 2

Name _____

	2	3	4		6	7	8	9	10
11	12	13	14	15		17	_8	19	20
21	22	23	24	25	26	27	_8	29	30
31	32	33	34				_8	39	40
41	42	43	44	45	46	47	_8	49	50

3 (fish icon) to the left of first row
4 (heart icon) to the left of third row
5 (hand icon) to the left of fifth row

6 (mug icon) _____

_____

7 (tree icon)

34 35 36   26 36 46   35 36 37

Directions Have students: **3** write the missing numbers in the first two rows, and then explain how they found the numbers; **4** color the boxes of the numbers that have 2 in the tens place; **5** find and mark an X on these numbers: *thirty-two, forty-four.* **6** **Vocabulary** Have students complete the numbers in the green column, explain the **pattern** they see in the tens place, and then write the number that is always the same in that column. **7** Have students find the blue boxes on the chart, and then circle the set of numbers that shows the missing numbers.

Topic 11 | Lesson 2   six hundred thirty-three **633**

8

1	2			5		7	8	9	
11		13	14	15	16		18	19	
21	22	23	24	25	26	27	28	29	
31	32	33	34	35	36	37	38	39	40
41	42	43	44	45	46	47	48	49	

9 10

※

Directions Have students: **8** write all the missing numbers in the chart, and then explain how they found the numbers; **9** color the boxes of the numbers that have 4 in the tens place; **10** find and mark an X on the following numbers: *thirty-five, forty-one, forty-eight.* **※ Higher Order Thinking** Have students look at the green column, write all the numbers that are in the column, and then explain how they used the number chart to find the answer.

Name _____

Another Look!

1	2	3	4	5	6	7	8	9	10
11	12	13	14	15	16	17	18	19	20
21	22	23	24	25	26	27	28	29	30
31	32	33	34	35	36	37	38	39	40
41	42	43	44	45	46	47	48	49	50

HOME ACTIVITY Tell your child a number under 50. Ask him or her to count from that number up to 50. Repeat with different numbers.

1	2	3	4	5	6	7	8	9	10
11	12	13	14	15	16	17	18	19	20
21	22	23	24	25	26	27	28	29	30
31	32	33	34	35	36	37	38	39	40
41	42	43	44	45	46	47	48	49	50

Directions Have students point to the fourth row. Say: *Listen to the following numbers, and then draw a circle around the numbers in the chart that you hear:* thirty-three, thirty-four, thirty-five, thirty-six, thirty-seven. *What number do you see in almost every box of this row? What number do you hear in those numbers?* Have students listen to the numbers, draw a circle around the numbers in the chart that they hear, and then tell what is repeated in each number: ⭐ *twenty-six, twenty-seven, twenty-eight, twenty-nine;* ❷ *forty-one, forty-two, forty-three, forty-four.*

3

①	②	③	④	5					10
11	12	13	14	15	16	17	18	19	20
21	22	23	24	25	26	27	28	29	30
31	32	33	34	35	36	37	38	39	40
41	42	43	44	45	46	47	48	49	50

4

5

Directions Have students: **3** write the missing numbers in the top row, say them aloud, and then explain how they know they are correct; **4** look at the numbers in the top row with a circle drawn around them. Then have them draw a circle around the tens place in each column that matches the pattern of those numbers. Have them count the numbers aloud, and then explain the pattern they hear. **5 Higher Order Thinking** Have students listen to the numbers, and then write the numbers they hear: *ten, twenty, thirty, forty, fifty*.

© Pearson Education, Inc. K **Topic 11** | Lesson 2

Name _____

Lesson 11-3
Count by Tens to 100

1	2	3	4	5	6	7	8	9	10
11	12	13	14	15	16	17	18	19	20
21	22	23	24	25	26	27	28	29	30
31	32	33	34	35	36	37	38	39	40
41	42	43	44	45	46	47	48	49	50
51	52	53	54	55	56	57	58	59	60
61	62	63	64	65	66	67	68	69	70
71	72	73	74	75	76	77	78	79	80
81	82	83	84	85	86	87	88	89	90
91	92	93	94	95	96	97	98	99	100

Directions Say: *Color all the boxes of the numbers that have a zero in the ones place as you count them aloud. Tell how you know which numbers to count.*

I can …
skip count by tens to 100.

© **Content Standards**
K.CC.A.1
Mathematical Practices
MP.2, MP.3, MP.4, MP.7

1	2	3	4	5	6	7	8	9	10
11	12	13	14	15	16	17	18	19	20
21	22	23	24	25	26	27	28	29	30
31	32	33	34	35	36	37	38	39	40
41	42	43	44	45	46	47	48	49	50
51	52	53	54	55	56	57	58	59	60

10
20
30
40
50
60

☆ Guided Practice

1

1	2	3	4	5	6	7	8	9	10
11	12	13	14	15	16	17	18	19	20
21	22	23	24	25	26	27	28	29	(30)
31	32	33	34	35	36	37	38	39	40
41	42	43	44	45	46	47	48	49	50
51	52	53	54	55	56	57	58	59	60

2

51	52	53	54	55	56	57	58	59	60
61	62	63	64	65	66	67	68	69	
71	72	73	74	75	76	77	78	79	80
81	82	83	84	85	86	87	88	89	90
91	92	93	94	95	96	97	98	99	100

50   60   (70)

Directions Have students: **1** draw a circle around the decade number that comes before 40 but after 20; **2** look at the chart, and then draw a circle around the missing number.

© Pearson Education, Inc. K

Name _____

3

1	2	3	4	5	6	7	8	9	10
11	12	13	14	15	16	17	18	19	20
21	22	23	24	25	26	27	28	29	30
31	32	33	34	35	36	37	38	39	40
41	42	43	44	45	46	47	48	49	50
51	52	53	54	55	56	57	58	59	60
61	62	63	64	65	66	67	68	69	70
71	72	73	74	75	76	77	78	79	80
81	82	83	84	85	86	87	88	89	90
91	92	93	94	95	96	97	98	99	100

4

20   30   50

5

40   60   70

6

80   90   100

Directions Have students: **3** draw a circle around the missing numbers in the following pattern: *ten, twenty, thirty, _____, fifty, _____, seventy, _____, _____, one hundred*; **4**–**6** count the cubes, and then draw a circle around the number that tells how many.

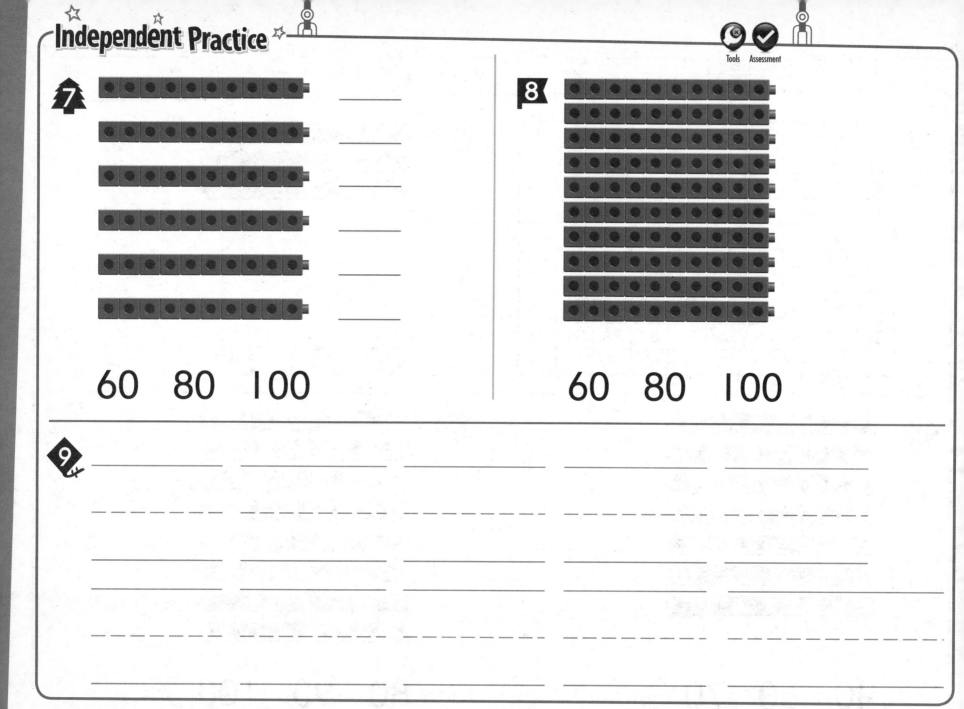

7

_____
_____
_____
_____
_____
_____

60 80 100

8

60 80 100

9

Directions **7 Algebra** Have students count the cube trains by tens, write the decade numbers as they count, and then circle the number that tells how many. **8** Have students count the cubes, and then draw a circle around the number that tells how many. **9 Higher Order Thinking** Have students write all the decade numbers in order.

640 six hundred forty
© Pearson Education, Inc. K
Topic 11 | Lesson 3

Help · Tools · Games

Another Look!

1	2	3	4	5	6	7	8	9	10
11	12	13	14	15	16	17	18	19	20
21	22	23	24	25	26	27	28	29	30
31	32	33	34	35	36	37	38	39	40
41	42	43	44	45	46	47	48	49	50
51	52	53	54	55	56	57	58	59	60
61	62	63	64	65	66	67	68	69	70
71	72	73	74	75	76	77	78	79	80
81	82	83	84	85	86	87	88	89	90
91	92	93	94	95	96	97	98	99	100

HOME ACTIVITY Arrange 30 objects, such as pennies, beads, or other small objects, in groups of 10 on a table. Ask your child to use decade numbers to count the number of objects aloud. Repeat with up to 10 groups of objects.

1	2	3	4	5	6	7	8	9	10
11	12	13	14	15	16	17	18	19	20
21	22	23	24	25	26	27	28	29	30
31	32	33	34	35	36	37	38	39	40
41	42	43	44	45	46	47	48	49	50
51	52	53	54	55	56	57	58	59	60
61	62	63	64	65	66	67	68	69	70
71	72	73	74	75	76	77	78	79	80
81	82	83	84	85	86	87	88	89	90
91	92	93	94	95	96	97	98	99	100

Directions Say: *Color green the boxes of the following decade numbers:* ten, forty, fifty, sixty, ninety. ⭐ Have students color orange the boxes of the following decade numbers: *twenty, thirty, fifty, seventy, eighty, one hundred.*

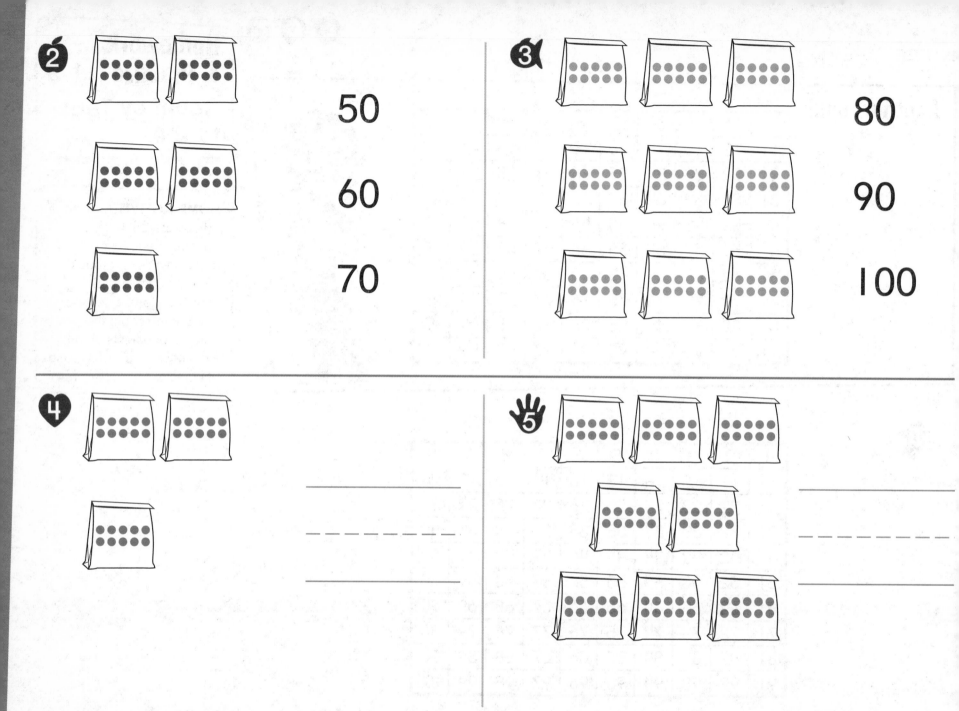

2 50 60 70

3 80 90 100

4

_ _ _ _ _ _ _ _ _

5

_ _ _ _ _ _ _ _ _

© Pearson Education, Inc. K

Solve & Share

Name _____

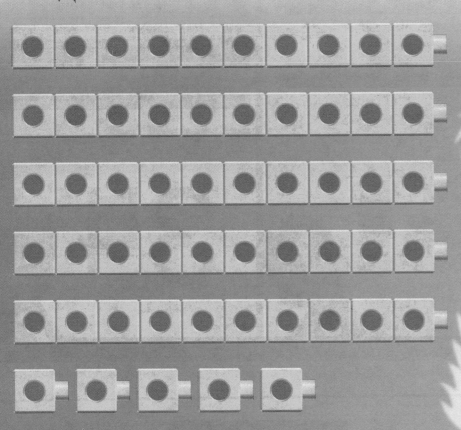

_____

- - - - - - - - - - -

_____

Directions Say: *Carlos has some cubes. How many cubes does Carlos have? What would be a quick way to count all of the cubes? Write the number to tell how many.*

I can ...
count to the number 100
by using tens and ones.

© **Content Standards**
K.CC.A.1, K.CC.A.2
Mathematical Practices
MP.1, MP.2, MP.3, MP.6

10
20
30

31 32 33 34

34

☆ Guided Practice

1.
77

(87)

97

2.
46

47

48

Directions 🌟 and ② Have students count by tens and by ones, and then draw a circle around the number that tells how many. Remind students that they can use a hundred chart to count by tens and by ones.

644 six hundred forty-four © Pearson Education, Inc. K **Topic 11** | Lesson 4

3

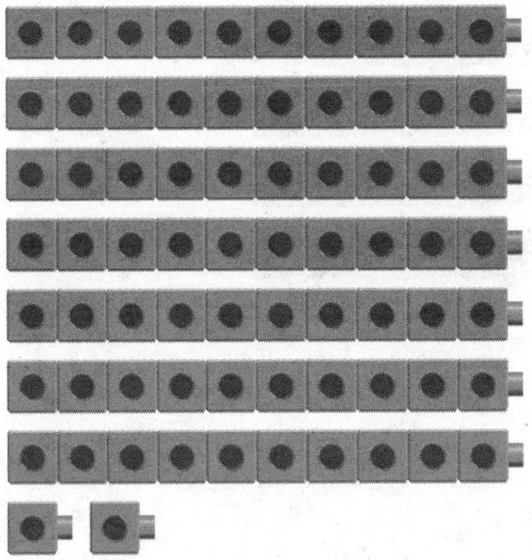

52

62

72

4

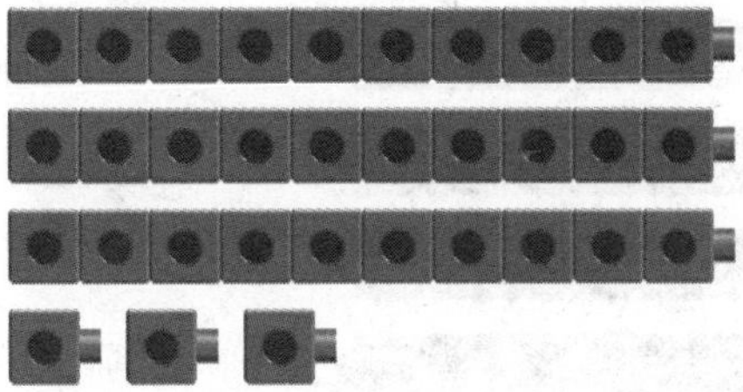

23

32

33

5

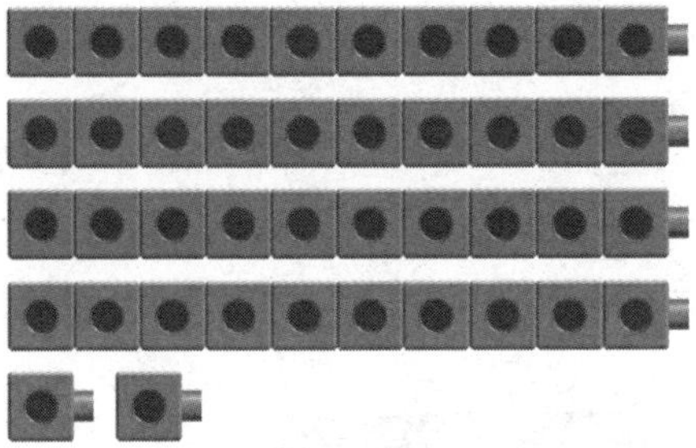

42

43

52

6

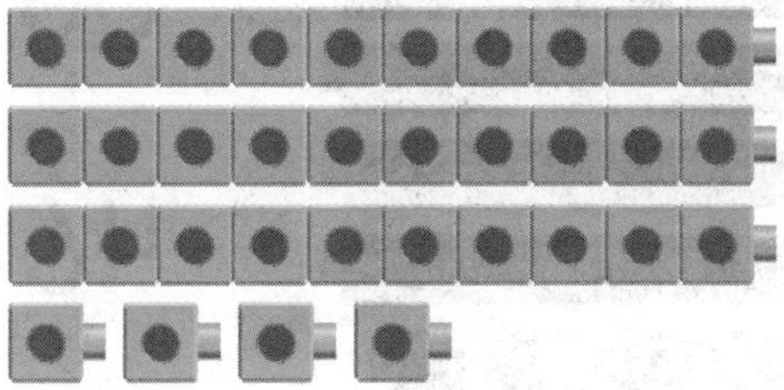

33

34

35

Directions **3**–**6** Have students count by tens and by ones, and then draw a circle around the number that tells how many. If needed, allow students to use a hundred chart.

Independent Practice

7

68

77

86

8

51

52

61

9

36

46

56

10

25

Directions **7–9** Have students count by tens and by ones, and then draw a circle around the number that tells how many. **10 Higher Order Thinking** Have students draw cubes to show how to arrange the number 25 for easy counting.

© Pearson Education, Inc. K

Topic 11 | Lesson 4

Help   Tools   Games

Another Look!

10
20
30
31

21   (31)   41

HOME ACTIVITY Set out a large number of pennies, beads, or other small objects. Have your child arrange the objects in groups of 10 for fast counting. Then have him or her count by tens and by ones to find how many.

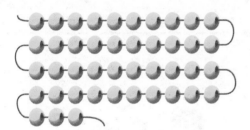

34   42   43

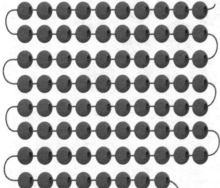

78   87   88

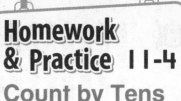

Directions Say: *Alex arranged his counting beads into groups of 10 for easy counting. Count the beads by tens and then by ones. How many beads are there? Draw a circle around the number that tells how many.* ⭐ and ② Have students count the beads by tens and by ones, and then draw a circle around the number that tells how many.

3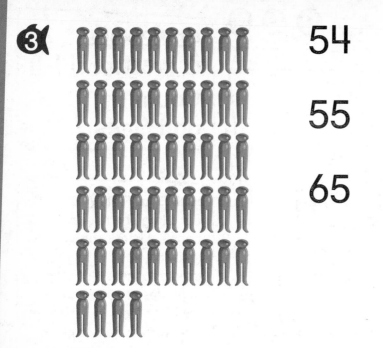

54

55

65

4

38

39

49

5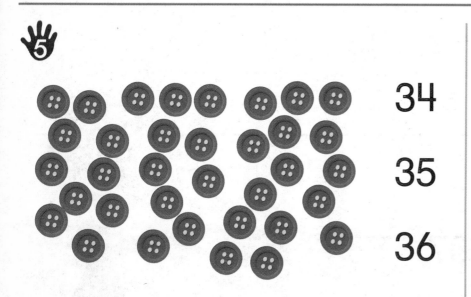

34

35

36

6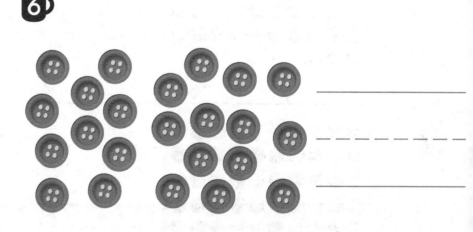

_____

- - - - - - - - -

_____

Topic 11 | Lesson 4

Name _____

 Solve

Lesson 11-5
Count Forward from Any Number to 100

1	2	3	4	5	6	7	8	9	10
11	12	13	14	15	16	17	18	19	20
21	22	23	24	25	26	27	28	29	30
31	32	33	34	35	36	37	38	39	40
41	42	43	44	45	46	47	48	49	50
51	52	53	54	55	56	57	58	59	60
61	62	63	64	65	66	67	68	69	70
71	72	73	74	75	76	77	78	79	80
81	82	83	84	85	86	87	88	89	90
91	92	93	94	95	96	97	98	99	100

Directions Say: *Count forward from the yellow number. Stop at the red number. Tell how many numbers you counted aloud. Color the boxes of the numbers you counted aloud to show your work.*

I can ...
count forward from any number to 100 by ones.

© **Content Standards**
K.CC.A.1, K.CC.A.2
Mathematical Practices
MP.1, MP.5, MP.7, MP.8

72

91

71	72→	73→	74→	75→	76→	77→	78→	79→	80→
81→	82→	83→	84→	85→	86→	87→	88→	89→	90→
91	92	93	94	95	96	97	98	99	100

☆ Guided Practice

1

21	22	23	24	25	26	27	28	29	30
31	32	33	34	35	36	37	38	39	40
41	42	43	44	45	46	47	48	49	50
51	52	53	54	55	56	57	58	59	60

2

1	2	3	4	5	6	7	8	9	10
11	12	13	14	15	16	17	18	19	20
21	22	23	24	25	26	27	28	29	30
31	32	33	34	35	36	37	38	39	40

Directions ⭐ and **2** Have students color the boxes of the numbers as they count aloud, starting at the yellow box and ending at the red box.

© Pearson Education, Inc. K

Topic 11 | Lesson 5

Name _____

 3

1	2	3	4	5	6	7	8	9	10
11	12	13	14	15	16	17	18	19	20
21	22	23	24	25	26	27	28	29	30
31	32	33	34	35	36	37	38	39	40
41	42	43	44	45	46	47	48	49	50
51	52	53	54	55	56	57	58	59	60
61	62	63	64	65	66	67	68	69	70
71	72	73	74	75	76	77	78	79	80
81	82	83	84	85	86	87	88	89	90
91	92	93	94	95	96	97	98	99	100

 4 ♥

1	2	3	4	5	6	7	8	9	10
11	12	13	14	15	16	17	18	19	20
21	22	23	24	25	26	27	28	29	30
31	32	33	34	35	36	37	38	39	40
41	42	43	44	45	46	47	48	49	50
51	52	53	54	55	56	57	58	59	60
61	62	63	64	65	66	67	68	69	70
71	72	73	74	75	76	77	78	79	80
81	82	83	84	85	86	87	88	89	90
91	92	93	94	95	96	97	98	99	100

 5

1	2	3	4	5	6	7	8	9	10
11	12	13	14	15	16	17	18	19	20
21	22	23	24	25	26	27	28	29	30
31	32	33	34	35	36	37	38	39	40
41	42	43	44	45	46	47	48	49	50
51	52	53	54	55	56	57	58	59	60
61	62	63	64	65	66	67	68	69	70
71	72	73	74	75	76	77	78	79	80
81	82	83	84	85	86	87	88	89	90
91	92	93	94	95	96	97	98	99	100

6

1	2	3	4	5	6	7	8	9	10
11	12	13	14	15	16	17	18	19	20
21	22	23	24	25	26	27	28	29	30
31	32	33	34	35	36	37	38	39	40
41	42	43	44	45	46	47	48	49	50
51	52	53	54	55	56	57	58	59	60
61	62	63	64	65	66	67	68	69	70
71	72	73	74	75	76	77	78	79	80
81	82	83	84	85	86	87	88	89	90
91	92	93	94	95	96	97	98	99	100

Directions **3–6** Have students color the boxes of the numbers as they count aloud, starting at the yellow box and ending at the red box.

Independent Practice

 7

1	2	3	4	5	6	7	8	9	10
11	12	13	14	15	16	17	18	19	20
21	22	23	24	25	26	27	28	29	30
31	32	33	34	35	36	37	38	39	40
41	42	43	44	45	46	47	48	49	50
51	52	53	54	55	56	57	58	59	60
61	62	63	64	65	66	67	68	69	70
71	72	73	74	75	76	77	78	79	80
81	82	83	84	85	86	87	88	89	90
91	92	93	94	95	96	97	98	99	100

 8

1	2	3	4	5	6	7	8	9	10
11	12	13	14	15	16	17	18	19	20
21	22	23	24	25	26	27	28	29	30
31	32	33	34	35	36	37	38	39	40
41	42	43	44	45	46	47	48	49	50
51	52	53	54	55	56	57	58	59	60
61	62	63	64	65	66	67	68	69	70
71	72	73	74	75	76	77	78	79	80
81	82	83	84	85	86	87	88	89	90
91	92	93	94	95	96	97	98	99	100

 9

1	2	3	4	5	6	7	8	9	10
11	12	13	14	15	16	17	18	19	20
21	22	23	24	25	26	27	28	29	30
31	32	33	34	35	36	37	38	39	40
41	42	43	44	45	46	47	48	49	50
51	52	53	54	55	56	57	58	59	60
61	62	63	64	65	66	67	68	69	70
71	72	73	74	75	76	77	78	79	80
81	82	83	84	85	86	87	88	89	90
91	92	93	94	95	96	97	98	99	100

 10

51	52	53	54	55	56	57	58	59	
61	62	63	64	65	66	67	68	69	
71	72	73	74	75	76	77	78	79	
81	82	83	84	85	86	87	88	89	
91	92	93	94	95	96	97	98	99	

Directions **7**–**9** Have students color the boxes of the numbers as they count aloud, starting at the yellow box and ending at the red box.
10 Higher Order Thinking Have students write the numbers as they count by tens aloud, starting at the yellow box and ending at the red box.

     Topic 11 | Lesson 5

Name _____

Another Look!

1	2	3	4	5	6	7	8	9	10
11	12	13	14	15	16	17	18	19	20
21	22	23	24	25	26	27	28	29	30
31	32	33	34	35	36	37	38	39	40
41	42	43	44	45	46	47	48	49	50
51	52	53	54	55	56	57	58	59	60
61	62	63	64	65	66	67	68	69	70
71	72	73	74	75	76	77	78	79	80
81	82	83	84	85	86	87	88	89	90
91	92	93	94	95	96	97	98	99	100

HOME ACTIVITY Point to a number on a hundred chart, such as 27. Have your child count from that number to another number you have chosen. Repeat with other numbers.

 1

1	2	3	4	5	6	7	8	9	10
11	12	13	14	15	16	17	18	19	20
21	22	23	24	25	26	27	28	29	30
31	32	33	34	35	36	37	38	39	40
41	42	43	44	45	46	47	48	49	50
51	52	53	54	55	56	57	58	59	60
61	62	63	64	65	66	67	68	69	70
71	72	73	74	75	76	77	78	79	80
81	82	83	84	85	86	87	88	89	90
91	92	93	94	95	96	97	98	99	100

 2

1	2	3	4	5	6	7	8	9	10
11	12	13	14	15	16	17	18	19	20
21	22	23	24	25	26	27	28	29	30
31	32	33	34	35	36	37	38	39	40
41	42	43	44	45	46	47	48	49	50
51	52	53	54	55	56	57	58	59	60
61	62	63	64	65	66	67	68	69	70
71	72	73	74	75	76	77	78	79	80
81	82	83	84	85	86	87	88	89	90
91	92	93	94	95	96	97	98	99	100

Directions Say: *You can count forward from any number. Find and draw a circle around the number* eighteen. *Count aloud until you reach the red box. Color the boxes of the numbers you counted aloud.* Have students draw a circle around the given number, and then color the boxes of the numbers as they count aloud, starting at the circled number and ending at the red box. Have them: **1** draw a circle around the number *eighty*; **2** draw a circle around the number *thirty-six*.

3

1	2	3	4	5	6	7	8	9	10
11	12	13	14	15	16	17	18	19	20
21	22	23	24	25	26	27	28	29	30
31	32	33	34	35	36	37	38	39	40
41	42	43	**44**	45	46	47	48	49	50
51	52	53	54	55	56	57	58	59	60
61	62	63	64	65	66	67	68	69	70
71	72	73	74	75	76	77	78	79	80
81	82	83	84	85	86	87	88	89	90
91	92	93	94	95	96	97	98	99	100

4

1	2	3	4	5	6	7	8	9	10
11	12	13	14	15	16	17	18	19	20
21	22	23	24	25	26	27	28	29	30
31	32	33	34	35	36	37	38	39	40
41	42	43	44	45	46	47	48	49	50
51	52	53	54	55	56	57	58	59	60
61	62	63	64	65	66	67	68	69	**70**
71	72	73	74	75	76	77	78	79	80
81	82	83	84	85	86	87	88	89	90
91	92	93	94	95	96	97	98	99	100

5

1	2	3	4	5	6	7	8	9	10
11	12	13	14	15	16	17	18	19	20
21	22	23	24	25	26	27	28	29	30
31	32	33	34	35	36	37	38	39	40
41	42	43	44	45	46	47	48	49	50
51	52	53	54	55	56	57	58	59	60
61	62	63	64	65	66	67	68	69	70
71	72	73	74	75	76	77	78	79	80
81	82	83	84	85	86	87	88	89	90
91	92	93	94	95	96	97	98	99	100

6

1	2	3	4	5	6	7	8	9	
11	12	13	14	15	16	17	18	19	
21	22	23	24	25	26	27	28	29	
31	32	33	34	35	36	37	38	39	
41	42	43	44	45	46	47	48	49	
51	52	53	54	55	56	57	58	59	
61	62	63	64	65	66	67	68	69	
71	72	73	74	75	76	77	78	79	
81	82	83	84	85	86	87	88	89	
91	92	93	94	95	96	97	98	99	

Directions Have students draw a circle around the given number, and then color the boxes of the numbers as they count aloud, starting at the circled number and ending at the red box. Have them: **3** draw a circle around the number *twenty-two*; **4** draw a circle around the number *fifty-one*. **5 Higher Order Thinking** Have students draw a circle around the number that comes after *sixteen*, the number that comes after *forty-eight*, and the number that comes after *eighty*. **6 Higher Order Thinking** Have students write the numbers as they count aloud by tens, starting at the yellow box and ending at the red box.

Name _____

1	2	3	4	5	6	7	8	9	10
11	12	13	14	15	16	17	18	19	20
21	22	23	24	25	26	27	28	29	30
31	32	33	34	35	36	37	38	39	40
41	42	43	44	45	46	47	48	49	50
51	52	53	54	55	56	57	58	59	60
61	62	63	64	65	66	67	68	69	70
71	72	73	74	75	76	77	78	79	80
81	82	83	84	85	86	87	88	89	90
91	92	93	94	95	96	97	98	99	100

Directions Say: *Carlos looks at the chart. He knows 21 comes just after 20. Draw a circle around the numbers that come just after each decade number. How do you know you are correct? What patterns do you see?*

I can ...
count by tens and ones from any number up to 100.

© **Content Standards**
K.CC.A.1, K.CC.A.2
Mathematical Practices
MP.2, MP.5, MP.6, MP.7

41	42	43	44	45	46	47	48	49	50
51	52	53	54	55	56	57	58	59	60
61	62	63	64	65	66	67	68	69	70
71	72	73	74	75	76	77	78	79	80
81	82	83	84	85	86	87	88	89	90
91	92	93	94	95	96	97	98	99	100

61	62	63	64	65	66	67	68	69	70
71	72	73	74	75	76	77	78	79	80
81	82	83	84	85	86	87	88	89	90
91	92	93	94	95	96	97	98	99	100

☆ Guided Practice

1

1	2	3	4	5	6	7	8	9	10
11	12	13	14	15	16	17	18	19	20
21	22	23	24	25	26	27	28	29	30

2

1	2	3	4	5	6	7	8	9	10
11	12	13	14	15	16	17	18	19	20
21	22	23	24	25	26	27	28	29	30

Directions 1 and 2 Have students count forward to find and write the missing numbers.

Topic 11 | Lesson 6

Name _____

 3

61	62	63	64	65				69	70
71	72	73	74	75	76	77	78	79	80
81	82	83	84	85	86	87	88	89	90

66   76   86

67   68   69

66   67   68

 4

42	43	44	45	46	47	48	49	50
52	53	54	55	56	57	58	59	60
62	63	64	65	66	67	68	69	70

41   42   43

41   51   61

41   43   45

 5

31	32	33	34	35	36	37	38	39	
41	42	43	44	45	46	47	48	49	
51	52	53	54	55	56	57	58	59	

40   50   60

40   41   42

38   39   40

6

11	12	13	14	15	16	17	18	19	20
21	22	23	24	25	26	27	28	29	
		33	34	35	36	37	38	39	40

20   30   40

28   29   30

30   31   32

Directions **3**–**6** Have students count forward, and then draw a circle around the row that shows the missing set of numbers.

Independent Practice

Tools Assessment

7

71	72	73	74	75	76	77	78	79	80
81	82	83	84	85	86	87	88	89	90
91	92	93	94	95	96	97			

80   90   100

98   99   100

89   99   100

8

51	52	53	54	55	56	57	58	59	60
61	62	63	64	65	66	67	68	69	70
71	72	73				77	78	79	80

74   84   94

74   64   54

74   75   76

9

1	2	3	4	5		7	8	9	10
11	12	13	14	15		17	18	19	20
21	22	23	24	25		27	28	29	30

6   7   8

6   16   26

6   17   28

10

31	32	33	34	35	36	37	38	39	40
41	42	43	44	45	46	47	48	49	50
51						57	58	59	60
61	62	63	64	65	66	67	68	69	70
71	72	73	74	75	76	77	78	79	80

Directions 7–9 Have students count forward, and then draw a circle around the row that shows the missing set of numbers. 10 **Higher Order Thinking** Have students count forward to find the missing numbers, write the missing numbers in the chart, and then draw a circle around the column that has 3 in the ones place.

© Pearson Education, Inc. K

Topic 11 | Lesson 6

Name _____

Another Look!

1	2	3	4	5	6	7	8	9	10
11	12	13	14	15	16	17	18	19	20
21	22	23	24	25	26	27	28	29	30
31	32	33	34	35	36	37	38	39	40
41	42	43	44	45	46	47	48	49	50

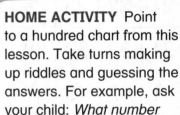

HOME ACTIVITY Point to a hundred chart from this lesson. Take turns making up riddles and guessing the answers. For example, ask your child: *What number comes just after 31 and just before 33?* (32)

⭐ 1

1	2	3	4	5	6	7	8	9	10
11	12	13	14	15	16	17	18	19	20
21	22	23	24	25	26	27	28	29	30
31	32	33	34	35	36	37	38	39	40
41	42	43	44	45	46	47	48	49	50

🍎 2

1	2	3	4	5	6	7	8	9	10
11	12	13	14	15	16	17	18	19	20
21	22	23	24	25	26	27	28	29	30
31	32	33	34	35	36	37	38	39	40
41	42	43	44	45	46	47	48	49	50
51	52	53	54	55	56	57	58	59	60

Directions Say: *Draw a circle around the column with the numbers:* seven, seventeen, twenty-seven, thirty-seven, forty-seven. *What pattern do you see and hear?* Have students: ⭐ draw a circle around the column that has 9 in the ones place, count the numbers aloud, and then explain the pattern they see and hear; 🍎 draw a circle around the numbers that have 3 in the tens place, count the numbers aloud, and then explain the pattern they see and hear.

1	2	3	4	5	6	7	8	9	10
11	12	13	14	15	16	17	18	19	20
21	22	23	24	25	26	27	28	29	30
31	32	33	34	35	36	37	38	39	40
41	42	43	44	45	46	47	48	49	50

41	42	43	44	45	46	47	48	49	50
51	52	52	54	55	56	57	58	59	60
61	62	63	64	65	66	67	68	69	70
71	72	73	74	75	76	77	78	79	80
81	82	83	84	85	86	87	88	89	90
91	92	93	94	95	96	97	98	99	100

11		13		15	16	17	18	19	20
	22	23	24	25	26	27	28		30
	32		34	35	36	37	38		40
41	42	43		45	46	47	48		
51		53	54	55	56	57		59	60

51	52	53	54	55	56	57	58	59	60
61	62	63	64	65	66	67	68	69	70
71	72	73	74	75	76	77	78	79	80
81	82	83	84	85	86	87	88	89	90
91	92	93	94	95	96	97	98	99	100

Directions Have students: **3** draw a circle around the row that starts with the number *twenty-one*, count the numbers aloud, and then explain the pattern they see and hear; **4** draw a circle around the column that has 9 in the ones place, count the numbers aloud, and then explain the pattern they see and hear. **5 Higher Order Thinking** Have students count by ones to write the missing numbers, and then draw a circle around the column that has 4 in the ones place. **6 Higher Order Thinking** Have students draw a circle around the number that is 1 more than 72, and then mark an X on the number that is 1 less than 90.

Topic 11 | Lesson 6

Solve & Share

Name _____

Solve

1	2	3	4	5	6	7	8	9	10
11	12	13	14	15	16	17	18	19	20
21	22	23	24	25	26	27	28	29	30

1	2	3	4	5	6	7	8	9	10
11	12	13	14	15	16	17	18	19	20
21	22	23	24	25	26	27	28	29	30

Think.

Directions Say: *Carlos's teacher gives the class a challenge. Is there more than one way to solve it? Begin at 3. Use arrows and show how you could count up 15 places. Color the number red to show where you end. Show another way to use arrows on the second chart.*

I can ...
count on from any number counting by tens and by ones.

© **Mathematical Practices**
MP.7 Also MP.6, MP.8
Content Standards
K.CC.A.1, K.CC.A.2

Both ways end at 33.

☆ Guided Practice

 1

1	2	3	4	5	6	7	8	9	10
11	12	13	14	15	16	17	18	19	20
21	22	23	24	25	26	27	28	29	30
31	32	33	34	35	36	37	38	39	40

 2

1	2	3	4	5	6	7	8	9	10
11	12	13	14	15	16	17	18	19	20
21	22	23	24	25	26	27	28	29	30
31	32	33	34	35	36	37	38	39	40

Directions Have students: **1** start at 22 and make a path to show how to count up 15 using only ones. Have them circle the number where they end, and then explain how they used the number chart to find the answer; **2** start at 12 and make a path to show how to count up 14 using tens and then ones. Have them circle the number where they end, and then explain how they used the number chart to find the answer.

Independent Practice

3

41	42	43	44	45	46	47	48	49	50
51	52	53	54	55	56	57	58	59	60
61	62	63	64	65	66	67	68	69	70
71	72	73	74	75	76	77	78	79	80

4

41	42	43	44	45	46	47	48	49	50
51	52	53	54	55	56	57	58	59	60
61	62	63	64	65	66	67	68	69	70
71	72	73	74	75	76	77	78	79	80

5

61	62	63	64	65	66	67	68	69	70
71	72	73	74	75	76	77	78	79	80
81	82	83	84	85	86	87	88	89	90
91	92	93	94	95	96	97	98	99	100

6

61	62	63	64	65	66	67	68	69	70
71	72	73	74	75	76	77	78	79	80
81	82	83	84	85	86	87	88	89	90
91	92	93	94	95	96	97	98	99	100

Directions Have students: **3** start at 42 and make a path to show how to count up 21 using ones and then tens. Have them circle the number where they end, and then explain how they used the number chart to find the answer; **4** start at 56 and make a path to show how to count up 15 using tens and ones. Have them circle the number where they end, and then explain how they used the number chart to find the answer; **5** start at 72 and make a path to show how to count up 27 in any way they choose. Have them circle the number where they end, and then explain how they used the number chart to find the answer; **6** start at 63 and make a path to show how to count up 22 in any way they choose. Have them draw a circle around the number where they end, and then explain how they know they are correct.

1	2	3	4	5	6	7	8	9	10
11	12	13	14	15	16	17	18	19	20
21	22	23	24	25	26	27	28	29	30
31	32	33	34	35	36	37	38	39	40

Directions Read the problem aloud. Then have students use multiple math practices to solve the problem. Say: *Start at 7 and count up 18 in any way you choose. Make a path to show how you counted, and then draw a circle around the number where you ended.* 🌲 **MP.6 Be Precise** *How many tens are in 18?* 🎁 **MP.7 Use Structure** *What numbers would you say if you only counted by ones? What numbers would you say if you counted by tens first and then by ones?* 🔷 **MP.8 Generalize** *What number would you end on if you counted by ones first and then by tens? How do you know you are correct if you did NOT count again?*

Topic 11 | Lesson 7

Name _____

Help   Tools   Games

Another Look!

61	62	63	64	65	66	67	68	69	70
71	72	73	74	75	76	77	78	79	80
81	82	83	84	85	86	87	88	89	90
91	92	93	94	95	96	97	98	99	100

61	62	63	64	65	66	67	68	69	70
71	72	73	74	75	76	77	78	79	80
81	82	83	84	85	86	87	88	89	90
91	92	93	94	95	96	97	98	99	100

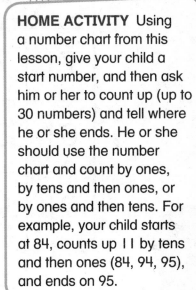

HOME ACTIVITY Using a number chart from this lesson, give your child a start number, and then ask him or her to count up (up to 30 numbers) and tell where he or she ends. He or she should use the number chart and count by ones, by tens and then ones, or by ones and then tens. For example, your child starts at 84, counts up 11 by tens and then ones (84, 94, 95), and ends on 95.

1

1	2	3	4	5	6	7	8	9	10
11	12	13	14	15	16	17	18	19	20
21	22	23	24	25	26	27	28	29	30
31	32	33	34	35	36	37	38	39	40

2

41	42	43	44	45	46	47	48	49	50
51	52	53	54	55	56	57	58	59	60
61	62	63	64	65	66	67	68	69	70
71	72	73	74	75	76	77	78	79	80

Directions Say: *Make a path to count up 25 from 72 by tens and ones. First count up by tens and then ones. Then count up by ones and then tens. Draw a circle around the number where you end.* Have students: **1** start at 19 and make a path to show how to count up 13 using only ones. Have them draw a circle around the number where they end, and then explain how they used the number chart to find the answer; **2** start at 41 and make a path to show how to count up 19 using tens and ones. Have them draw a circle around the number where they end, and then explain how they used the number chart to find the answer.

61	62	63	64	65	66	67	68	69	70
71	72	73	74	75	76	77	78	79	80
81	82	83	84	85	86	87	88	89	90
91	92	93	94	95	96	97	98	99	100

Directions Read the problem aloud. Then have students use multiple math practices to solve the problem. Say: *Start at 62 and count up 25 in any way you choose. Make a path to show how you counted, and then draw a circle around the number where you ended.*
③ MP.6 Be Precise *How many tens are in 25?* **④ MP.7 Use Structure** *How would you use the number chart to help you count first by tens and then by ones?* **✋ MP.8 Generalize** *What number would you end on if you counted by ones first and then by tens? How do you know you are correct if you did NOT count again?*

1

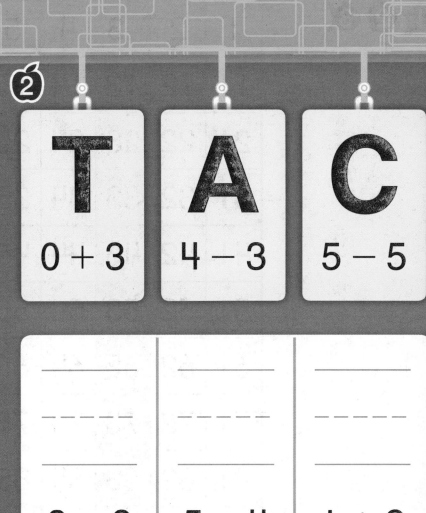

G	B	I
4 + 1	2 + 2	3 − 1

3 + 1	4 − 2	2 + 3

2

T	A	C
0 + 3	4 − 3	5 − 5

3 − 3	5 − 4	1 + 2

Directions 1 and 2 Have students find a partner. Have them point to a clue in the top row, and then solve the addition or subtraction problem in the clue. Then have them look at the clues in the bottom row to find a match, and then write the clue letter above the match. Have students find a match for every clue.

I can ...
add and subtract fluently within 5.

© **Content Standard** K.OA.A.5

1	2	3	4	5	6	7	8	9	10
11	12	13	14	15	16	17	18	19	20
21	22	23	24	25	26	27	28	29	30
31	32	33	34	35	36	37	38	39	40
41	42	43	44	45	46	47	48	49	50
51	52	53	54	55	56	57	58	59	60
61	62	63	64	65	66	67	68	69	70
71	72	73	74	75	76	77	78	79	80
81	82	83	84	85	86	87	88	89	90
91	92	93	94	95	96	97	98	99	100

Directions **Understand Vocabulary** Have students: ⭐ draw a circle around the part of the number in the orange column that is the **ones** place; ❷ draw a circle around the part of the number in the blue column that is the **tens** place; ❸ color the **decade** numbers yellow.

© Pearson Education, Inc. K

Set A

①	②	③	④	⑤	⑥	⑦	⑧	⑨	⑩
⑪	⑫	⑬	⑭	⑮	⑯	⑰	⑱	⑲	20
21	22	23	24	25	26	27	28	29	30

1	2	3	4	5	6	7	8	9	10
11	12	13	14	15	16	17	18	19	20
21	22	23	24	25	26	27	28	29	30

Set B

41	42	43	44	45	46	47	48	49	50
51	52	53	54	55	56	57	58	59	60
61	62	63	64	65	66	67	68	69	70
71	72	73	74	75	76	77	78	79	80
81	82	83	84	85	86	87	88	89	90
91	92	93	94	95	96	97	98	99	100

2

73

83

84

Directions Have students: ⭐ count aloud the numbers in the top row. Then have them count aloud the numbers in the bottom row and draw a circle around the number in the top row and the part of the number in the bottom row that sound the same; ② count by tens and ones, and then draw a circle around the number that tells how many.

1	2	3	4	5	6	7	8	9	10
11	12	13	14	15	16	17	18	19	20
21	22	23	24	25	26	27	28	29	30
31	32	33	34	35	36	37	38	39	40
41	42	43	44	45	46	47	48	49	50

3

51	52	53	54	55	56	57	58	59	60
61	62	63	64	65	66	67	68	69	70
71	72	73	74	75	76	77	78	79	80
81	82	83	84	85	86	87	88	89	90
91	92	93	94	95	96	97	98	99	100

1	2	3	4	5	6	7	8	9	10
11	12	13	14	15	16	17	18	19	20
21	22	23	24	25	26	27	28	29	30
			34	35	36	37	38	39	40
41	42	43	44	45	46	47	48	49	50

31   32   33

4

51	52	53	54	55	56	57	58	59	60
61	62	63	64	65	66	67	68	69	70
71	72	73	74	75		77	78	79	80
81	82	83	84	85		87	88	89	90
91	92	93	94	95		97	98	99	100

75   76   77

76   86   90

76   86   96

Directions Have students: **3** color the boxes of the numbers as they count aloud by ones, starting at the yellow box and ending at the red box; **4** count forward, and then draw a circle around the row that shows the missing set of numbers.

Name _____

© Assessment

 1

Ⓐ 60

Ⓑ 70

Ⓒ 80

Ⓓ 90

 2

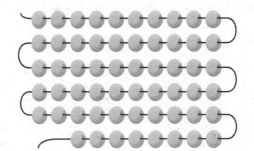

Ⓐ 56

Ⓑ 57

Ⓒ 58

Ⓓ 59

3

61	62	63	64	65	66	67	68	69	70
71	72	73	74	75	76	77	78	79	
81	82	83	84	85	86	87	88	89	
91	92	93	94	95	96	97	98	99	

Ⓐ 80 90 100

Ⓑ 80 80 99

Ⓒ 81 91 100

Ⓓ 85 95 100

Directions Have students mark the best answer. **1** Which number tells how many cubes? **2** Count the beads by tens and then by ones. Which number tells how many? **3** Which set of numbers shows the set of missing numbers in the number chart?

4

1	2	3	4	5	6	7	8	9	10
11	12	13	14	15	16	17	18	19	20
21	22	23	24	25	26	27	28	29	30

5

51	52	53	54	55	56	57	58	59	60
61	62	63	64	65	66	67	68	69	70
71	72	73	74	75	76	77	78	79	80
81	82	83	84	85	86	87	88	89	90
91	92	93	94	95	96	97	98	99	100

6

1	2	3	4	5	6	7	8	9	10
11	12	13	14	15	16	17	18	19	20
21	22	23	24	25	26	27	28	29	30
31	32	33	34	35	36	37	38	39	40
41	42	43	44	45	46	47	48	49	50
51	52	53	54	55	56	57	58	59	60
61	62	63	64	65	66	67	68	69	70
71	72	73	74	75	76	77	78	79	80
81	82	83	84	85	86	87	88	89	90
91	92	93	94	95	96	97	98	99	100

7

11	12	13	14	15		17	18	19	
21		23	24	25	26	27	28	29	
31	32		34	35	36	37	38		
	42	43	44	45	46			49	50
51	52	53	54			57	58	59	60

21	22	28	30
33	35	39	40
41	46	47	48
51	55	56	60

Directions Have students: ♥ color the boxes of the numbers that have the number *eight* in the ones place; ✋ look at the row beginning with 61. Have them draw a circle around the tens place of the numbers to show the pattern, and then draw a circle around the column that has 0 in the ones place; ☕ color the boxes of the numbers as they count by ones, starting at the yellow box and ending at the red box, and then explain any patterns they might see or hear; 🌲 count by ones to write the missing numbers in the top row, and then draw a circle around the missing numbers in the remaining rows.

© Pearson Education, Inc. K

Topic 11 | Assessment

Name _____

★ 1

1	2	3	4	5	6	7	8	9	10
11	12	13	14	15	16	17	18	●	20
21	22	23	24	25	26	27	28	29	30
31	32	33	34	35	36	37	38	39	40
41	42	43	44	45	46	47	48	49	50

9   19   20

🍎 2

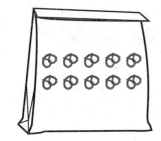 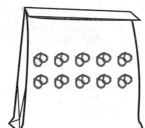  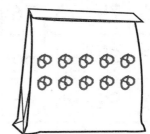 

50   60   70

Directions **School Snacks** Say: *It's snack time for the Kindergarten class!* ★ Say: *Keisha puts a grape on the hundred chart to show how many grapes she has in her snack bag.* Have students look at the numbers that come just before and just after the grape, and then at the numbers that are just above and just below it. Have them draw a circle around the missing number that tells how many grapes Keisha has. ② Have students count the pretzels that Liam and his friends share for their snack. Have them draw a circle around the number that tells how many. If needed, students can use the hundred chart to help.

3

65   66   67

4

51	52	🍒	🍒	🍒	56	57	58	59	60
61	62	63	[64]	65	66	67	68	69	70
71	72	73	74	75	76	77	78	79	80
81	82	83	84	85	86	87	88	89	90
91	92	93	94	95	96	97	98	99	100

50   60   70

53   54   55

50   51   52

Directions ❸ Say: *Chen brings crackers for snack time. How many does he bring?* Have students draw circles around groups of crackers for easy counting by tens and ones. Then have them draw a circle around the number that tells how many. ❹ Say: *Zoe counts the cherries that she gives to her friends. She puts cherries on the number chart for the last three numbers that she counts.* Have students find the cherries in the chart. Then have them look at the numbers to the right of the chart, and then draw a circle around the set of missing numbers to show how Zoe counted the cherries. ❺ Say: *Ty has 64 raisins in one bag. He has 18 raisins in another bag. Help Ty count his raisins.* Have students start at 64 on the number chart and make a path to show how to count up 18 in any way they choose. Then have them draw a circle around the number where they stopped, and then explain how they counted up.

© Pearson Education, Inc. K

Topic 11 | Performance Assessment

TOPIC 12

Identify and Describe Shapes

Essential Question: How can two- and three-dimensional shapes be identified and described?

Wheels help push and pull objects!

Wheels

Math and Science Project: Pushing and Pulling Objects

Directions Read the character speech bubbles to students. **Find Out!** Have students investigate different kinds of wheels. Say: *Not all wheels look alike, but they are all the same shape. Talk to your friends and relatives about the shape of a wheel and ask them how it can help when you need to push and pull objects.* **Journal: Make a Poster** Have students make a poster that shows various objects with wheels. Have them draw up to 5 different kinds of objects that have wheels.

Name _____

★1

10 20 30 40 50

10 12 15 21 30

2

1	2	3	4	5	6	7	8	9	10
11	12	13	14	15	16	17	18	19	20
21	22	23	24	25	26	27	28	29	30
31	32	33	34	35	36	37	38	39	40
41	42	43	44	45	46	47	48	49	50
51	52	53	54	55	56	57	58	59	60
61	62	63	64	65	66	67	68	69	70
71	72	73	74	75	76	77	78	79	80
81	82	83	84	85	86	87	88	89	90
91	92	93	94	95	96	97	98	99	100

3

51	52	53	54	55	56	57	58	59	60
61	62	63	64	65	66	67	68	69	70
71	72	73	74	75	76	77	78	79	80
81	82	83	84	85	86	87	88	89	90
91	92	93	94	95	96	97	98	99	100

4

_____   _____

5

_ _ _ _ _ _ _

6

23   8   13

Directions Have students: **★1** draw a circle around the set of numbers that show a pattern of counting by tens; **2** draw a circle around the hundred chart; **3** draw a circle around the numbers *fifty-five* and *ninety-nine*; **4** count the objects, write the numbers, and then draw a circle around the number that is greater than the other number; **5** count the objects, and then write the number; **6** draw a circle around the number that tells how many counters.

Topic 12

A-Z Glossary

sort

two-dimensional shape

three-dimensional shape

circle

triangle

side

Directions Review the definitions and have students study the cards. Extend learning by having students draw pictures for each word on a separate piece of paper.

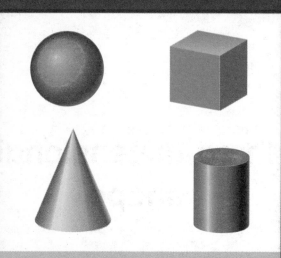

Point to the shapes.
Say: *Solid figures are also called* **three-dimensional shapes**.

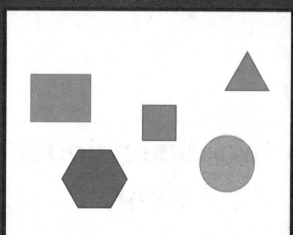

Point to the shapes.
Say: *Flat shapes are also called* **two-dimensional shapes**.

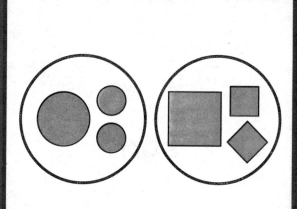

Point to the groups.
Say: *You can* **sort** *objects by shape.*

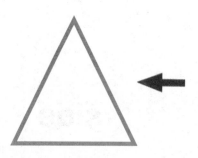

Point to the side of the triangle.
Say: *This is one* **side** *of the triangle. It has 3 sides in all.*

Point to the shape.
Say: *This shape is a* **triangle**.

Point to the shape.
Say: *This shape is a* **circle**.

My Word Cards

Directions Have students cut out the vocabulary cards. Read the front of the card, and then ask them to explain what the word or phrase means.

A-Z
Glossary

vertex (vertices)

square

rectangle

hexagon

sphere

cube

My Word Cards

Point to the shape.
Say: *This shape is a **rectangle**.*

Point to the shape.
Say: *This shape is a **square**.*

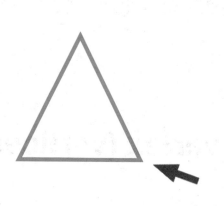

Point to the vertex of the triangle.
Say: *Another word for corner is **vertex**. All triangles have 3 **vertices**.*

Point to the shape.
Say: *This solid figure is a **cube**.*

Point to the shape.
Say: *This solid figure is a **sphere**.*

Point to the shape.
Say: *This shape is a **hexagon**.*

My Word Cards

Directions Have students cut out the vocabulary cards. Read the front of the card, and then ask them to explain what the word or phrase means.

A-Z Glossary

cone

cylinder

in front of

behind

next to

above

My Word Cards

Point to the orange.
Say: *The orange is **in front of** the basket.*

Point to the shape.
Say: *This solid figure is a **cylinder**.*

Point to the shape.
Say: *This solid figure is a **cone**.*

Point to the picture.
Say: *The picture is **above** the table.*

Point to the white dog.
Say: *The white dog is **next to** the brown dog.*

Point to the lamp.
Say: *The lamp is **behind** the table.*

My Word Cards

Directions Have students cut out the vocabulary cards. Read the front of the card, and then ask them to explain what the word or phrase means.

A-Z
Glossary

below

beside

My Word Cards

Point to the dog.
Say: *The dog is* **beside** *the dog house.*

Point to the ball.
Say: *The ball is* **below** *the table.*

© Pearson Education, Inc. K

Solve & Share

Name _____

Solve

Directions Say: *Pick 6 shapes from a bag. Put the shapes into two groups. Tell how the groups are different. Then draw a picture of the shapes you put on each table.*

I can ...
name shapes as flat or solid.

© **Content Standards**
K.G.A.3
Mathematical Practices
MP.3, MP.6, MP.7

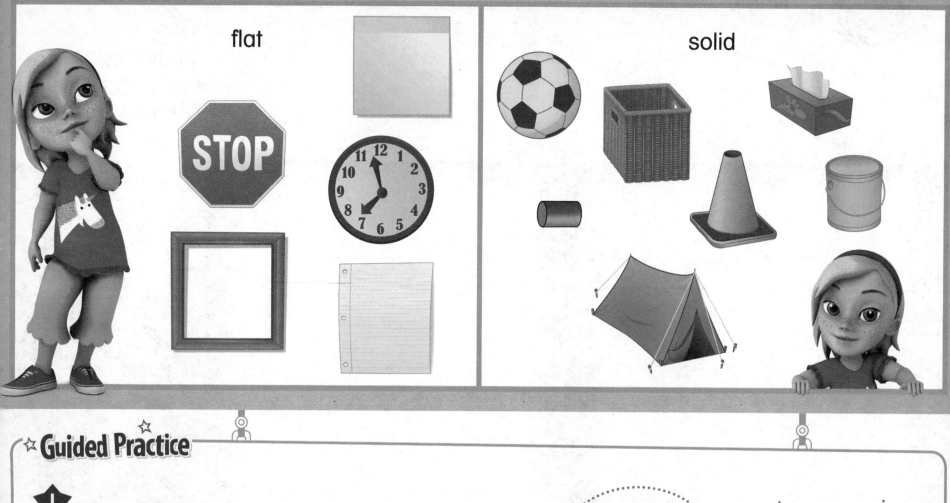

flat

solid

☆ Guided Practice

1

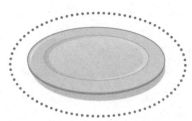

Directions ☆ Have students draw a circle around the objects that are flat, and mark an X on the objects that are solid.

Name _____

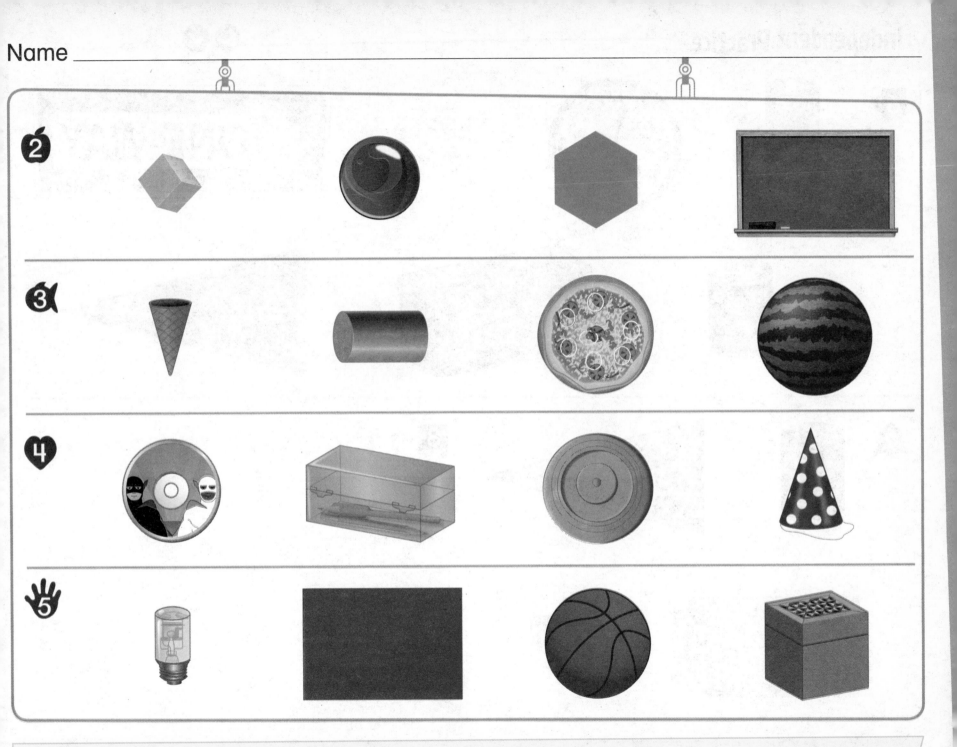

Directions Have students: 🍎 and 🐟 draw a circle around the objects that are flat in each row, and then mark an X on the objects that are solid; ♥ mark an X on the objects that are NOT flat; ✋ mark an X on the objects that are NOT solid.

Independent Practice

 6

 **7**

 8

Directions Have students: **6** mark an X on the objects that are solid. Then have them draw a circle around the objects that are flat; **7** mark an X on the objects that are NOT solid. **8** **Higher Order Thinking** Have students draw a picture of an object that is solid.

688 six hundred eighty-eight

© Pearson Education, Inc. K

Topic 12 | Lesson 1

Name _____

Another Look!

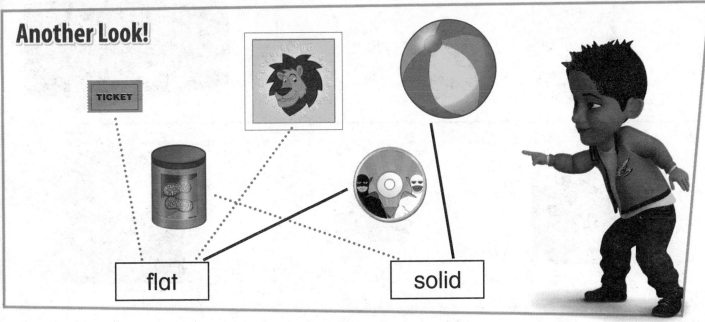

flat

solid

HOME ACTIVITY Point to various objects throughout your house. Have your child tell whether the object is flat or solid. Then have him or her draw a flat object and a solid object that can be found in the kitchen.

 1

Directions Say: *The DVD is flat. What other objects are flat? Draw a line from the objects that are flat to the box labeled* flat. *The beach ball is solid. Draw a line from other objects that are solid to the box labeled* solid. 🟊 Have students draw a circle around the objects that are flat, and then mark an X on the objects that are solid.

♥ 4

✋ 5

Topic 12 | Lesson 1

Name _____

Directions Say: *The zoo has a polar animals exhibit. There are polar bears and penguins. Place the shapes in the animal pens that are the same shape. Tell how the shapes you placed in the pen on the left are different from the shapes you placed in the pen on the right.*

I can ...
identify and describe circles and triangles.

© **Content Standards**
K.G.A.2, K.G.B.4
Mathematical Practices
MP.2, MP.5, MP.6, MP.7

☆ Guided Practice

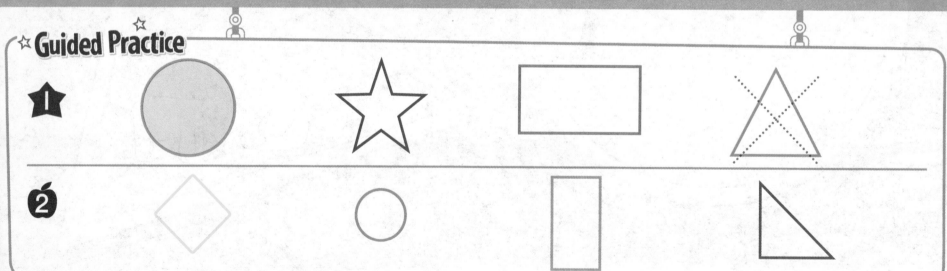

1

2

Directions ⭐ and 🍎 Have students color the circle in each row, and then mark an X on each triangle.

© Pearson Education, Inc. K

Name _____

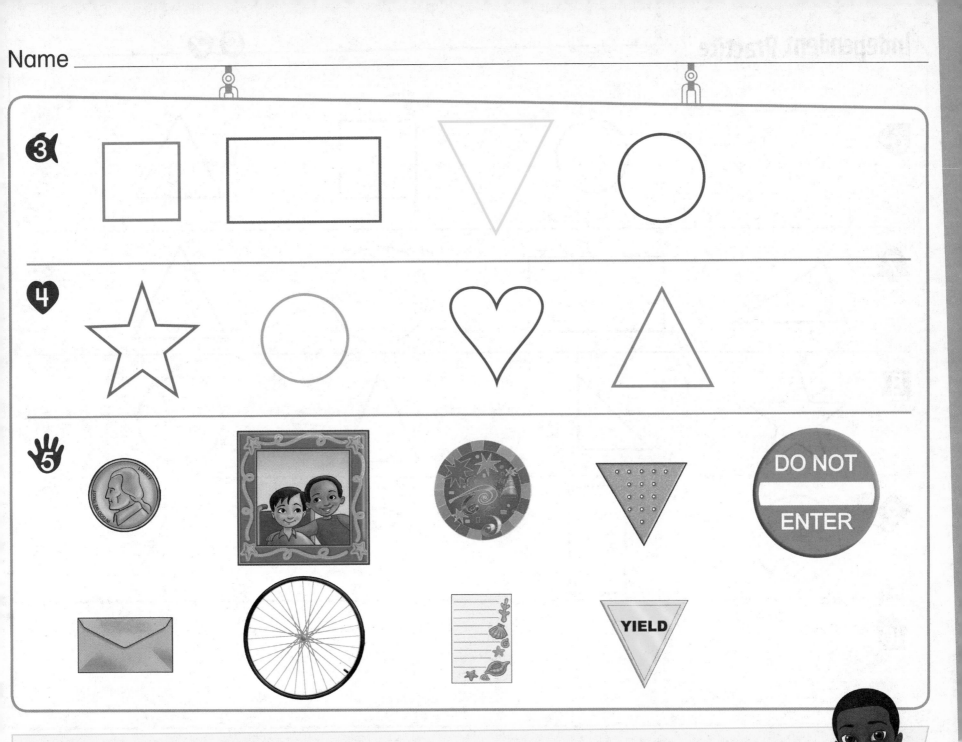

Directions ❸ Have students color the circle and mark an X on the triangle. ❹ **Number Sense** Have students mark an X on the shape that has 3 sides. ❺ Have students draw a circle around the objects that look like a triangle, and then mark an X on the objects that look like a circle.

Topic 12 | Lesson 2

six hundred ninety-three **693**

Independent Practice

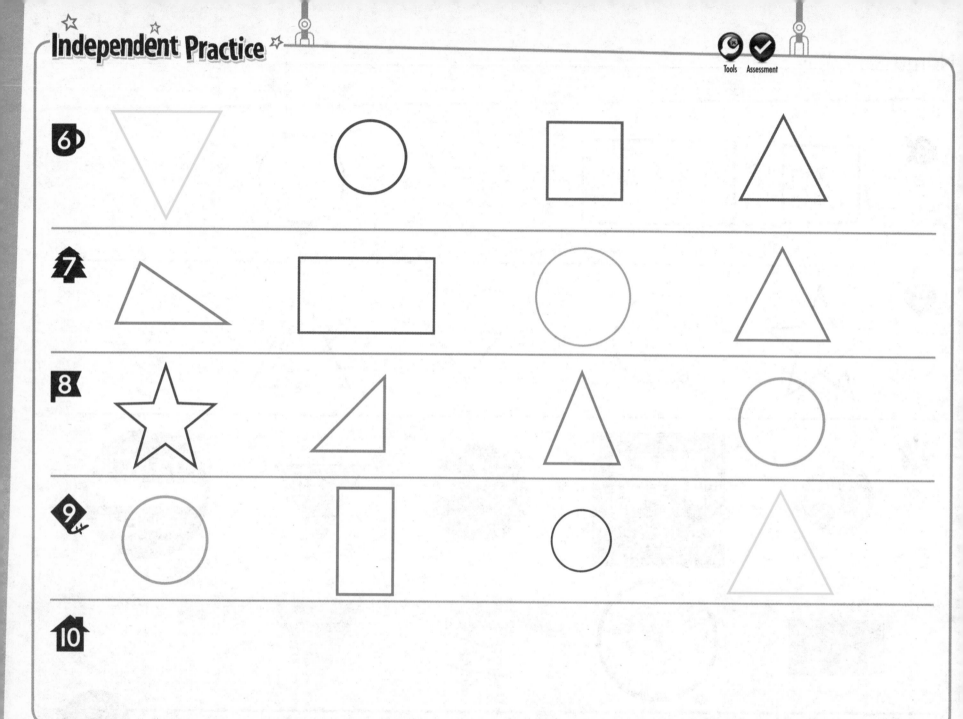

6

7

8

9

10

Directions 6–9 Have students color the circles and mark an X on the triangles in each row. 10 **Higher Order Thinking** Have students draw a picture of an object that is shaped like a triangle.

Name _____

Another Look!

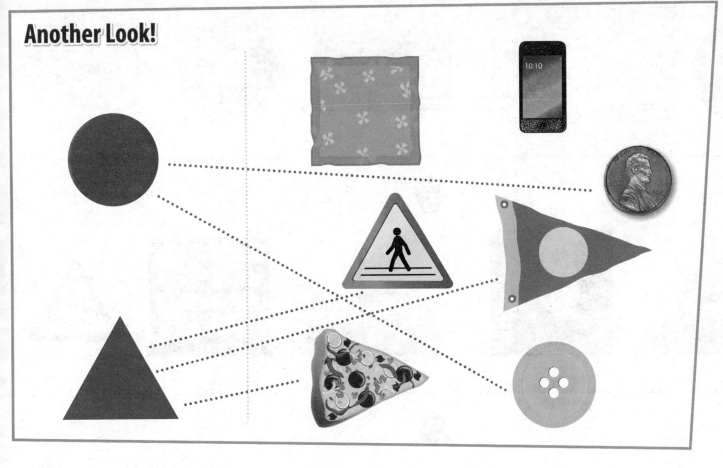

HOME ACTIVITY Look through a magazine with your child. Ask him or her to find pictures of objects that look like a circle or a triangle.

Directions Say: *A circle is round. Draw a line from the objects that look like a circle to the blue circle on the left. A triangle has 3 sides and 3 vertices. Draw a line from the objects that look like a triangle to the blue triangle on the left.* ⭐ Have students draw a circle around the objects that look like a triangle and mark an X on the objects that look like a circle.

2

 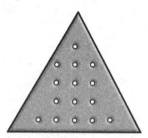 

 3

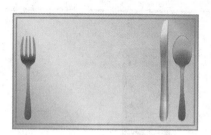  

4

5

6

7

Directions Have students: **2** and **3** mark an X on the objects that look like a circle; **4** and **5** draw a circle around the objects that look like a triangle. **6** **Higher Order Thinking** Have students draw a large red circle and a small blue triangle. **7** **Higher Order Thinking** Have students draw a picture using at least 2 circles and 1 triangle. Have them tell a partner what they drew using the names of the shapes.

© Pearson Education, Inc. K

Name _____

Solve

Lesson 12-3
Squares
and Other
Rectangles

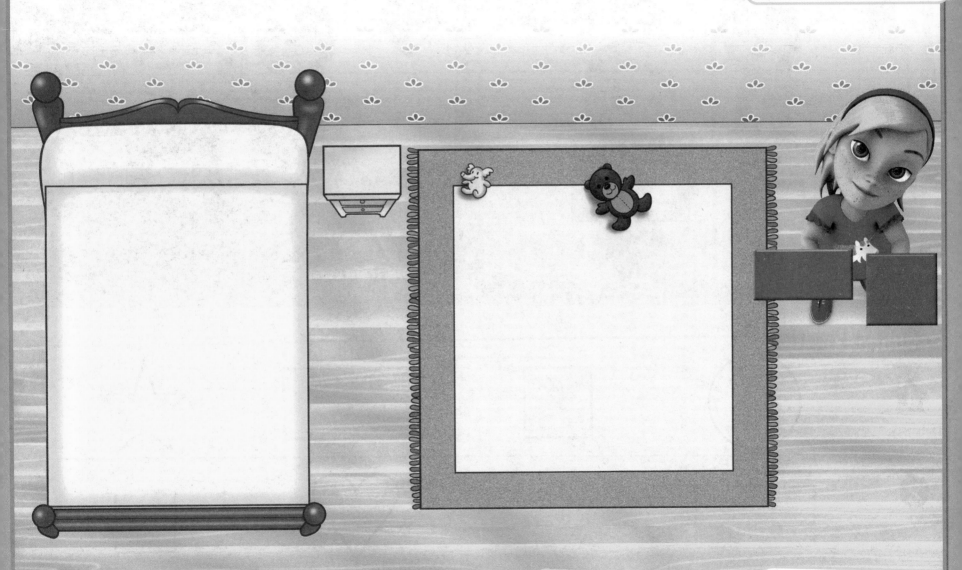

Directions Say: *Emily is holding 2 shapes. Pick either the red or the blue shape. Draw a line from that shape to something in the room that has the same shape.*

I can ...
identify and describe squares
and other rectangles.

© **Content Standards**
K.G.A.2, K.G.B.4
Mathematical Practices
MP.2, MP.6, MP.7, MP.8

☆ **Guided Practice**

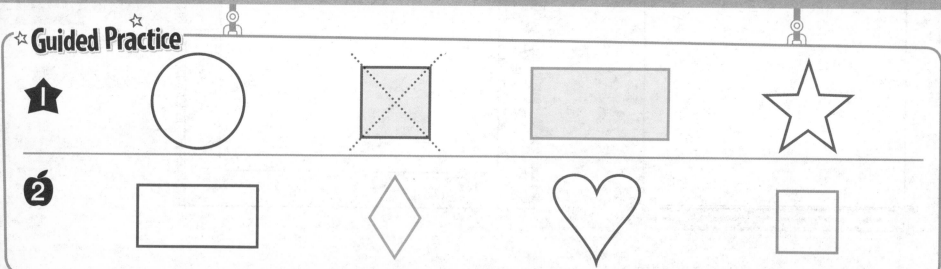

1

2

Directions 🌟 and 🍎 Have students color the rectangles in each row, and then mark an X on each rectangle that is also a square.

698 six hundred ninety-eight

© Pearson Education, Inc. K

Topic 12 | Lesson 3

Name _____

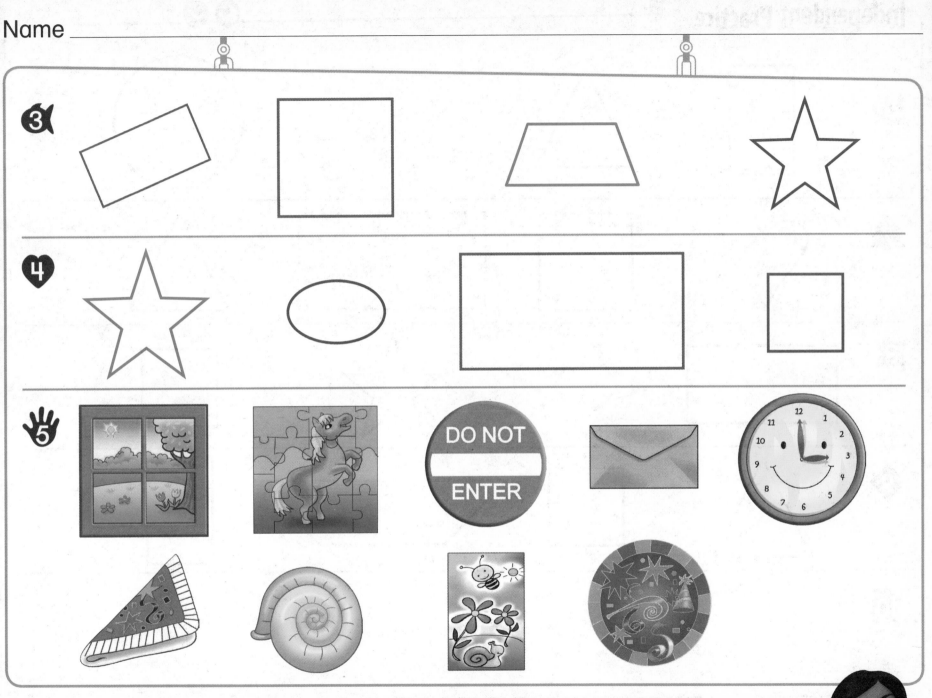

Directions Have students: ❸ and ❹ color the rectangles in each row, and then mark an X on each rectangle that is also a square; ✋⃝5 draw a circle around the objects that look like a rectangle, and then mark an X on each object that also looks like a square.

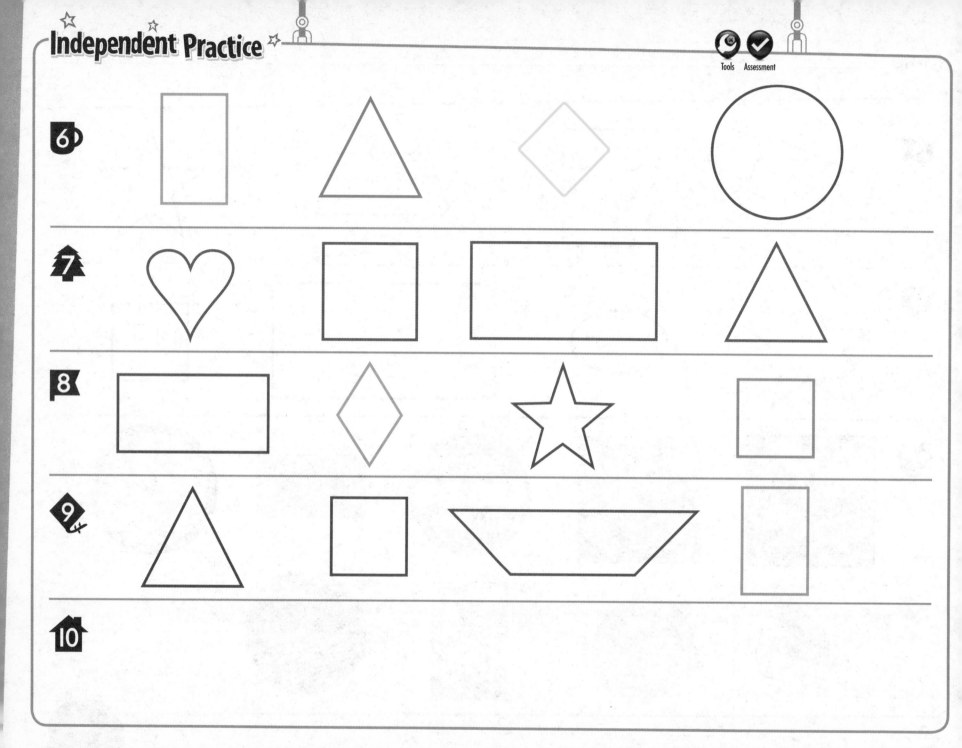

6

7

8

9

10

Directions 6–9 Have students color the rectangles in each row, and then mark an X on each rectangle that is also a square.
10 **Higher Order Thinking** Have students draw a green rectangle, and then draw a yellow square.

700 seven hundred   © Pearson Education, Inc. K   **Topic 12** | Lesson 3

Name ______________________

Help Tools Games

Homework & Practice 12-3

Squares and Other Rectangles

HOME ACTIVITY Take a walk around your home or neighborhood. Ask your child to look for windows that have the shape of a rectangle or a square.

Another Look!

1

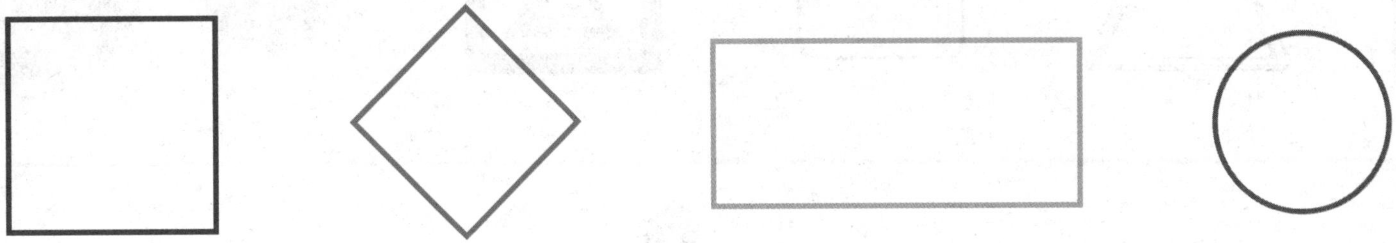

2

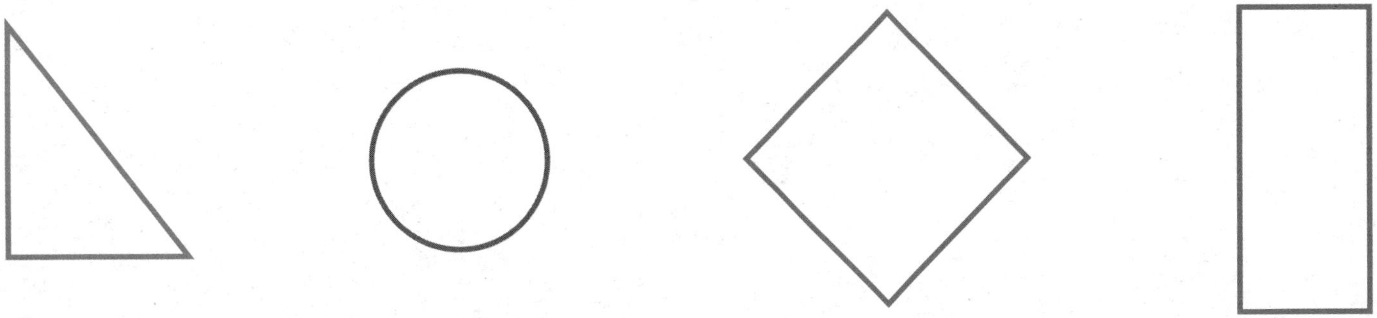

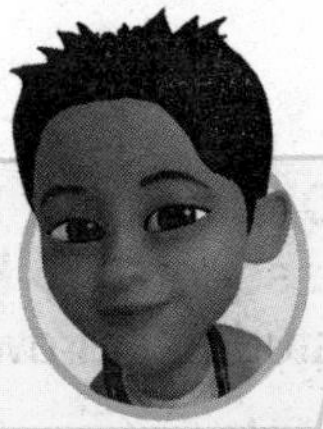

Directions Say: *Look at the shapes. What is the name of each shape? Color the square.* Have students: 1 look at the shapes, name them, and then color the squares; 2 look at the shapes, name them, and then color the rectangles.

3

 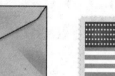 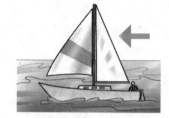

 4

 5

  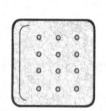  

 6

 7

Directions Have students: **3** and **4** mark an X on the objects that look like a rectangle; **5** draw a circle around the objects that look like a square. **6** **Higher Order Thinking** Have students draw an object that is both a rectangle and a square. **7** **Higher Order Thinking** Have students draw a picture using at least 2 rectangles and 2 squares.

Topic 12 | Lesson 3

Solve & Share

I can ...
describe and identify hexagons.

© **Content Standards**
K.G.A.2, K.G.B.4
Mathematical Practices
MP.3, MP.5, MP.6, MP.7

Directions Say: *Emily wants to buy art that has six-sided shapes in it like the yellow pattern block. Draw a circle around all the pieces of art that she can buy.*

✩ Guided Practice

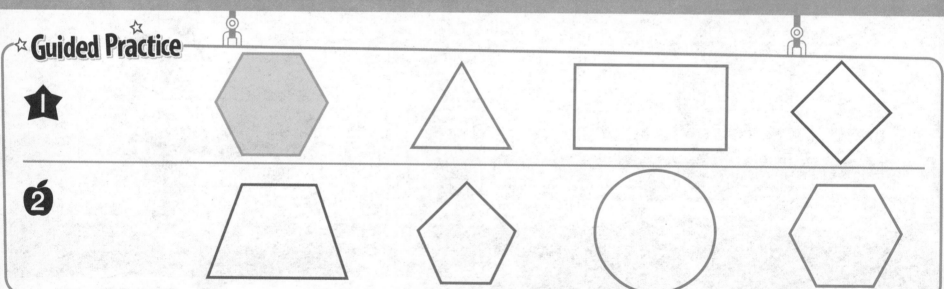

1

2

Directions **1** and **2** Have students color the hexagon in each row.

© Pearson Education, Inc. K

Name _____

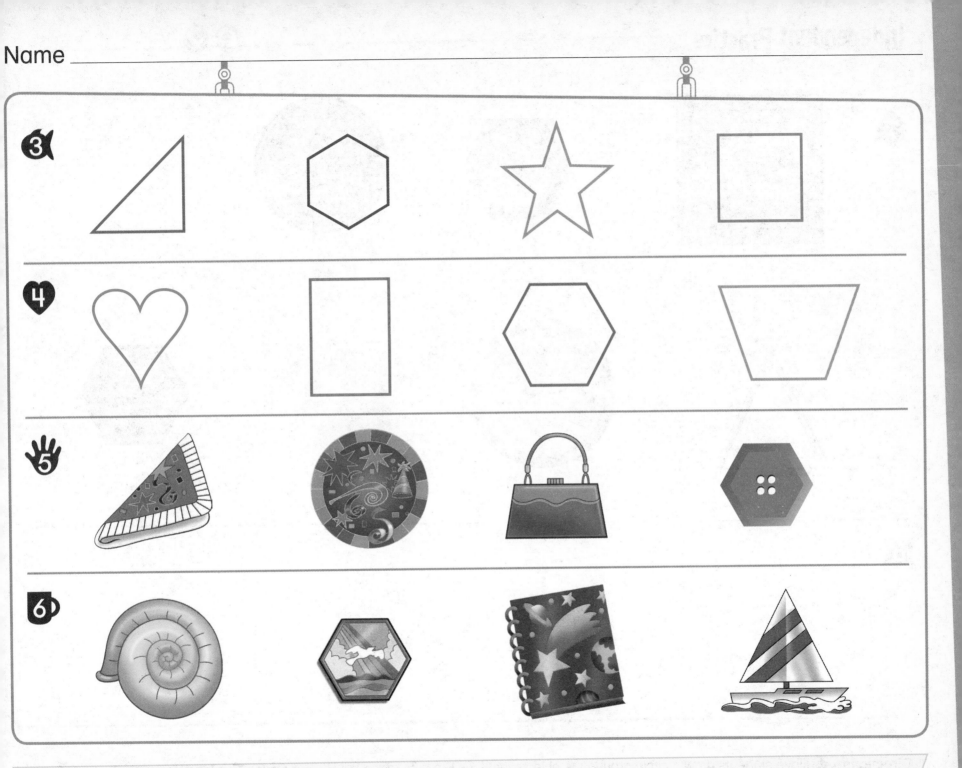

Directions Have students: 3 and 4 color the hexagon; 5 and 6 draw a circle around the object that looks like a hexagon.

Topic 12 | Lesson 4

seven hundred five **705**

7

8

Directions ✌ Have students draw a circle around the objects that look like a hexagon. **8 Higher Order Thinking** Have students draw a picture using at least 1 hexagon.

Topic 12 | Lesson 4

Name _____

Another Look!

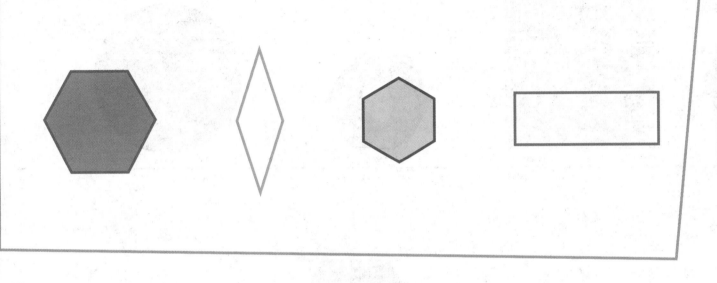

HOME ACTIVITY Have your child look through newspapers and magazines to identify pictures of objects that look like a hexagon. Then have them draw an object shaped like a hexagon.

  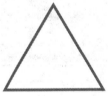

 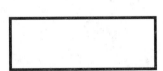 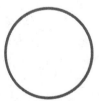 

Directions Say: *Look at the shapes. What is the name of each shape? Color the hexagons.* and ❷ Have students color the hexagons in each row.

3

4

Directions **3** and **4** Have students draw a circle around the objects that look like a hexagon. **5 Higher Order Thinking** Have students draw a picture of an object that is shaped like a hexagon.

© Pearson Education, Inc. K

Name _____

 Solve

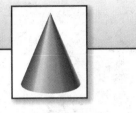

Directions Say: *Jackson wants to find objects that have the same shape as the solid figures. How can he find objects that have the same shape? Draw objects below each solid figure that have the same shape.*

I can ...
describe and identify solid figures.

© **Content Standards**
K.G.A.2, K.G.B.4
Mathematical Practices
MP.2, MP.4, MP.6, MP.7

1

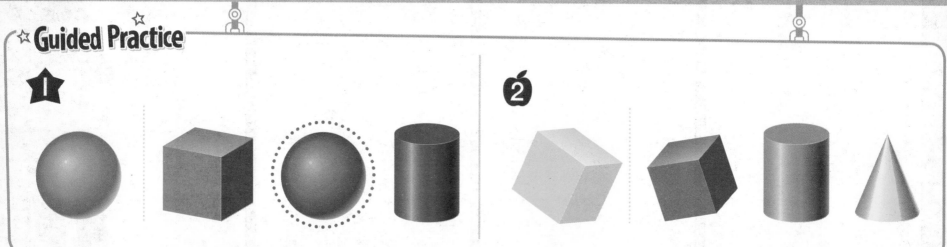

2

Directions ★ and ② Have students name the solid figure on the left, and then draw a circle around the solid figure on the right that is the same shape.

© Pearson Education, Inc. K

3

4

5

6

7

8

Directions **3** and **4** Have students name the solid figure on the left, and then draw a circle around the solid figure on the right that is the same shape. **5**—**8** Have students name the solid figure on the left, and then draw a circle around the object on the right that looks like that shape.

Independent Practice

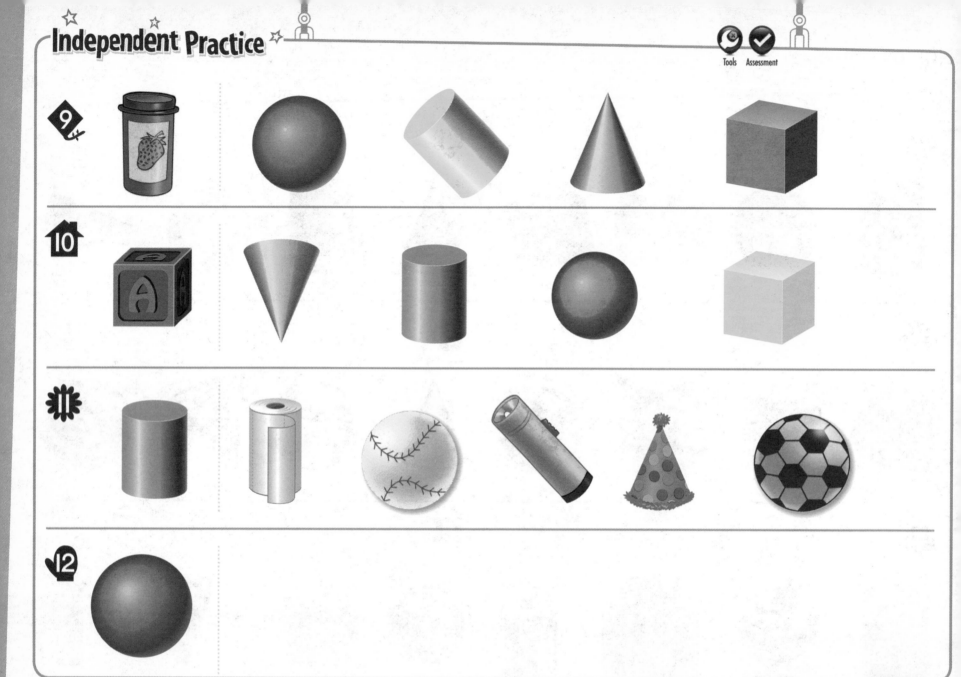

9

10

11

12

Directions Have students: **9** and **10** look at the object on the left, and then draw a circle around the solid figure on the right that looks like that shape; **11** name the solid figure on the left, and then draw a circle around the objects on the right that look like that shape. **12 Higher Order Thinking** Have students name the solid figure on the left, and then draw 2 more objects that look like that shape.

© Pearson Education, Inc. K **Topic 12** | Lesson 5

Name _____

Another Look!

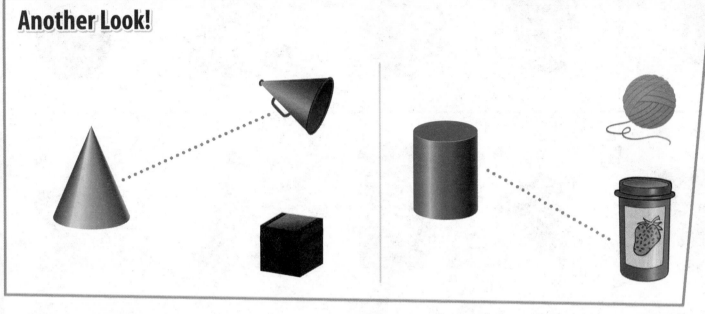

HOME ACTIVITY Show your child several objects that look like cubes, cylinders, spheres, or cones. Ask him or her to name the solid figure that it looks like. For example, show your child a ball and ask him or her to name the shape (sphere).

⭐1

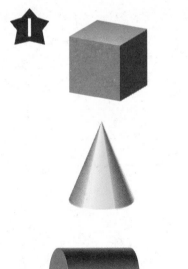

🍎2

Directions Have students point to the blue cone. Say: *This solid figure is a cone. Draw a line from the cone to the object that looks like that shape. Draw a line from the cylinder to the object that looks like that shape.* Have students: ⭐ and 🍎 draw a line from each solid figure to the object that looks like that shape.

6

Directions **3** and **4** Have students draw a circle around the 4 objects in each row that look like the same shape, and then name the shape. **Math and Science** Say: *Pushing on an object can make it move. Some shapes are easier to push than others.* Have students draw a circle around the object that is easier to push. **6 Higher Order Thinking** Have students draw 2 objects that do NOT look like a sphere. Tell a partner what shapes the objects look like.

714 seven hundred fourteen

© Pearson Education, Inc. K

Topic 12 | Lesson 5

Name _____

Directions Say: *Draw a circle around one of the shapes on the workmat. Name the shape. Can you find that shape in your classroom? Draw a picture of the object and its surroundings.*

I can ...
describe shapes in the environment.

© **Content Standards**
K.G.A.1, K.G.A.2, K.G.A.3
Mathematical Practices
MP.1, MP.3, MP.6, MP.7

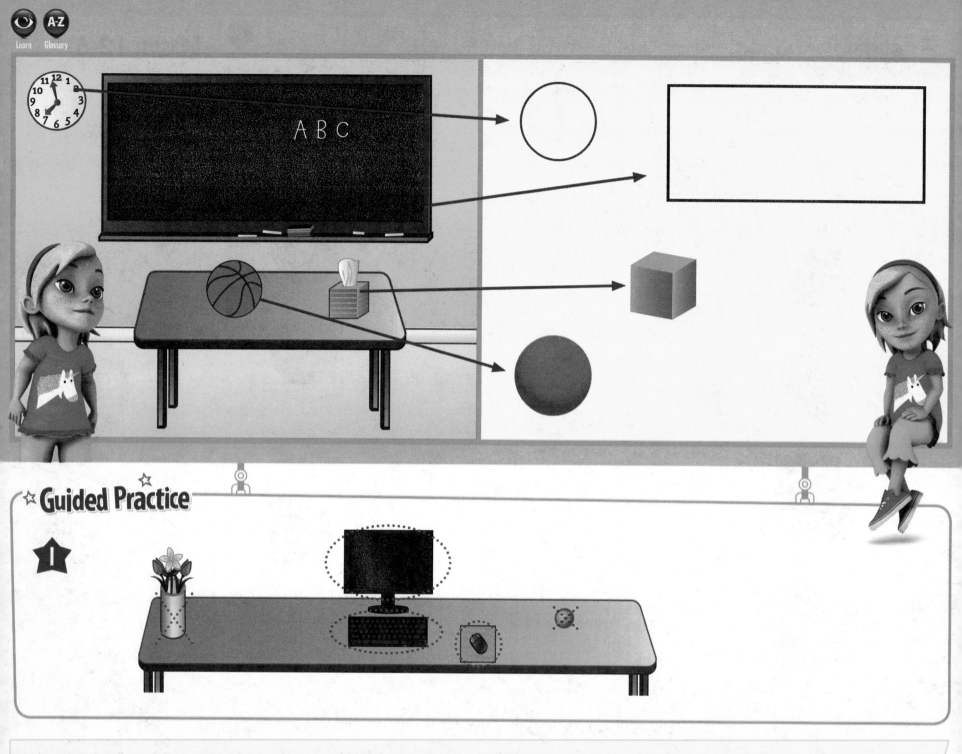

A B C

☆ **Guided Practice**

1

Directions ⭐ Have students point to objects in the picture and name their shape. Then have them draw a circle around objects that are flat, and then mark an X on the objects that are solid.

Topic 12 | Lesson 6

2

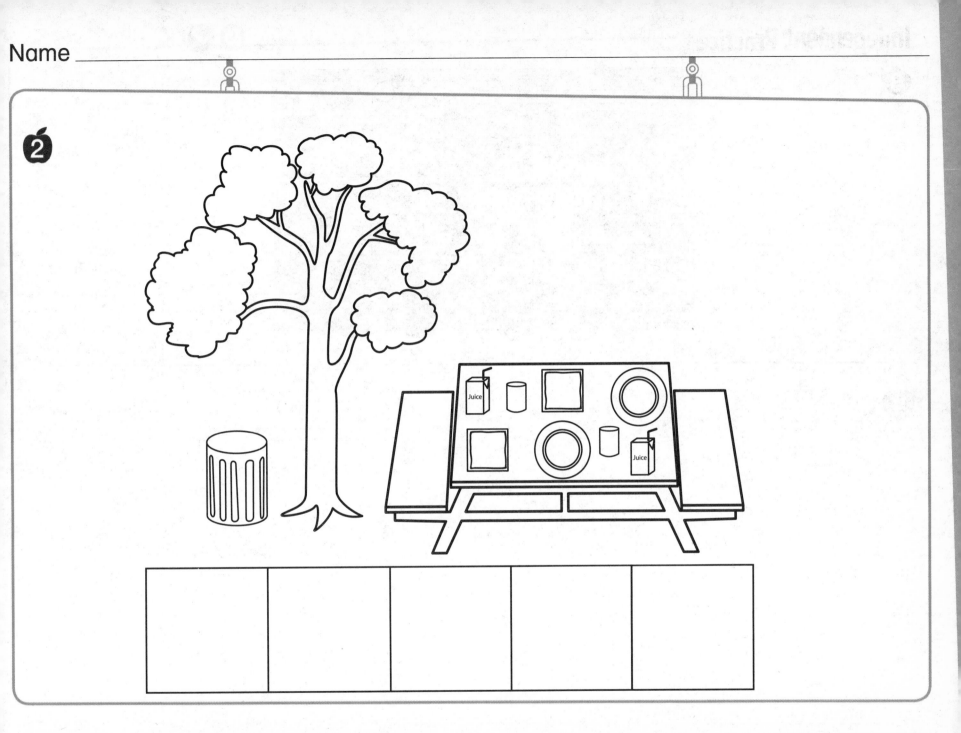

Directions ❷ Vocabulary Have students point to objects in the picture and name their shape. Then have them color the objects that look like a **square** blue, objects that look like a **cylinder** yellow, and objects that look like a **circle** red.

3

4

Directions ❸ Have students point to objects in the picture and name each shape. Then have them draw a circle around the objects that look like a cylinder, and mark an X on the objects that look like a cone. ❹ **Higher Order Thinking** Have students draw a picture of a park. Have them include 1 or more objects in the park that look like a rectangle.

© Pearson Education, Inc. K

Name _____

Another Look!

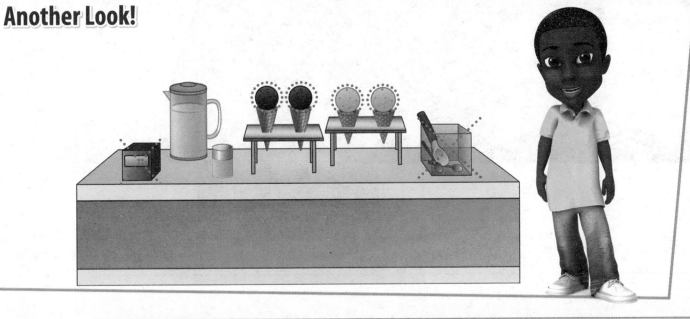

HOME ACTIVITY Have your child identify and name objects in your house that look like a circle, square, rectangle, triangle, hexagon, sphere, cube, cylinder, and cone. Have them tell where each object is located in the house.

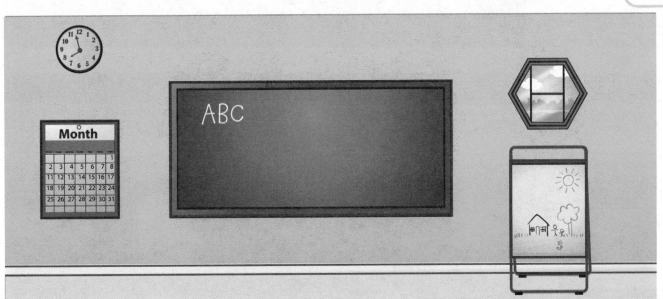

Directions Say: *Point to a scoop of ice cream. What shape is the scoop of ice cream? Find other objects in the picture that look like a sphere and draw a circle around them. Can you find an object that looks like a cube? Mark an X on the objects that look like a cube.*
⭐ Have students point to objects in the picture and name each shape. Then have them draw a circle around the objects that look like a rectangle, and then mark an X on the object that looks like a hexagon.

Topic 12 | Lesson 6   Digital Resources at PearsonRealize.com   seven hundred nineteen **719**

Directions ❷ Have students point to objects in the picture and name their shape. Have them draw a circle around objects that are flat, and then mark an X on objects that are solid. ❸ **Higher Order Thinking** Have students draw a picture of a playground. Have them draw at least 1 object that looks like a sphere and 1 object that looks like a rectangle.

720 seven hundred twenty   © Pearson Education, Inc. K   **Topic 12** | Lesson 6

Solve & Share

Name _____

Directions Say: Emily feeds the animals on the farm. Look at the objects in the picture. Color and name the shapes you see. Draw a horse on the farm. Describe the position of the horse.

I can ...
describe positions of shapes in the environment.

© **Content Standards**
K.G.A.1
Mathematical Practices
MP.1, MP.2, MP.3, MP.6

Guided Practice

1

Directions ⭐ Have students mark an X on the object next to the pencil that looks like a rectangle. Have students draw an object that looks like a square in front of the mug. Then have them draw an object that looks like a cone next to the table.

© Pearson Education, Inc. K

Name _____

Directions ② Have students name the shape of the objects in the picture and use position words to describe their location. Then have them draw an X on the object in front of the sandcastle that looks like a cylinder. Have students draw an object that looks like a sphere beside Jackson, and then an object that looks like a rectangle beside the sandbox.

3

Directions 3 **Higher Order Thinking** Have students mark an X on the object below the tree that looks like a rectangle. Have students draw an object that looks like a sphere above the tree, and then an object that looks like a triangle behind the fence. Then have them name the shape of the objects in the picture and use position words to describe their location.

© Pearson Education, Inc. K

Name _____

Another Look!

HOME ACTIVITY Have your child name the shapes of several items in the kitchen, and then tell where they are located using the following position words: *above, below, in front of, behind, next to,* and *beside.*

Directions Say: *Look at the shapes on the left. Then look at the picture. Find the object that is below the tree, and then mark an X on the shape that it looks like. Then draw circles around the objects in the picture that look like circles.* ⭐ Have students find the object that is behind the cone, and then mark an X on the solid figure that it looks like on the left. Then have students draw circles around the objects in the picture that are shaped like spheres.

2

3

© Pearson Education, Inc. K

 **Solve & Share**

Name _____

Solve

Think.

Directions Say: *Emily's teacher teaches her class a game. She uses 1 blue cube, 1 red cube, 1 yellow counter, and 1 red counter and puts each of them somewhere on the farm picture. Play this game with a partner. Place the tools on the page, and then describe where one of them is located. Do NOT tell your partner which one you are talking about. How can your partner tell which one you are describing? Change places and play again.*

I can ...
describe positions of shapes in the environment.

© **Mathematical Practices**
MP.6 Also MP.3, MP.2
Content Standards
K.G.A.1

Topic 12 | Lesson 8

Digital Resources at PearsonRealize.com

seven hundred twenty-seven **727**

☆ Guided Practice

⭐ **1**

Directions ⭐ Have students mark an X on the object above the bed that looks like a cube. Then have them explain how they know they are correct. Then have them draw a shape that looks like a rectangle next to the bed.

© Pearson Education, Inc. K

Tools Assessment

Independent Practice

2

3

Directions **2** Have students name the shapes of the objects in the picture. Then have them mark an X on the object that is behind another object, and is next to the object that looks like a cylinder. Have them explain how they decided which shape to mark. **3** Have students find the object in the picture that is NOT beside the box of tissues, and then mark an X on the solid it looks like on the left. Have them explain why a sphere is NOT the right answer. Then have them name the shape of the objects in the picture.

4 5 6

Directions Read the problem to students. Then have them use multiple math practices to solve the problem. Say: *Carlos wants to tell a friend about different things in the locker room and where they are located. What words can he use?* 4 **MP.6 Be Precise** *Mark an X on the object that looks like a cylinder that is beside the object that looks like a cube. What words helped you find the correct object?* 5 **MP.2 Reason** *Carlos says the soccer ball is behind the water bottle. What is another way to explain where the water bottle is?* 6 **MP.3 Explain** *Carlos describes the rectangle poster as being above the circle clock. Do you agree or disagree? Explain how you know you are correct.*

© Pearson Education, Inc. K

Name _____

Another Look!

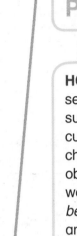

HOME ACTIVITY Place several items on a table, such as a plate, spoon, fork, cup, and napkin. Have your child tell the position of each object using the following words: *above, below, beside, next to, in front of,* and *behind*. For example, a child might say, "The spoon is beside the plate."

1

Directions Say: *Look at the objects in the picture. Name the shapes of the objects you see. Now draw a circle around the shapes that you see. Name the object above the basketball. Mark an X on that object. Draw a circle around the object that is next to the basketball and below the block.* ⭐ Have students mark an X on the object that looks like a sphere below the picnic table. Then have them draw a circle around the object that looks like a cylinder beside the tree.

Directions Read the problem to students. Then have them use multiple math practices to solve the problem. Say: *Marta wants to tell a friend about different things in the kitchen and where they are located. What words can she use?* ❷ **MP.6 Be Precise** *Mark an X on the object that looks like a cylinder that is behind the object that looks like a cone. What words helped you find the correct object?* ❸ **MP.2 Reason** *The ice cream cone is next to the sugar cube. What is another way to explain where the ice cream cone is?* ❹ **MP.3 Explain** *Marta describes the door as looking like a rectangle. She also says it is below the clock. Do you agree or disagree? Explain how you know you are correct.*

     Topic 12 | Lesson 8

1

5 − 2	3 − 1	1 − 1	2 + 0	5 − 4
5 − 0	0 + 2	3 + 1	2 − 0	1 + 2
1 + 4	2 + 0	4 − 2	5 − 3	4 − 0
0 + 1	1 + 1	4 − 3	3 − 1	4 − 1
3 + 2	4 − 2	0 + 3	1 + 1	4 − 4

2

_____

_ _ _ _ _

_____

I can ...
add and subtract fluently within 5.

© **Content Standard** K.OA.A.5

Directions Have students: ★ color each box that has a sum or difference that is equal to 2; ❷ write the letter that they see.

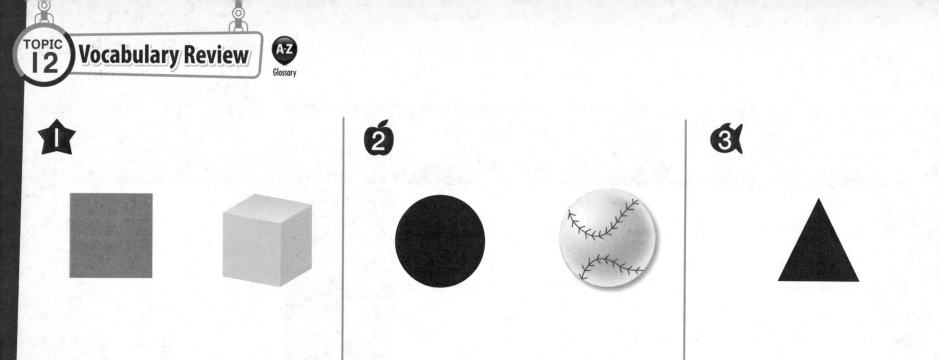
⭐ **1**

🍎 **2**

🐦 **3**

❤️ **4**

✋ **5**

Directions **Understand Vocabulary** Have students: ⭐ draw a circle around the **two-dimensional** shape; 🍎 draw a circle around the **three-dimensional** shape; 🐦 draw a circle around the **vertices** of the triangle; ❤️ draw a **circle**; ✋ draw a shape that is NOT a **square**.

Name _____

Set A _____

⭐

Set B _____

🍎

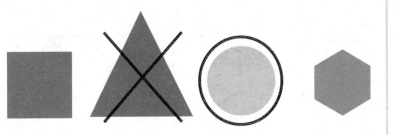

Directions Have students: ⭐ draw a circle around the objects that are flat, and then mark an X on the objects that are solid; 🍎 draw a circle around the objects that look like a circle, and then mark an X on the objects that look like a triangle.

Topic 12 | Reteaching

seven hundred thirty-five **735**

Set C

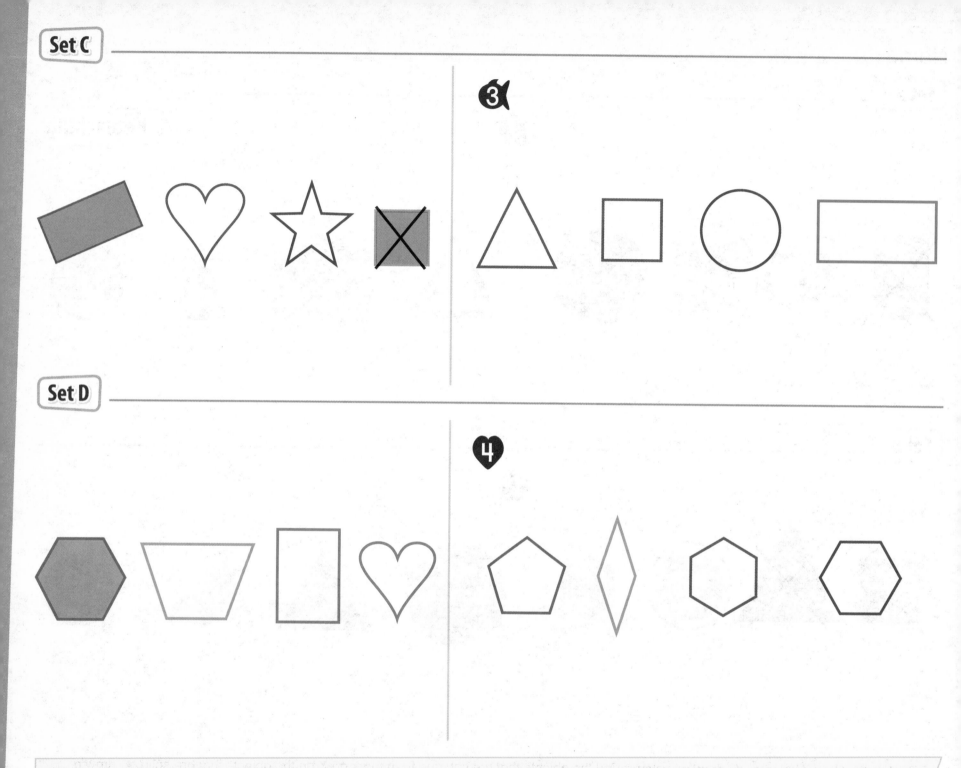

③

Set D

④

Directions Have students: ③ color the rectangles, and then mark an X on the rectangle that is a square; ④ color the hexagons.

Topic 12 | Reteaching

Name _____

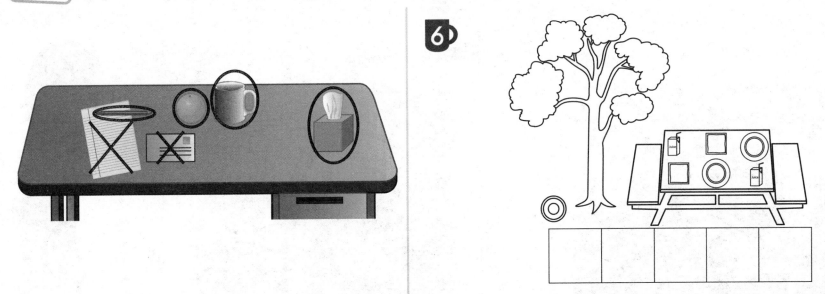

Directions Have students: ✋🖐 name the solid figure on the left, and then draw a circle around the solid figure that looks like that shape on the right; ☕ point to each object in the picture and tell what shape each looks like. Then have them draw a circle around the objects that are solid, and mark an X on objects that are flat.

Topic 12 | Reteaching

seven hundred thirty-seven **737**

Use Digital Tools.

Directions Have students: 7️⃣ mark an X on the object that is next to the blue book, and then draw a circle around the object that is below the object that is shaped like a sphere; 8️⃣ mark an X on the objects that look like a circle that are behind the object that is shaped like a sphere.

© Pearson Education, Inc. K

Name _____

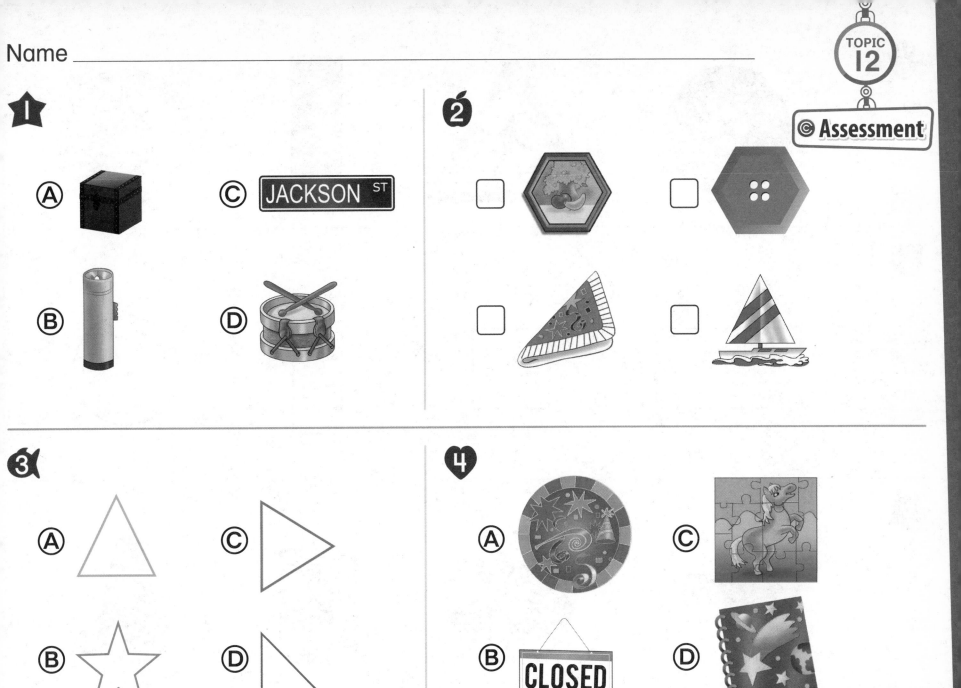

1

Ⓐ 　Ⓒ JACKSON ST

Ⓑ 　Ⓓ

2

☐ 　☐

☐ 　☐

3

Ⓐ 　Ⓒ

Ⓑ 　Ⓓ

4

Ⓐ 　Ⓒ

Ⓑ CLOSED 　Ⓓ

Directions Have students mark the best answer. ★ Which object is NOT solid? ② Mark all the objects that look like a hexagon. ③ Which object is NOT a triangle? ④ Which object looks like a square?

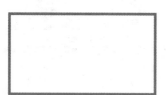  

Directions Have students: mark an X on the objects that do NOT look like a circle; name the shapes, color the rectangles, and then mark an X on the rectangle that is a square; look at the solid figure on the left, and then draw a circle around the object that looks like that shape.

© Pearson Education, Inc. K

Topic 12 | Assessment

Name _____

flat	solid
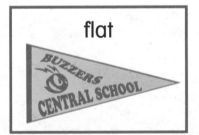	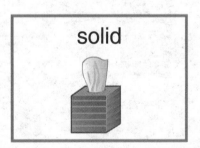

Directions Have students: 🔳 draw an object that looks like a cylinder in front of the vase. Then mark an X on the object that looks like a square next to the cat; 🔷 draw lines from the objects that are flat to the first box. Then have them draw lines from the objects that are solid to the second box.

Directions Have students: 🔟 draw a picture of an object that looks like a sphere below a book and next to a cup; 🕚 draw a picture of an object that is flat. Then have them draw an object that is solid; 🕛 draw a circle around the objects that look like a circle, and then mark an X on the objects that look like a rectangle.

© Pearson Education, Inc. K

Topic 12 | Assessment

Name _____

© Performance Assessment

1

2

Directions **Play Time!** Say: *Supna and her friends are playing with toys.* Have students: **1** draw a circle around the toys that look like a cube. Have students mark an X on the toys that look like a cylinder; **2** draw a circle around the toys that look like a rectangle. Then have them mark an X on the rectangles that are squares.

Directions Have students: ❸ mark an X on the object in the playroom that looks like a hexagon; ❹ draw an object next to the shelves that looks like a cone; ✋❺ listen to the clues, and then draw a circle around the object the clues describe. Say: *The object is above the blocks. It looks like a sphere. It is next to a green ball. The object is NOT yellow.*

Analyze, Compare, and Create Shapes

Essential Question: How can solid figures be named, described, compared, and composed?

Digital Resources

Solve Learn Glossary

Tools Assessment Help Games

Math and Science Project: How Do Objects Move?

Directions Read the character speech bubbles to students. **Find Out!** Have students observe and describe how objects move using the terms *roll*, *stack*, and *slide*. Say: *Objects move in different ways. Talk to your friends and relatives about everyday objects that are cones, cylinders, spheres, or cubes. Ask them how each one moves and whether they roll, stack, or slide.* **Journal: Make a Poster** Have students make a poster that shows everyday objects that are cones, cylinders, spheres, and cubes, and then tell how each one moves.

Name _____

1

○ □ △

2

▭ ○ △

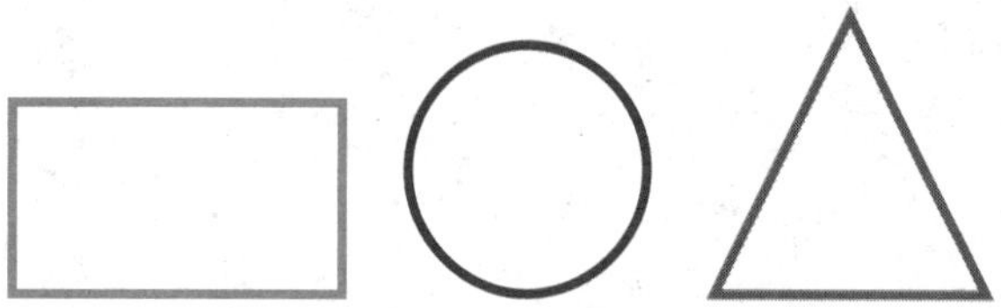

3

□ ▭ ○

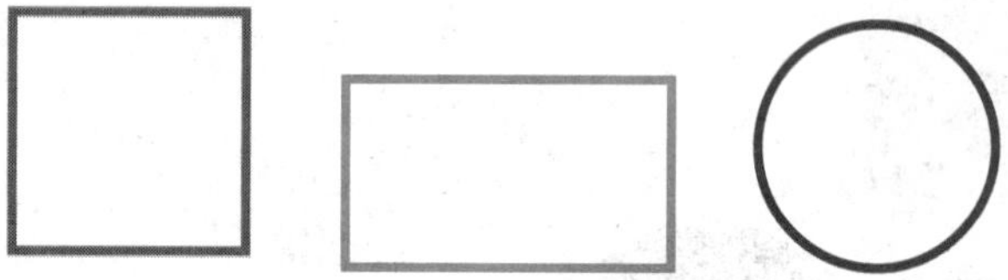

4

▶ ■
▲ ♥

5

■ ■
▲ ●

6

● ●
■ ●

Directions Have students: ★ draw a circle around the triangle; ② draw a circle around the circle; ③ draw a circle around the square; ④–⑥ draw a circle around the shapes that are the same shape.

© Pearson Education, Inc. K

Topic 13

My Word Cards

Directions Have students cut out the vocabulary cards. Read the front of the card, and then ask them to explain what the word or phrase means.

A-Z
Glossary

roll

slide

stack

flat surface

My Word Cards

Point to the shapes.
Say: *Some solid figures can* **stack** *on each other.*

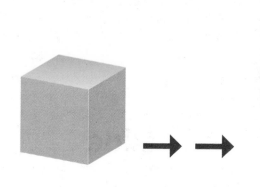

Point to the shape.
Say: *Solid figures with flat surfaces can* **slide**.

Point to the shape.
Say: *Some solid figures can* **roll**.

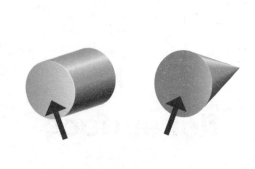

Point to the flat surface of each object.
Say: *Some solid figures have* **flat surfaces**.

Solve & Share

Name _____

Directions Say: *Emily wants to figure out what shape is behind the door. The shape has 4 vertices and 4 equal sides. Use the shapes above the door to help you find the mystery shape. Draw the shape on the door.*

I can ...
analyze and compare 2-D shapes.

© **Content Standards**
K.G.B.4
Mathematical Practices
MP.2, MP.4, MP.6, MP.7

Guided Practice

Directions Have students listen to the clues, mark an X on the shapes that do NOT fit the clues, draw a circle around the shape that the clues describe, and then tell how the shapes they marked with an X are different from the shape they drew a circle around. ⭐ *I have 4 sides. I do NOT have 4 sides that are the same length. What shape am I?* ② *I do NOT have 4 sides. I do NOT have any vertices. What shape am I?*

© Pearson Education, Inc. K

Topic 13 | Lesson 1

Name _____

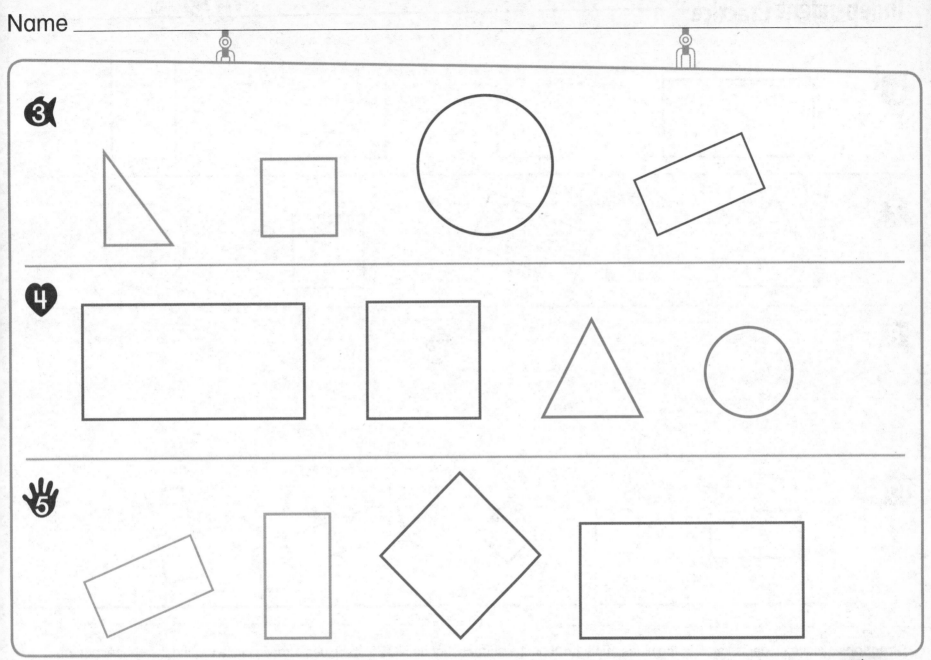

3

4

5

Directions Have students listen to the clues, mark an X on the shapes that do NOT fit the clues, draw a circle around the shape that the clues describe, and then tell how the shapes they marked with an X are similar to the shape they drew a circle around.
3 Number Sense *I am NOT round. I have less than 4 sides. What shape am I?* **4** *I am NOT a rectangle. I have 0 sides. What shape am I?* **5** *I have 4 vertices. I am a special kind of rectangle because all my sides are the same length. What shape am I?*

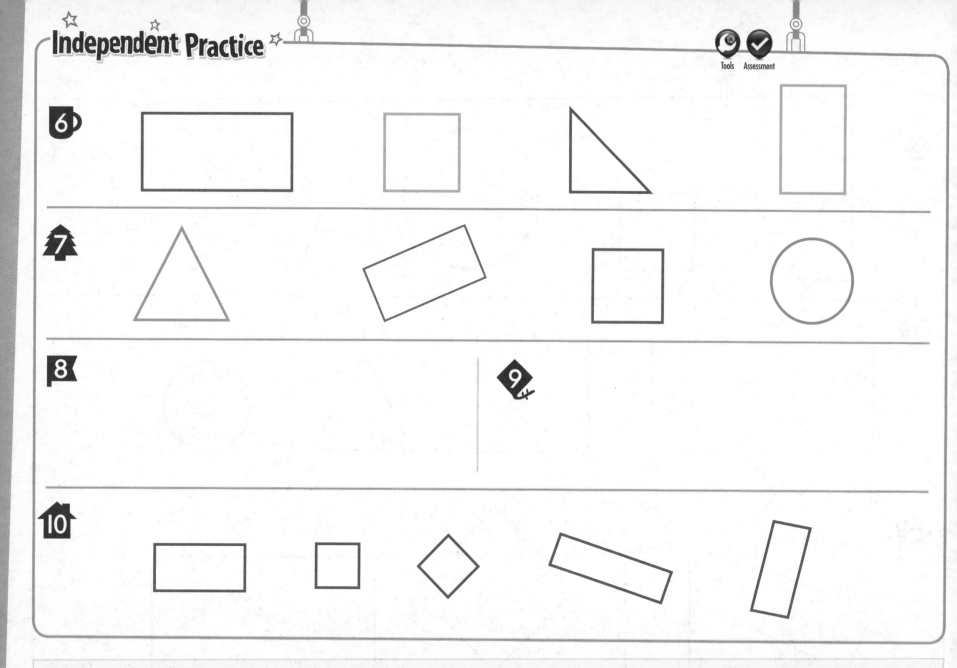

6

7

8

9

10

Directions Have students listen to the clues, mark an X on the shapes that do NOT fit the clues, draw a circle around the shape that the clues describe, and then tell how the shapes they marked with an X are different from the shape they drew a circle around. **6** *All of my sides are NOT the same length. I have 3 vertices. What shape am I?* **7** *I have 4 sides. I am the same shape as a classroom door. What shape am I?* **8** Have students listen to the clues, and then draw the shape the clues describe: *I have more than 3 sides. The number of vertices I have is less than 5. All of my sides are the same length. What shape am I?* **9** **Higher Order Thinking** Have students draw a shape with 4 sides and 4 vertices that is NOT a square or rectangle, and then explain why it is not. **10** **Higher Order Thinking** Have students draw a circle around the rectangles. Have them color all the squares, and then explain how the shapes are both similar and different from one another.

Topic 13 | Lesson 1

Name _____

Another Look!

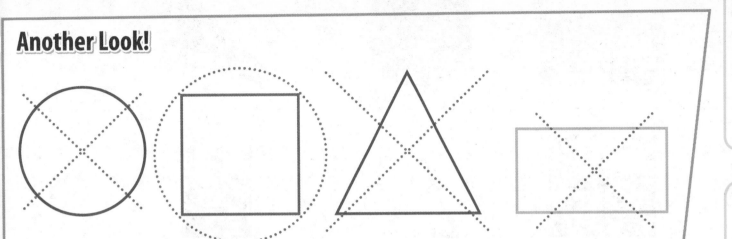

 1

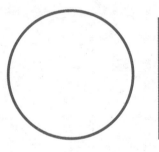 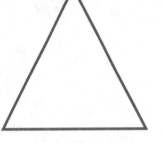  

 2

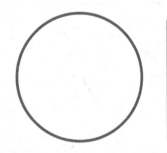 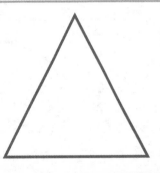  

HOME ACTIVITY Play *What Object Am I?* with your child. Think of an object in the house, such as a window or a door, and give clues about it. For example: "I have 4 sides and 4 vertices. All of my sides are the same length. What shape am I?" Then have your child give you clues about an object.

Directions Say: *Listen to the clues. After each clue, mark an X on any shape that does NOT fit the clue. I have 4 sides. I am a special kind of rectangle because all of my sides are the same length. Draw a circle around the shape that fits all of the clues.* Have students listen to the clues, mark an X on the shapes that do NOT fit the clues, draw a circle around the shape that the clues describe, and then tell how the shapes they marked with an X are similar to the shape they drew a circle around. ⭐ *I do NOT have 4 vertices. I have 3 sides. What shape am I?* ❷ *I have 4 vertices. My sides are NOT all the same length. What shape am I?*

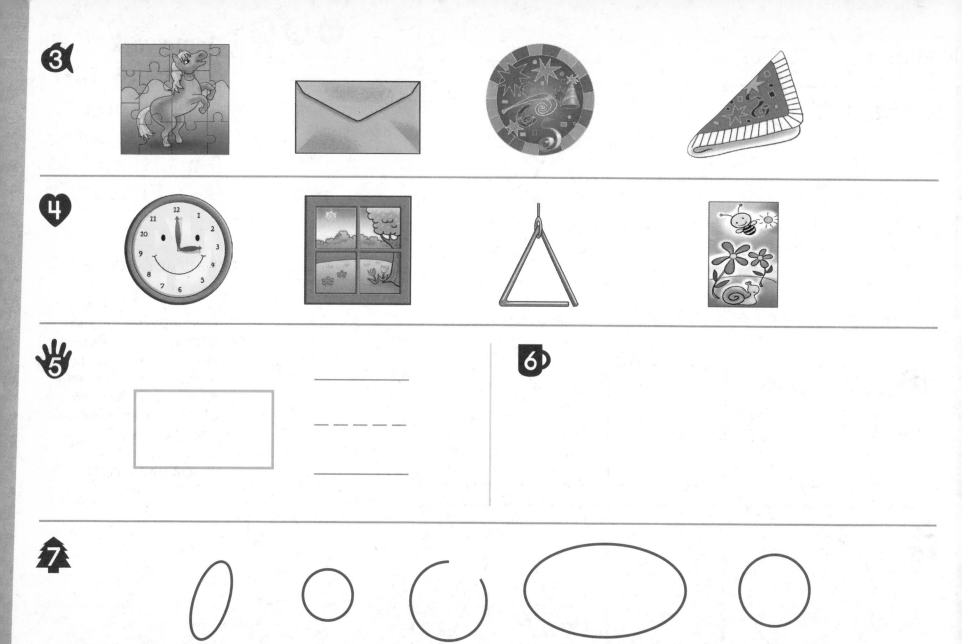

3

4

5

6

7

Directions Have students listen to the clues to find the mystery object in each row. Have students mark an X on the objects that do NOT fit the clues, draw a circle around the object that the clues describe, and then tell how the shape of the objects they marked with an X are different from the shape of the object they drew a circle around. **3** *I do NOT have 3 sides. I am round. What shape do I look like?* **4** *I am NOT round. I have 4 sides that are the same length. What shape do I look like?* **5** Have students write the number that tells how many vertices the shape has. **6** **Higher Order Thinking** Have students draw a picture of an object in the classroom that has 0 sides and 0 corners. **7** **Higher Order Thinking** Have students draw a circle around the circles, and then mark an X on the other shapes. Have them explain why the others are NOT circles.

Solve

Lesson 13-2

Analyze and
Compare
Three-
Dimensional
(3-D) Shapes

Name _____

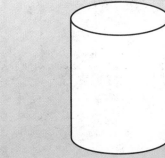

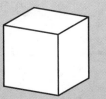

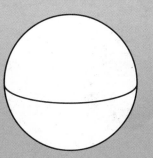

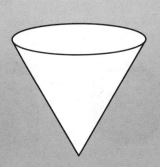

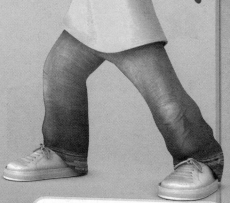

Directions Say: *Jackson wants to find a solid figure. The solid figure has flat sides and it rolls. Color the solid figures that match the description.*

I can ...
analyze and compare
3-D shapes.

© **Content Standards**
K.G.B.4
Mathematical Practices
MP.1, MP.2, MP.3, MP.7

☆ Guided Practice

1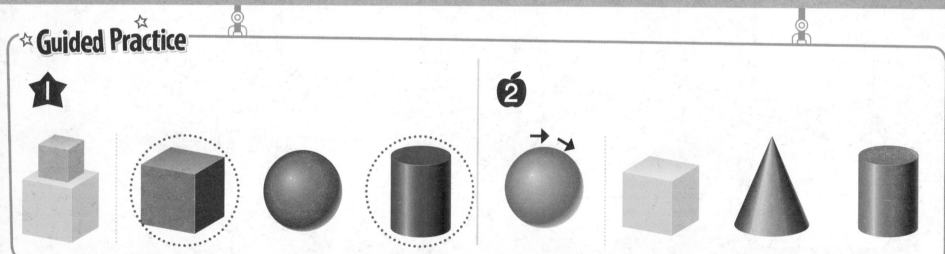

2

Directions Have students: **1** look at the stacked solid figures on the left, and then draw a circle around the other solid figures that stack; **2** look at the rolling solid figure on the left, and then draw a circle around the other solid figures that roll.

756 seven hundred fifty-six

© Pearson Education, Inc. K

Topic 13 | Lesson 2

Name _____

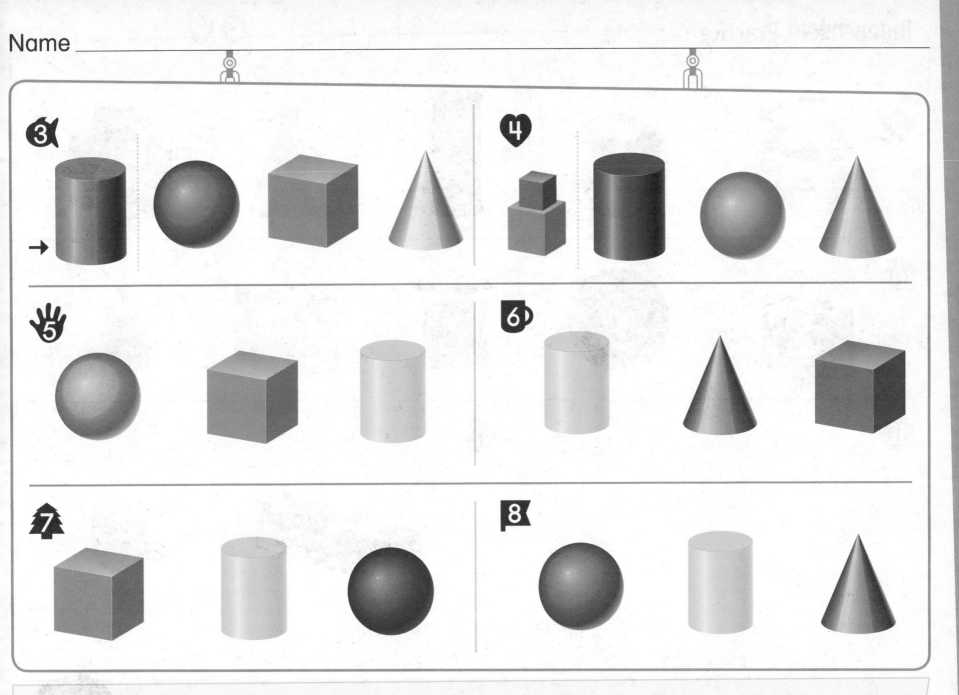

Directions Have students: ❸ look at the sliding solid figure on the left, and then draw a circle around the other solid figures that slide; ❹ look at the stacked solid figures on the left, and then draw a circle around the other solid figures that stack; ✋ draw a circle around the solid figure that rolls and stacks; ❻ draw a circle around the solid figures that slide and roll; 🌲 draw a circle around the solid figures that stack and slide. ⛳ **Math & Science** Have students draw a circle around the solid figure that does NOT stack or slide. Then ask them what motion would cause a sphere to roll.

Independent Practice

9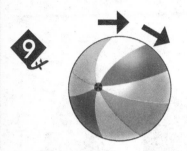

10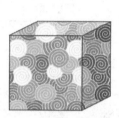

11

12

Directions Have students: **9** look at the rolling object on the left, and then draw a circle around the other objects that roll; **10** look at the sliding object on the left, and then draw a circle around the other objects that slide. **11 Higher Order Thinking** Have students draw 2 solid figures that can stack on each other. **12 Higher Order Thinking** Have students draw a circle around the cube, and then explain why the other solid is NOT a cube.

© Pearson Education, Inc. K **Topic 13 | Lesson 2**

Name _____

Another Look!

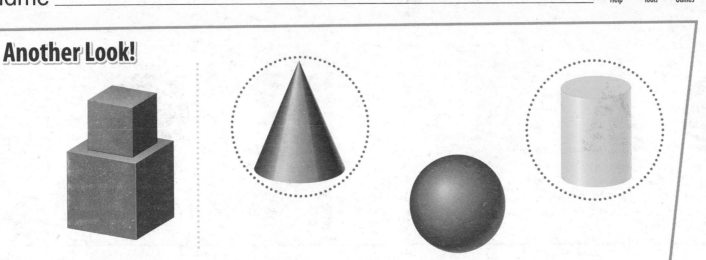

HOME ACTIVITY Show your child a ball, a can, and a cube-shaped block. Ask him or her to compare the features of each object, such as which objects can stack, which can roll, and which can slide. Have your child point to the flat surfaces on each of the objects.

 1

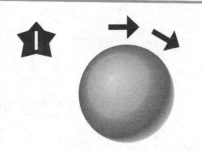  

2

   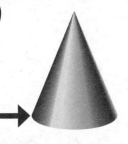

Directions Say: *A cube can stack on top of another cube. Draw a circle around the other solid figures that can also be stacked on top of a cube.* Have students: ⭐ look at the solid figure on the left that can roll, and then draw a circle around the other solid figures that can roll; ② look at the solid figure on the left that can slide, and then draw a circle around the other solid figures that can slide.

③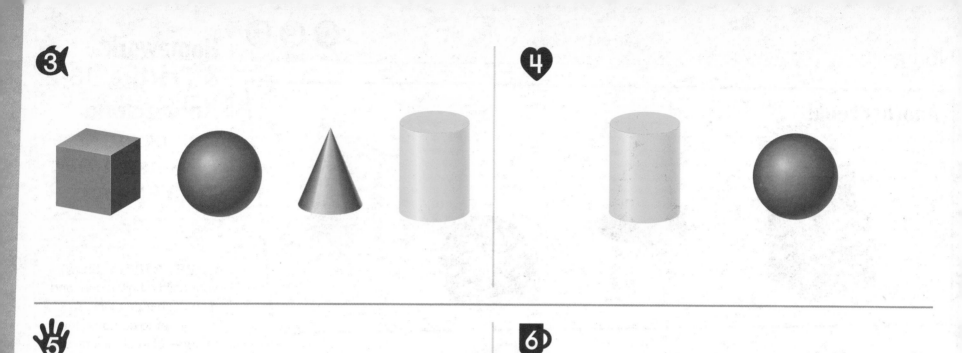

④

👋⑤

☕⑥

Directions Have students: **③** mark an X on the solid figures that can both roll and slide; **④** mark an X on the solid figure that is NOT a sphere, and then explain how it is similar to and different from a sphere. **👋⑤ Higher Order Thinking** Have students draw 2 solid figures that can roll. **☕⑥ Higher Order Thinking** Have students use all of the 3 solid figures that can stack to draw a castle made of blocks. Then have them explain why cones can only stack on top of other shapes.

760 seven hundred sixty

© Pearson Education, Inc. K

Topic 13 | Lesson 2

Name _____

Solve

Lesson 13-3

Compare
2-D and 3-D
Shapes

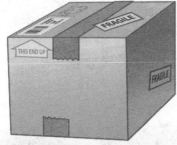

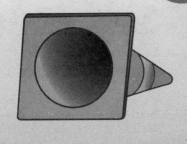

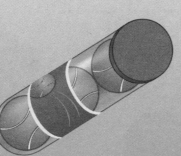

Directions Say: *Jackson needs to find a circle that is a flat surface of a solid figure. What solid figures have a circle as a part of the figure? Draw a circle around the solid figures that have a circle as a part. Mark an X on the solid figures that do NOT.*

I can ...
analyze and compare 2-D and 3-D shapes.

© **Content Standards**
K.G.B.4
Mathematical Practices
MP.2, MP.5, MP.6

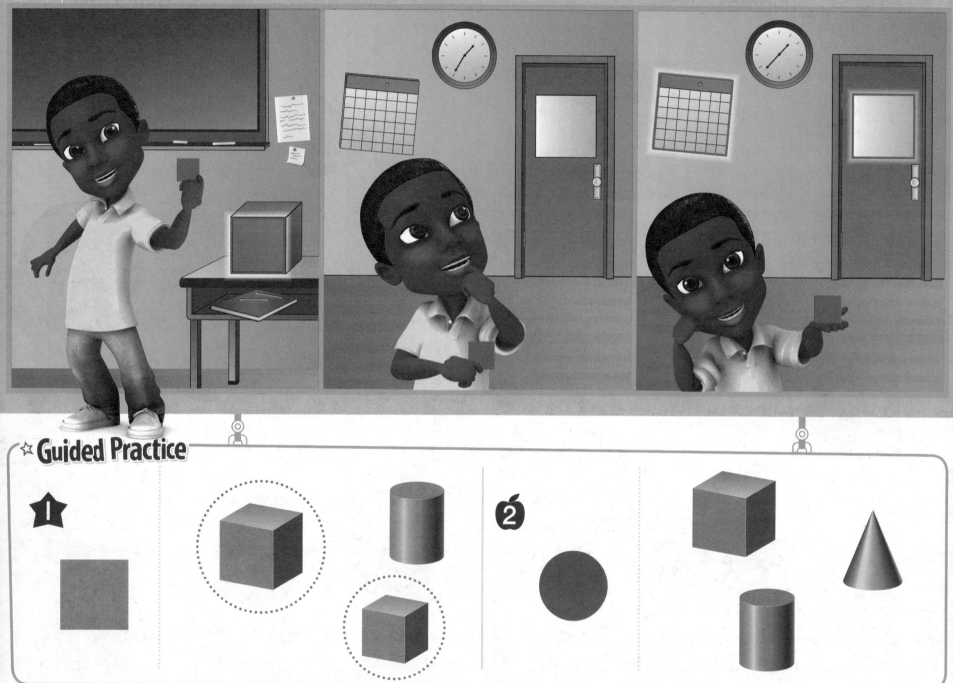

☆ Guided Practice

1

2

Directions Have students: **1** and **2** look at the shape on the left, and then draw a circle around the solid figures that have a flat surface with that shape.

© Pearson Education, Inc. K

Name _____

3

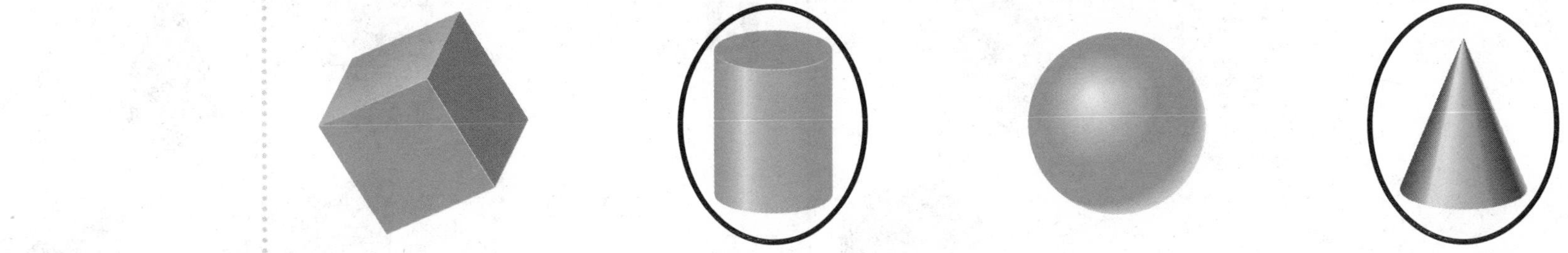

4

5

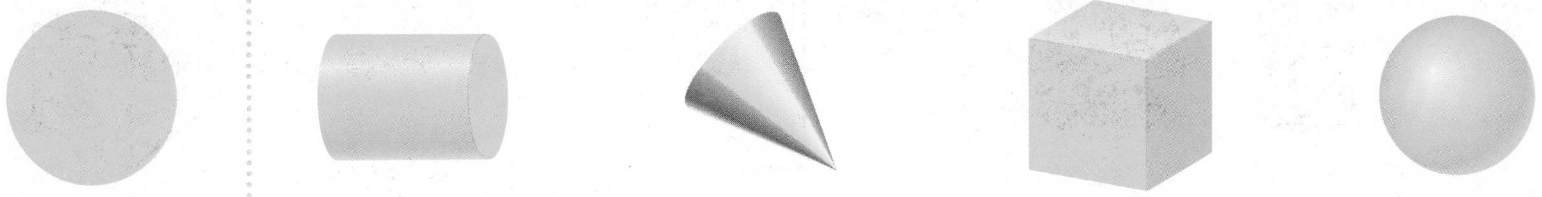

6

Directions **3** **Vocabulary** Have students draw the **flat surface** of the solid figures that have circles around them. **4**–**6** Have students look at the shape on the left, and then draw a circle around the solid figures that have a flat surface with that shape.

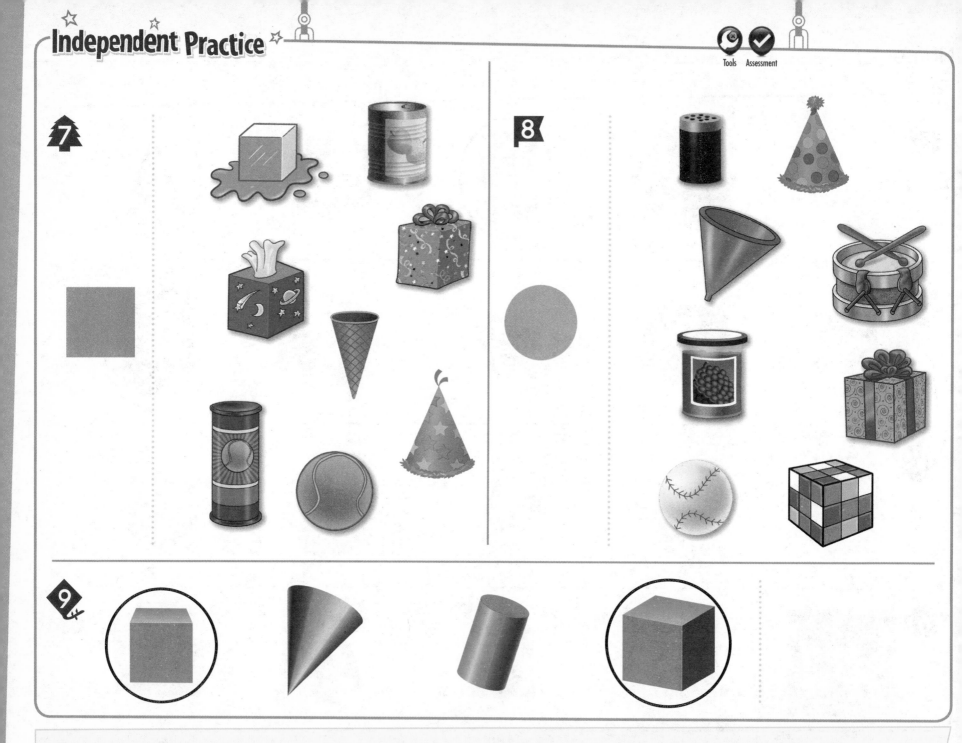

7

8

9

Directions Have students: **7** and **8** look at the shape on the left, and then draw a circle around the objects that have a flat surface with that shape. **9** **Higher Order Thinking** Have students look at the solid figures that have a circle around them, and then draw the shape of the flat surfaces of these solid figures.

764 seven hundred sixty-four   © Pearson Education, Inc. K   **Topic 13** | Lesson 3

Name _____

Another Look!

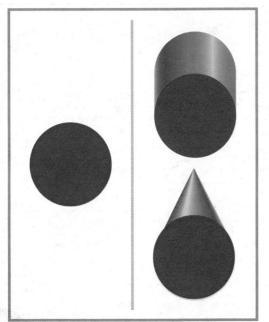

HOME ACTIVITY Show your child a can and ask him or her to identify the flat surfaces (circles). Show your child a box shaped like a cube and ask him or her to identify the flat surfaces (squares). Take turns identifying other objects that have flat surfaces that are circles or squares.

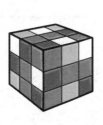

Directions Say: *A cube has square flat surfaces. Draw a circle around the objects that have a square flat surface.* ⭐ Have students look at the cylinder and cone in the blue box, identify the shape of their flat surfaces, and then mark an X on the objects that have a flat surface with that shape.

2

3

4

5

Directions Have students: **2** and **3** look at the object on the left, and then draw a circle around the shape of its flat surfaces; **4** and **5** look at the objects, and then draw the shape of their flat surfaces.

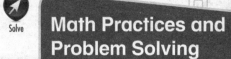

1

2

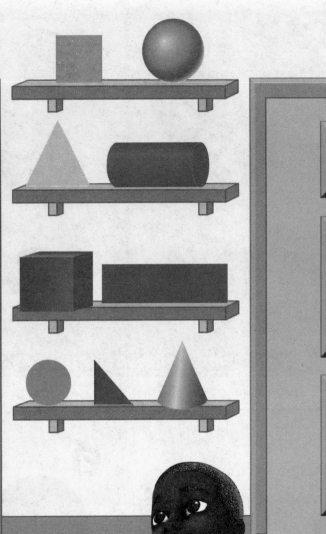

Think.

I can ...
analyze, compare, and make different 2-D and 3-D shapes using math.

© **Mathematical Practices**
MP.1 Also MP.3, MP.5, MP.6
Content Standards
K.G.A.3, K.G.B.4

Directions Say: *Jackson wants to put flat shapes behind Door 1 and solid figures behind Door 2. Draw a line from each shape to the correct door to show how he should sort the shapes.*

☆ Guided Practice

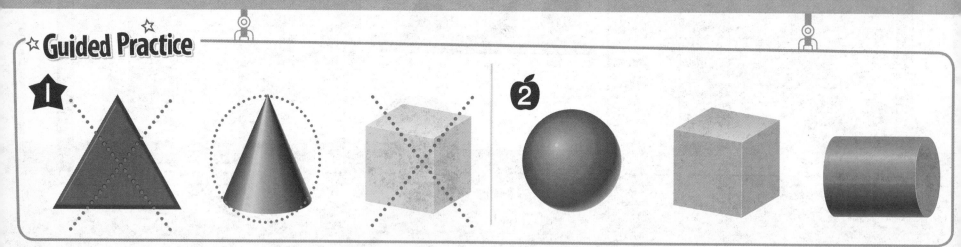

Directions Have students listen to the clues, mark an X on the shapes that do NOT fit the clues, and then draw a circle around the shape that the clues describe. Have students name the shape, and then explain their answers. ⭐ *I am a solid figure. I can roll. I have only 1 flat surface. What shape am I? Explain which clues helped you solve the mystery.* ❷ *I am a solid figure. I can roll. I can also stack. What shape am I? Explain which clues helped you solve the mystery.*

© Pearson Education, Inc. K

Independent Practice

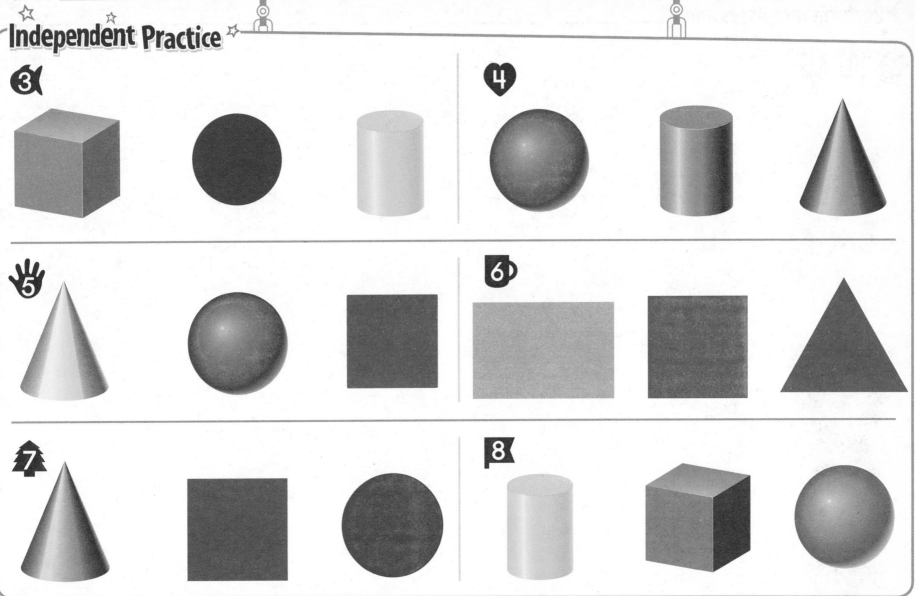

3

4

5

6

7

8

Directions Have students listen to the clues, mark an X on the shapes that do NOT fit the clues, and then draw a circle around the shape that the clues describe. Have students name the shape, and then explain their answers. **3** *I am a solid figure. I can stack and slide. I have 6 flat surfaces. What shape am I?* **4** *I am a solid figure. I can slide. I have only 1 flat surface. What shape am I?* **5** *I am a solid figure. I can roll. I do NOT have any flat surfaces. What shape am I?* **6** *I am a flat shape. I have 4 sides. All of my sides are the same length. What shape am I?* **7** *I am a flat shape. I do NOT have any straight sides. What shape am I?* **8** *I am a solid figure. I can roll. I have 2 flat surfaces. What shape am I?*

Directions Read the problem to students. Then have them use multiple math practices to solve the problem. Have students look at the shape at the top of the page. Say: *Emily's teacher teaches the class a game. They have to give a classmate clues about the mystery shape. What clues can Emily give about this shape?* ◆ **MP.1 Make Sense** *What is the shape? What makes it special?* ⑩ **MP.6 Be Precise** *What clues can you give about the shape? Think about how it looks, and whether or not it can roll, stack, or slide.* ✱ **MP.3 Explain** *What if your classmate gives you the wrong answer? Can you give more clues to help him or her?*

© Pearson Education, Inc. K

Name _____

Another Look!

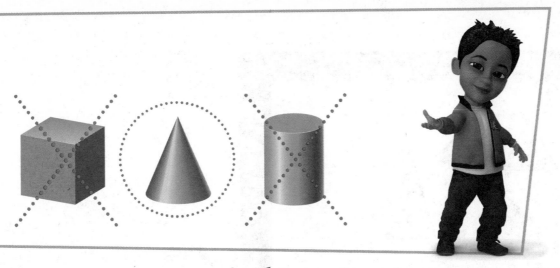

HOME ACTIVITY Pick an object in the room that is a cube, sphere, cone, or cylinder. Give your child clues about its shape, and ask him or her to guess which object you are thinking about. For example, a clue could be "Its flat surface is shaped like a square." (cube) Then invite your child to take a turn picking an object and giving you clues.

 1

 2

 3

 4

Directions Say: *Listen to the clues. After each clue, mark an X on any shape that does NOT fit the clue. I can roll. I do NOT have 2 flat surfaces. What shape am I? Draw a circle around the shape that fits all of the clues.* Read the clues to students. Have them mark an X on the shapes that do NOT fit the clues and draw a circle around the shape that the clues describe. Have students explain which clues helped them get the answer. **1** *I can roll. I CANNOT stack. What shape am I?* **2** *I can stack. I can slide. What shape am I?* **3** *I can roll. I have only 1 flat surface. What shape am I?* **4** *I can stack. I CANNOT roll. What shape am I?*

Directions Read the problem to students. Then have them use multiple math practices to solve the problem. Say: *Jackson is trying to solve a mystery. How are the shapes inside the frame similar? How can you find the answer?* ✋ **MP.1 Make Sense** *What shapes are outside of the frame? What shapes are inside the frame?* ☕ **MP.6 Be Precise** *What attribute do all of the shapes inside the frame have? Draw another shape like it inside the frame.* 🌲 **MP.5 Use Tools** *Listen to the clues, and then draw 3 shapes inside the bottom frame that match the clues. I have 4 sides and 4 vertices. My sides are NOT the same length. What shape am I?*

Name _____

Directions Say: *Emily has 2 triangles. She thinks she can use them to make a 2-D shape she has learned—a circle, triangle, square, or rectangle. Try to make one of these shapes with your triangles. Tell what shape you made.*

I can ...
make 2-D shapes using other 2-D shapes.

© Content Standards
K.G.B.6
Mathematical Practices
MP.1, MP.4, MP.5, MP.7, MP.8

☆ Guided Practice

1

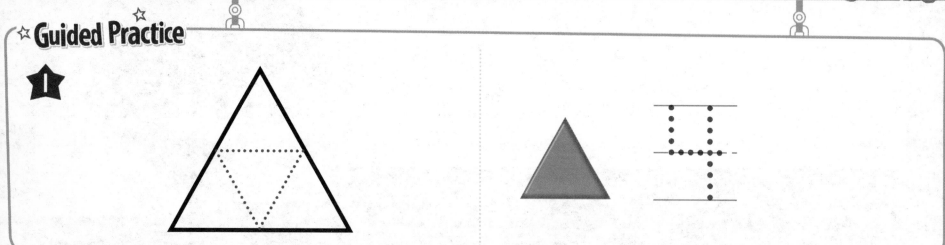

Directions ⭐ Have students use the pattern block shown to cover the shape, draw the lines, and then write the number that tells how many pattern blocks to use.

Topic 13 | Lesson 5

Name _____

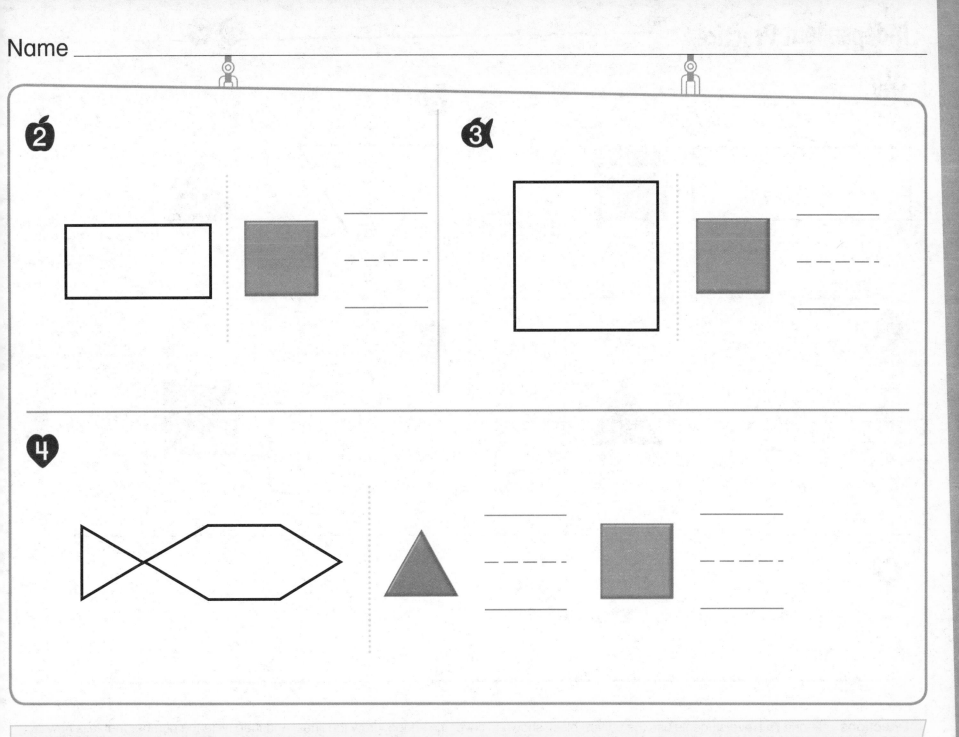

Directions ❷–❸ Have students use the pattern block shown to cover the shape, draw the lines, and then write the number that tells how many pattern blocks to use. ❹ Have students use the pattern blocks shown to create the fish, and then write the number that tells how many of each pattern block to use.

Topic I3 | Lesson 5   seven hundred seventy-five **775**

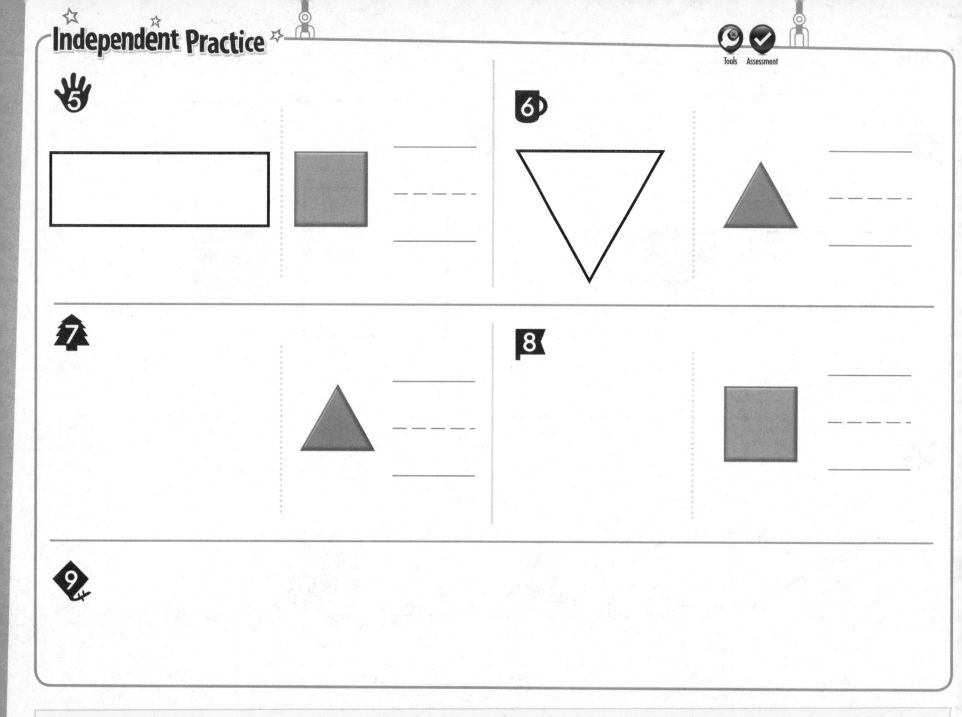

5

6

7

8

9

Directions ✋**5** and ☕**6** Have students use the pattern block shown to cover the shape, draw the lines, and then write the number that tells how many pattern blocks to use. 🌲**7** and 🚩**8** Have students use the pattern block shown to create a 2-D shape, draw the shape, and then write the number of pattern blocks used. 🥕**9 Higher Order Thinking** Have students use pattern blocks to create a picture, and then draw it in the space.

Name _____

Another Look!

 6

HOME ACTIVITY Give your child paper, pencil, and a small square shape, such as a square cracker or a square sticky-note. Ask him or her to draw another shape, such as a rectangle, using the square. Repeat with other shapes.

Directions Say: *What shape is the pattern block? Use 6 pattern blocks to make a rectangle. Draw the new shape you made.* Have students use 9 pattern blocks to make a triangle, and then draw the new 2-D shape.

2

3

4

Directions ✌ Have students use 5 pattern blocks to make a rectangle, and then draw the new 2-D shape. ✦ Have students use pattern blocks to create a tree, and then draw it in the space. ♥ **Higher Order Thinking** Have students use at least the pattern blocks shown to create a picture.

© Pearson Education, Inc. K

Solve & Share

Name _____

Solve

Lesson 13-6
Build 2-D
Shapes

Circle | NOT a Circle

Directions Say: *Use yarn, string, or pipe cleaners to build a circle. Then use yarn, string, pipe cleaners, or straws to build a shape that is NOT a circle, and then tell what shape you built. Explain how the shapes you built are different from one another.*

I can ...
build 2-D shapes that match given attributes.

© **Content Standards**
K.G.B.5, K.G.B.4
Mathematical Practices
MP.2, MP.3, MP.4, MP.7

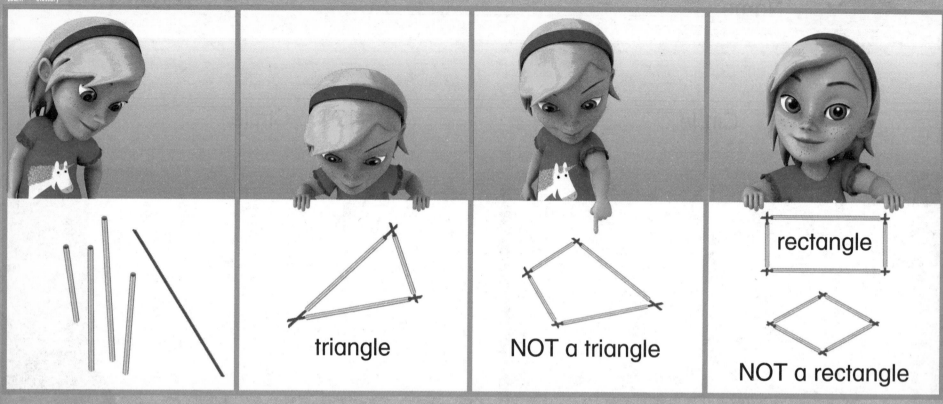

triangle

NOT a triangle

rectangle

NOT a rectangle

Guided Practice

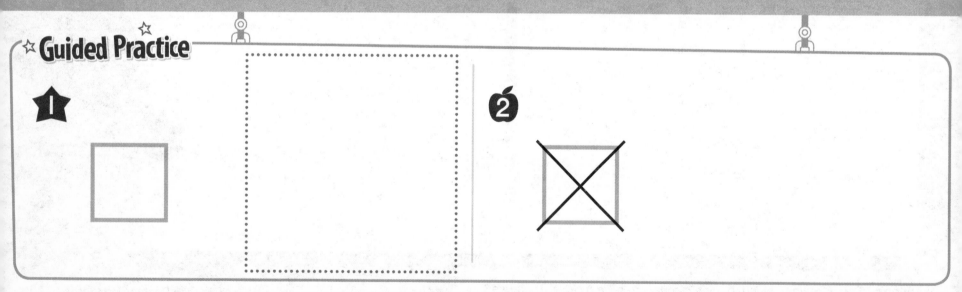

Directions Provide students with yarn, pipe cleaners, or straws to make each shape. Students should attach the shapes they make with materials to the page. Have students draw or build: ★ a square; ② a shape that is NOT a square.

780 seven hundred eighty   © Pearson Education, Inc. K   **Topic 13** | Lesson 6

Name _____

3

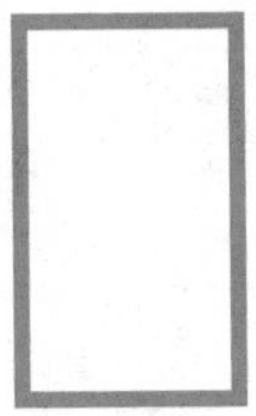

4

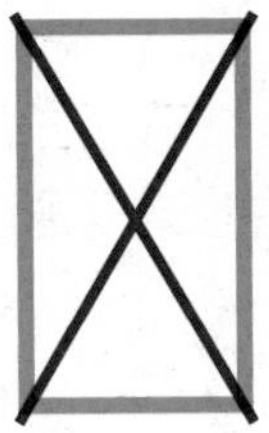

5

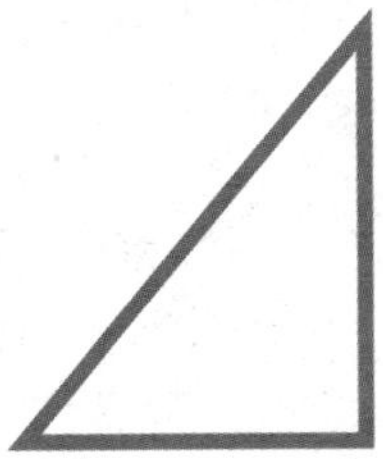

6

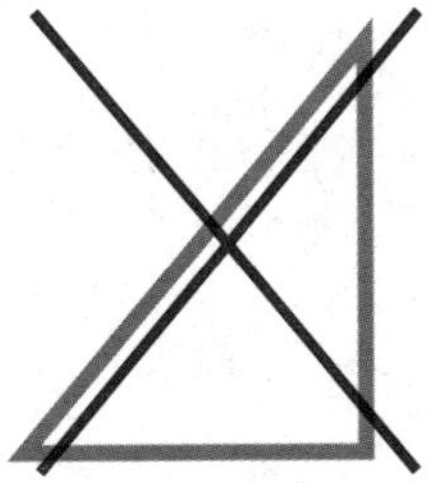

Directions Provide students with yarn, pipe cleaners, or straws to make each shape. Students should attach the shapes they make with materials to the page. Have students draw or build: **3** a rectangle; **4** a shape that is NOT a rectangle; **5** a triangle; **6** a shape that is NOT a triangle.

Topic 13 | Lesson 6   seven hundred eighty-one **781**

7

8

9

10

Directions Have students: **7** draw a rectangle; **8** draw a triangle; **9** draw a square. **10** **Higher Order Thinking** Have students choose yarn, string, pipe cleaners, or straws to build a circle. Have them attach it to this page, and then explain why some materials are better than others for building circles.

© Pearson Education, Inc. K

Name _____

Another Look!

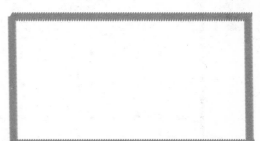

HOME ACTIVITY Take a look around your kitchen. With your child, look for materials that can be used to build different 2-D shapes. For example, your child can build shapes from dough, wooden spoons, or string.

 1

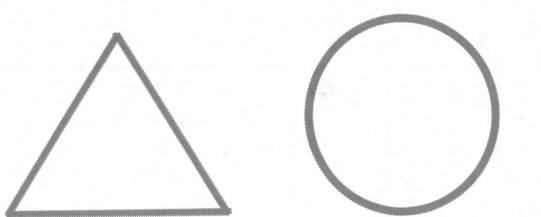

Directions Say: *This is a square. How do you know it is a square? Let's practice drawing a square.* Have students listen to the story:
⭐ Avery built shapes out of pipe cleaners. Mark an X on the triangle.

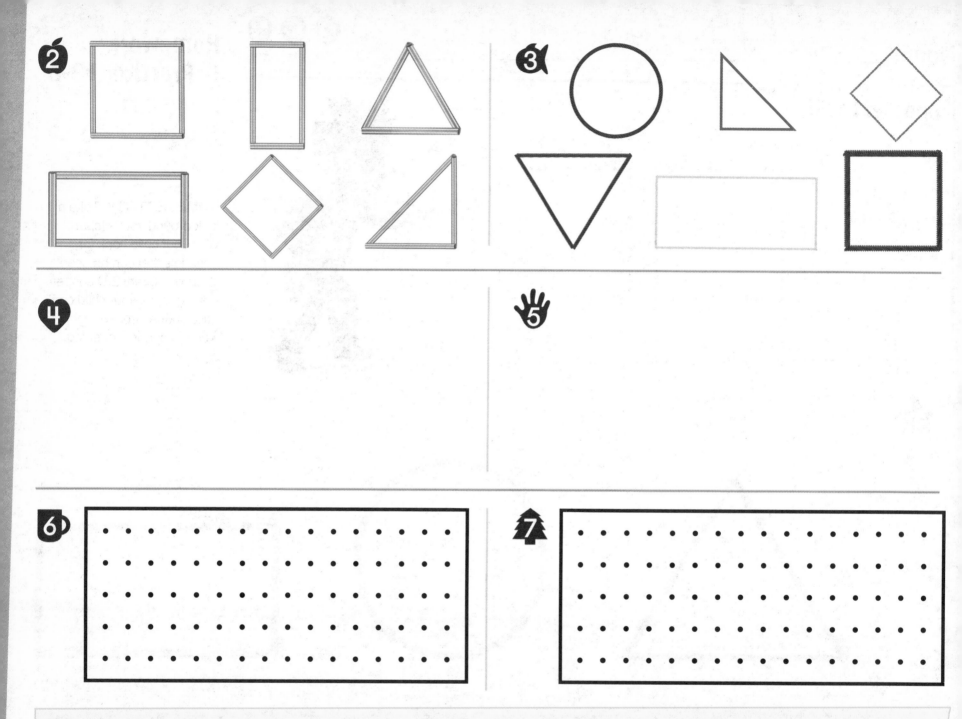

Directions Have students listen to each story: ❷ *Diego built 6 shapes out of straws. Mark an X on the shapes that are NOT rectangles.* ❸ *Destiny built 6 shapes out of pipe cleaners. Mark an X on the shapes that are NOT triangles.* Have students: ❹ draw a circle; ❺ draw a triangle. ❻ **Higher Order Thinking** Have students draw a rectangle that is NOT a square. ❼ **Higher Order Thinking** Have students draw a rectangle that is also a square.

© Pearson Education, Inc. K

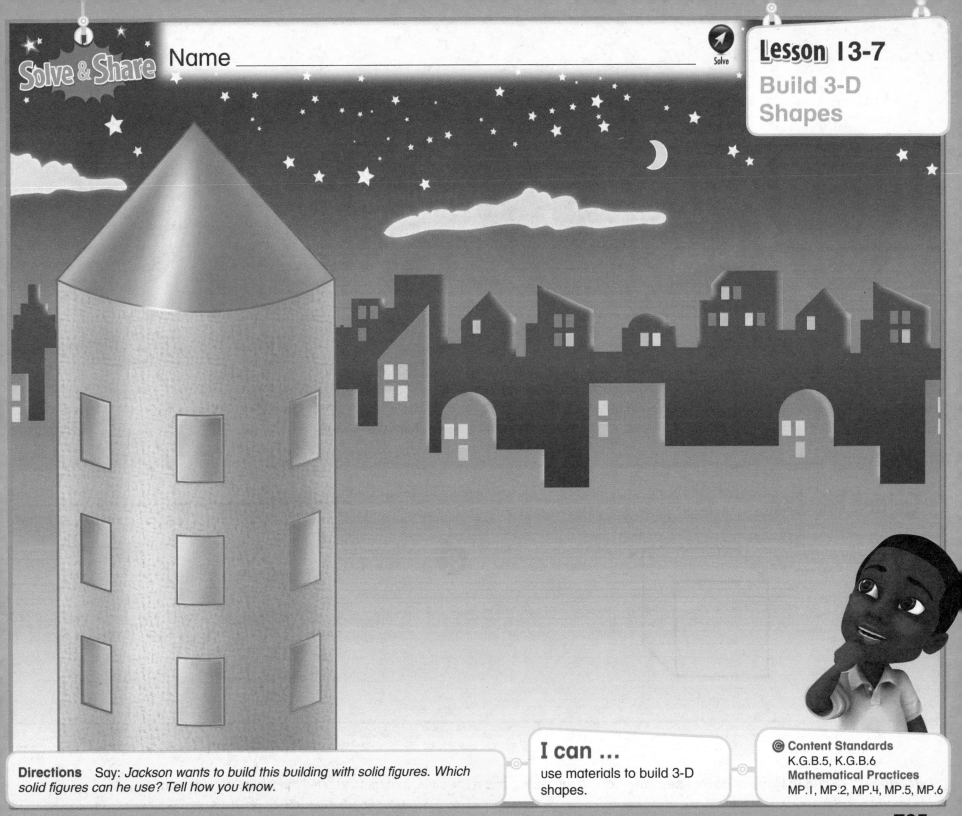

Directions Say: *Jackson wants to build this building with solid figures. Which solid figures can he use? Tell how you know.*

I can ...
use materials to build 3-D shapes.

© **Content Standards**
K.G.B.5, K.G.B.6
Mathematical Practices
MP.1, MP.2, MP.4, MP.5, MP.6

☆ Guided Practice

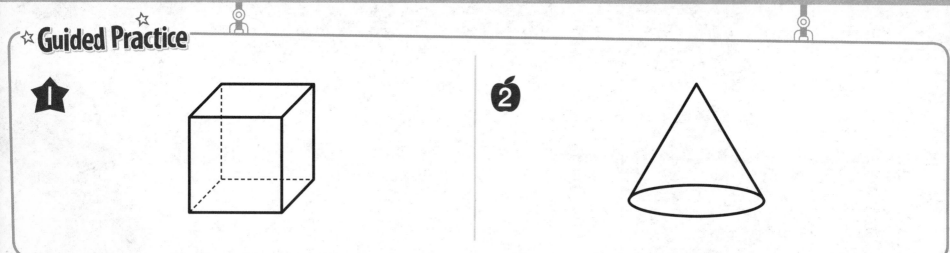

1

2

Directions ⭐ and ❷ Have students use straws, clay, craft sticks, paper, or other materials to build the solid figure shown.

Name

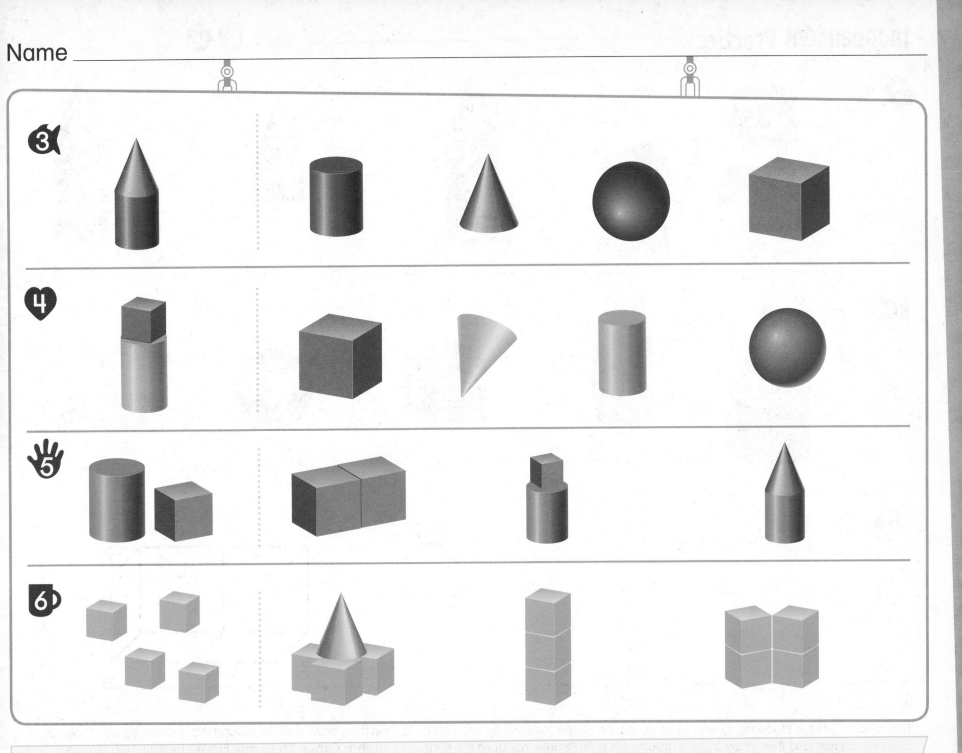

Directions Have students: ③ and ④ use tools to build the shape, and then draw a circle around the solid figures that build the shape; ⑤ and ⑥ use tools to find the shape the solid figures can build, and then draw a circle around the shape.

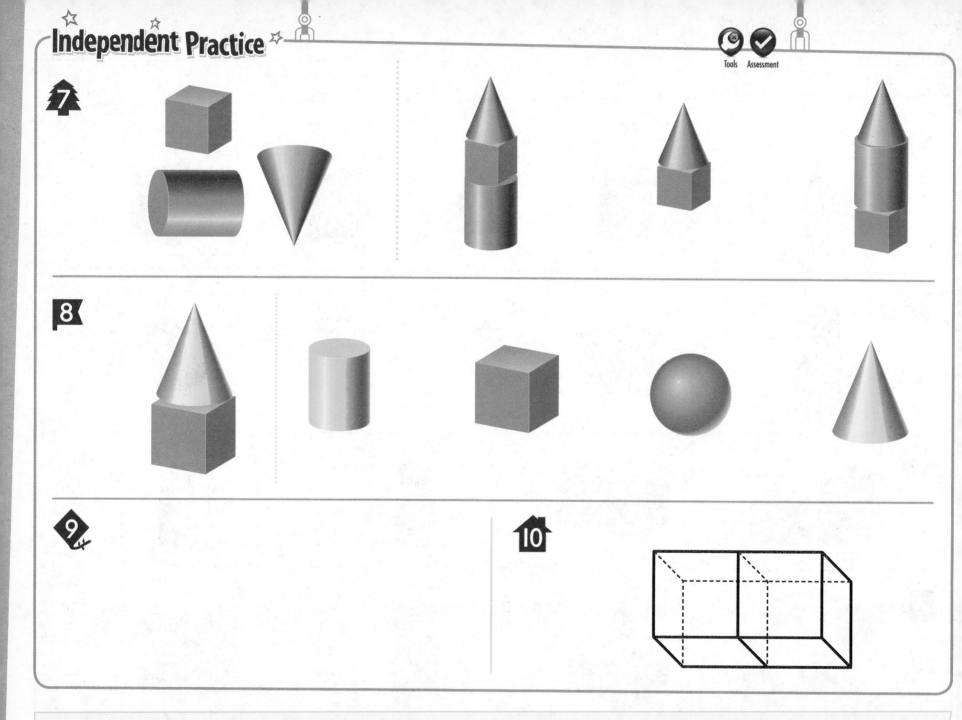

7

8

9

10

Directions Have students: **7** use tools to find the shape the solid figures can build, and then draw a circle around the shapes; **8** use tools to build the shape, and then draw a circle around the solid figures that build the shape. **9 Higher Order Thinking** Have students use straws, yarn, pipe cleaners, or other materials to build a solid figure that is NOT a cone. **10 Higher Order Thinking** Have students use straws, clay, craft sticks, paper, or other materials to build the shape shown.

© Pearson Education, Inc. K
Topic 13 | Lesson 7

Name _____

Another Look!

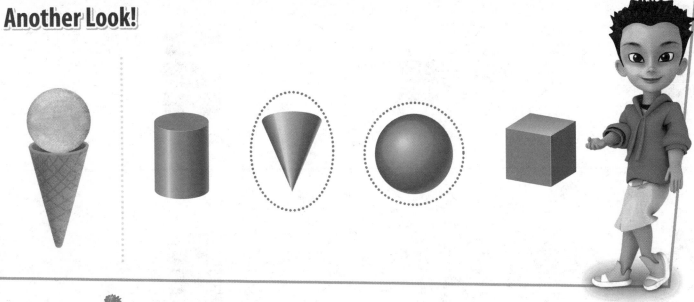

 HOME ACTIVITY Have your child use materials from your house to build a 3-D shape.

1

2

Directions Say: *Look at the object on the left. Draw a circle around the solid figures that make the shape.* Have students: **1** and **2** draw a circle around the solid figures that build the shape.

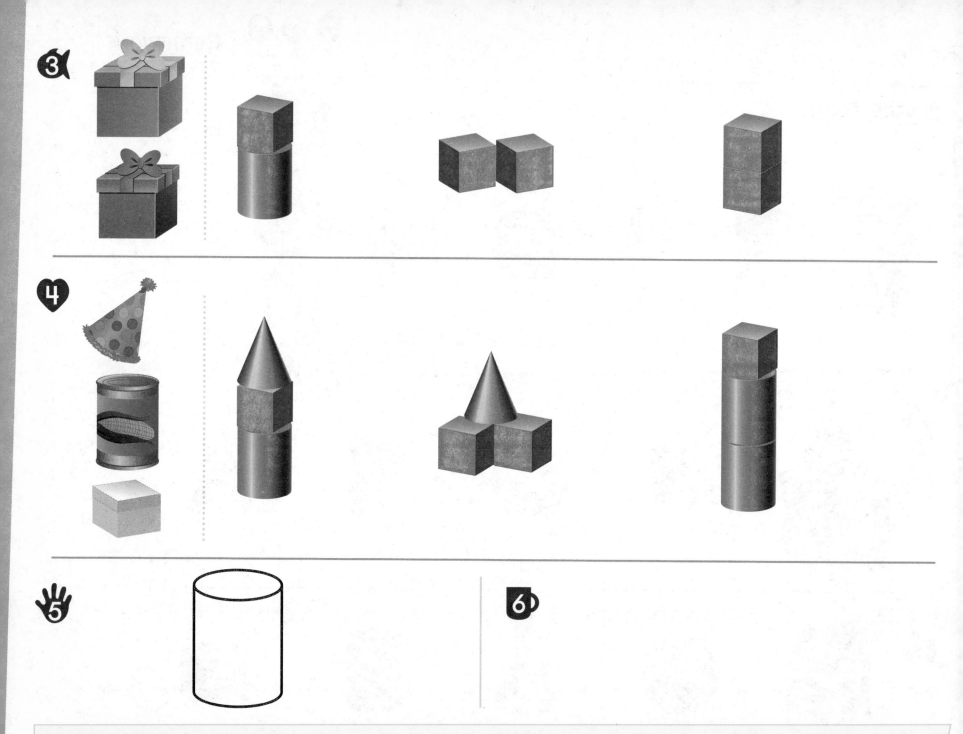

3

4

5

6

Directions Have students: **3** and **4** draw a circle around the shapes the solid figures can build. **5 Higher Order Thinking** Have students use pipe cleaners or paper to build the shape. **6 Higher Order Thinking** Have students use tools to build any shape, and then draw what they built.

© Pearson Education, Inc. K

①

P	T	O
1 + 0	5 − 2	3 + 2

②

T	H	A
5 − 1	1 + 1	2 − 2

1 + 2	4 + 1	4 − 3

3 − 1	5 − 5	2 + 2

Directions ① and ② Have students find a partner. Have them point to a clue in the top row, and then solve the addition or subtraction problem in the clue. Then have them look at the clues in the bottom row to find a match, and then write the clue letter above the match. Have students find a match for every clue.

I can ...
add and subtract fluently within 5.

© **Content Standard** K.OA.A.5

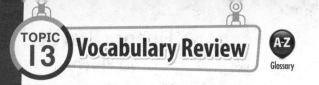

1

2

3

Directions **Understand Vocabulary** Have students: ✦ draw a circle around the solid figures that **roll**; ✦ draw a circle around the solid figures that **stack**; ✦ draw a circle around the solid figures that **slide**.

 Topic 13 | Vocabulary Review

Name _____

Set A

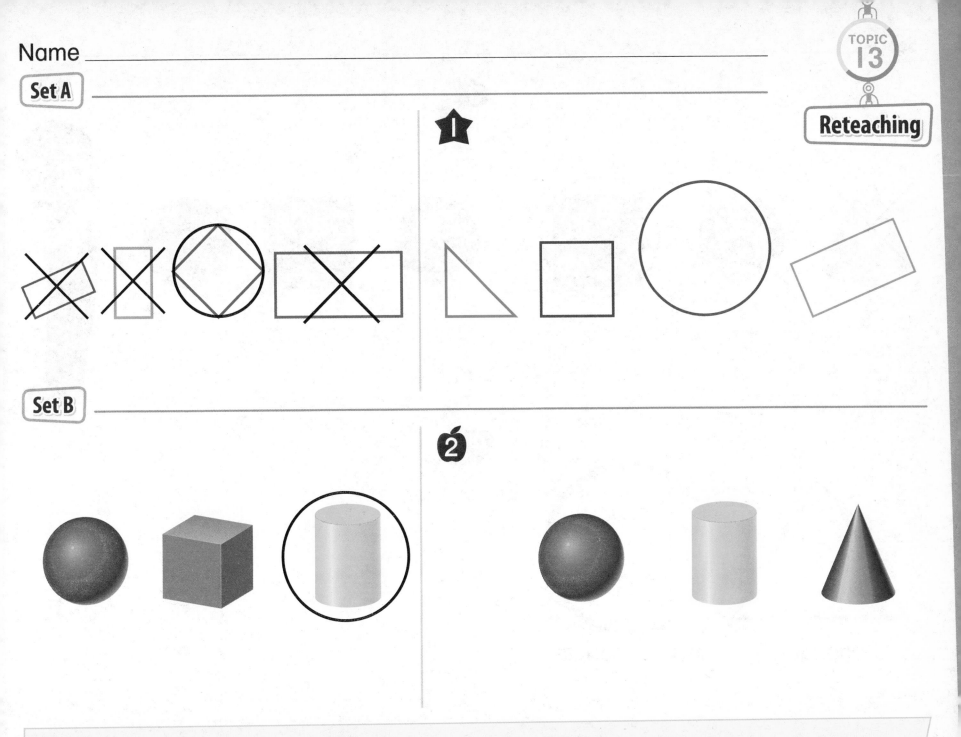

Set B

Directions Have students: ⭐ listen to the clues, mark an X on the shapes that do NOT fit the clues, draw a circle around the shape that the clues describe, and then tell how the shapes they marked with an X are similar to the shape they drew a circle around. *I am NOT round. I have 4 sides. They are NOT all the same length;* 🍎 draw a circle around the solid figure that does NOT stack and slide.

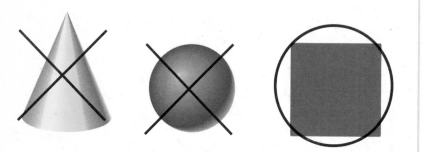

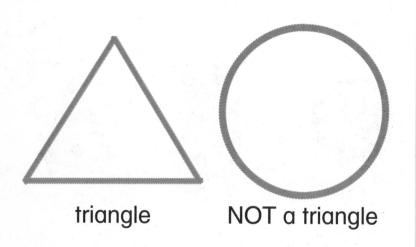

triangle   NOT a triangle

Directions Have students: ❸ mark an X on the shapes that do NOT fit the clues, and then draw a circle around the shape the clues describe: *I have no sides. I do NOT roll. Which shape am I?* ❹ draw or use yarn, pipe cleaners, or straws to make a triangle and a shape that is NOT a triangle, and then attach their shapes to this page.

© Pearson Education, Inc. K

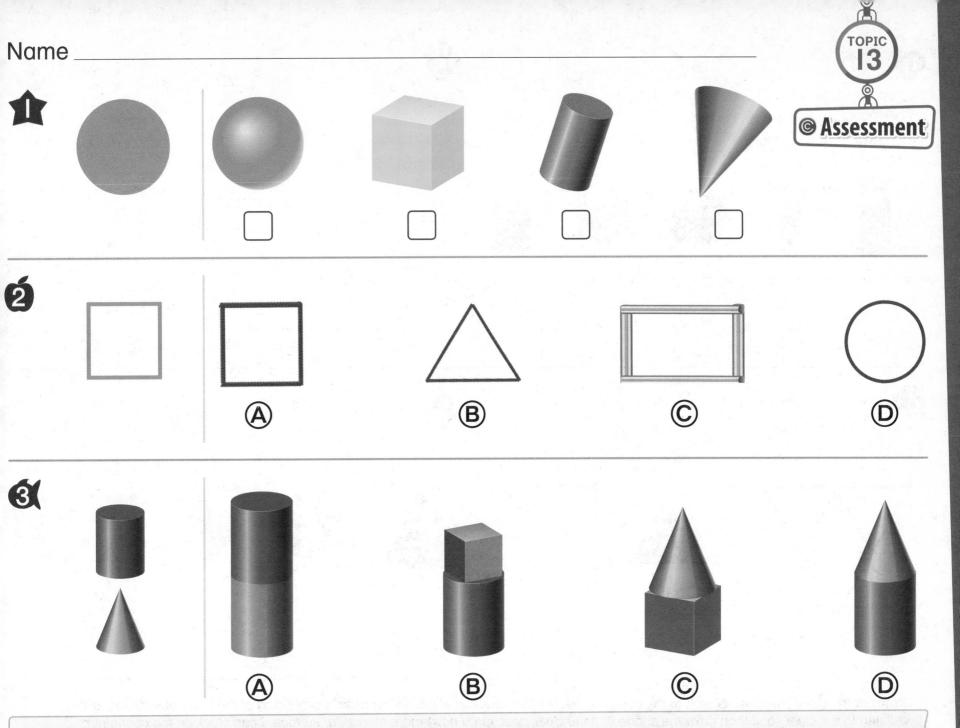

⭐ 1

② 2

Ⓐ   Ⓑ   Ⓒ   Ⓓ

★ 3

Ⓐ   Ⓑ   Ⓒ   Ⓓ

Directions Have students mark the best answer. ⭐ Look at the shape on the left. Mark all the solid figures that have a flat surface with that same shape. ② Which shape that was built using different materials or drawn matches the shape on the left? ★ Which shape can be built using the solid figures on the left?

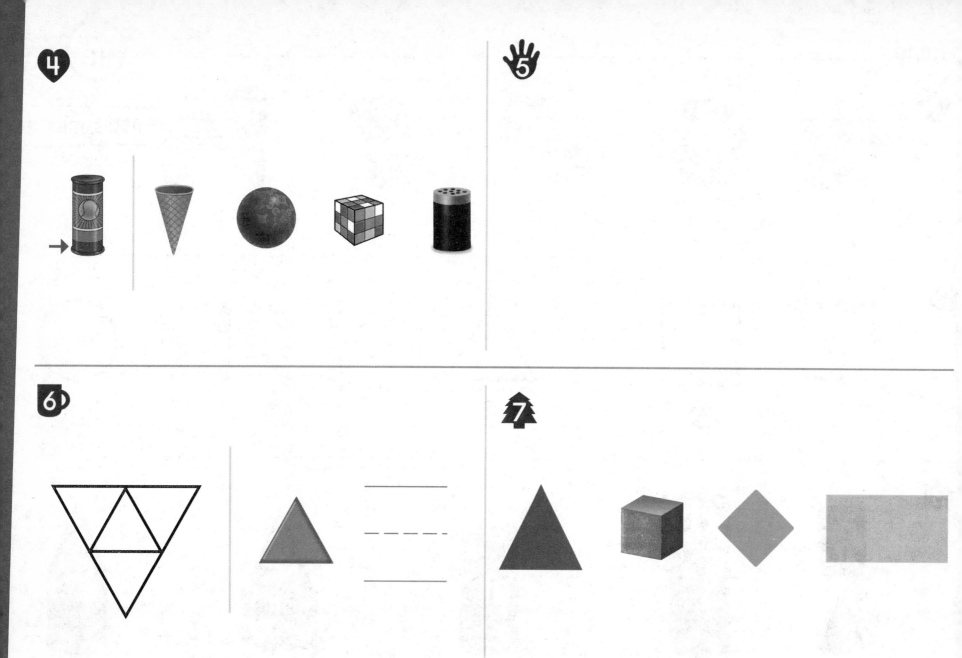

Directions Have students: ❤ look at the object on the left that slides, and then draw a circle around all of the other objects that slide; ✋ listen to the clues, and then draw the shape that the clues describe. *I have more than 1 flat surface. I can stack on top of another shape. I can roll. What solid figure am I?*; 6 write the number that tells how many triangle pattern blocks can cover the shape; 🌲 listen to the clues, mark an X on the shapes that do NOT fit the clues, and then draw a circle around the shape that the clues describe. *I am a flat shape. I have 4 straight sides. Two of my sides are shorter than the other 2 sides. What shape am I?*

Name _____

⭐ 1

🍎 2

★ 3

Directions **Bria's Bash** Say: *Bria has a party for her friends. These are some objects that are at her party.* Have students: ⭐ draw a circle around the objects that can slide. Have them tell how the shape of those objects are different from the shape of the other objects. Then have students mark an X on the objects that are cylinders. 🍎 draw what one flat surface of a cylinder looks like, and then name that shape. ★ Say: *Bria puts her party hat on top of a present.* Have students draw a circle around the solid figures that could be used to build the same shape. If needed, have students use tools to help them.

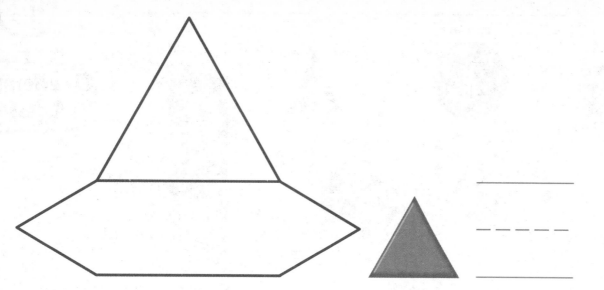

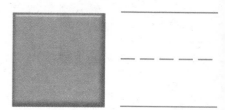

© Pearson Education, Inc. K

Topic 13 | Performance Assessment

Describe and Compare Measurable Attributes

Essential Question: How can objects be compared by length, height, capacity, and weight?

Digital Resources

Solve · Learn · Glossary

Tools · Assessment · Help · Games

Math and Science Project: Using Materials to Create Shade

Directions Read the character speech bubbles to students. **Find Out!** Have students find out different ways to create shade. Say: *We can use materials to create shade. Talk to your friends and relatives about different ways humans create shade from the sun.* **Journal: Make a Poster** Have students make a poster that shows various objects humans use to create shade. Have them draw three different ways humans create shade.

Name _____

 1

 2

 3

4

 5

 6

Directions Have students: ⭐ draw a circle around the cube; 🍎 draw a circle around the cylinder; 🔄 draw a circle around the cone;
✋ draw a circle around the solid figure that can stack; ✋ draw a circle around the solid figure that can roll; ☕ draw a circle around the
solid figure that can slide.

My Word Cards

Directions Have students cut out the vocabulary cards. Read the front of the card, and then ask them to explain what the word or phrase means.

A-Z
Glossary

length

longer

shorter

height

taller

capacity

Directions Review the definitions and have students study the cards. Extend learning by having students draw pictures for each word on a separate piece of paper.

Point to the shorter string.
Say: *The bottom string is **shorter** than the top string.*

Point to the longer string.
Say: *The top string is **longer** than the bottom string.*

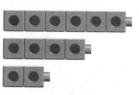

Point to the cube trains.
Say: ***Length*** *measures how long something is. These cube trains are different lengths.*

Point to the cup that holds more.
Say: *The cup that holds more has a larger **capacity** than the cup that holds less.*

Point to the cube tower on the left.
Say: *This cube tower is **taller** than the other two towers.*

Point to the cube towers.
Say: ***Height*** *measures how tall something is. These cube towers are different heights.*

My Word Cards

Directions Have students cut out the vocabulary cards. Read the front of the card, and then ask them to explain what the word or phrase means.

Glossary

weight

weighs

heavier

lighter

attribute

balance scale

eight hundred three **803**

Directions Review the definitions and have students study the cards. Extend learning by having students draw pictures for each word on a separate piece of paper.

Point to the apple.
Say: *The apple weighs more than the cherry. It is **heavier** than the cherry.*

Point to the apple.
Say: *The apple **weighs** more than the cherry.*

Point to the balance scale.
Say: *A balance scale can be used to compare the **weights** of objects. These objects are the same weight.*

Point to the balance scale.
Say: *A **balance scale** is a tool we use to compare weight.*

Point to the vase.
Say: *The measurable **attributes** of an object can be weight, capacity, length, and height.*

Point to the apple.
Say: *The apple weighs less than the watermelon. It is **lighter** than the watermelon.*

Name _____

Solve & Share

Solve

Directions Say: *Marta makes a cube train with 4 cubes. Is her cube train bigger or smaller than the crayon? Is her cube train bigger or smaller than the pencil? How can you find out?*

I can ...
compare objects by length and height.

© **Content Standards**
K.MD.A.2
Mathematical Practices
MP.2, MP.5, MP.6, MP.7

Topic 14 | Lesson 1

Digital Resources at PearsonRealize.com

eight hundred five **805**

☆ Guided Practice

Directions Have students: ★ mark an X on the shorter object; 🍎 draw a circle around the taller object.

Name _____

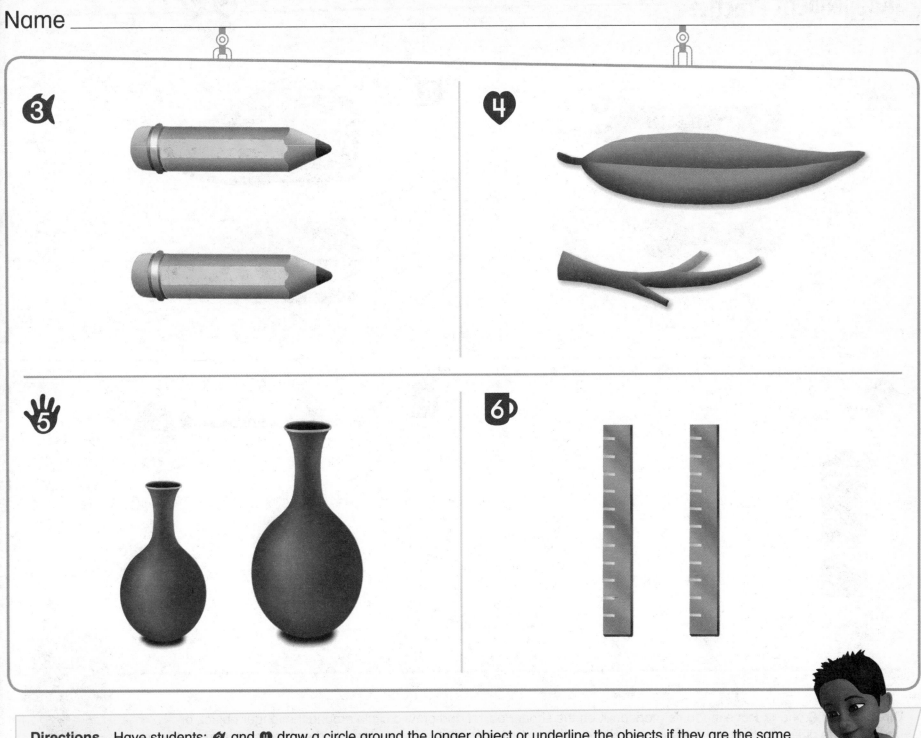

Directions Have students: ❸ and ❹ draw a circle around the longer object or underline the objects if they are the same length; ❺ and ❻ mark an X on the shorter object or underline the objects if they are the same height.

Topic 14 | Lesson 1   eight hundred seven **807**

Tools Assessment

7

8

9

10

Directions ✿ and **8** Have students mark an X on the shorter object and draw a circle around the longer object, or underline the objects if they are the same length. ✿ **Higher Order Thinking** Have students draw an object that is shorter than the cube tower. **10** **Higher Order Thinking** Have students draw an object that is the same length as the spoon.

Topic 14 | Lesson 1

Name _____

Another Look!

HOME ACTIVITY Set a kitchen spoon on a table. Ask your child to find 2 kitchen items that are longer than the spoon and 2 kitchen items that are shorter than the spoon. Then set a vase on the table. Ask your child to find 2 household objects that are taller than the vase and 2 household objects that are shorter than the vase.

⭐ 1

🍎 2

Directions Say: *Compare the objects on the left by length. Which object is longer? Draw a circle around the longer object. Now compare the objects by height. Draw a circle around the taller object. How are length and height related?* Have students: ⭐ mark an X on the shorter object or underline the objects if they are the same length; 2 draw a circle around the taller object or underline the objects if they are the same height.

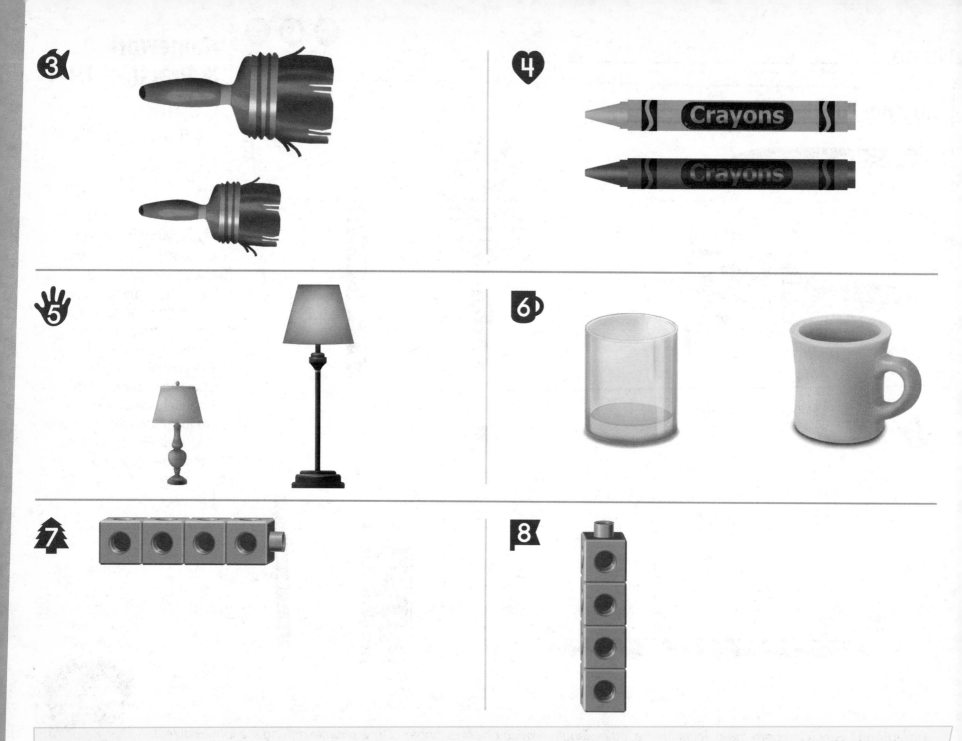

© Pearson Education, Inc. K

Directions Say: *Marta has 2 cups. She wants to use the cup that holds more. How can she find out which cup holds more? Glue the cup that holds less on the left side of the workmat and the cup that holds more on the right side.*

I can ...
compare objects by capacity.

© **Content Standards**
K.MD.A.2
Mathematical Practices
MP.2, MP.3, MP.6, MP.8

Topic 14 | Lesson 2

Digital Resources at PearsonRealize.com

eight hundred eleven **811**

☆ Guided Practice

Directions ⭐ and 🍎 Have students draw a circle around the cup that holds more and mark an X on the cup that holds less, or underline the cups if they hold the same amount.

Name _____

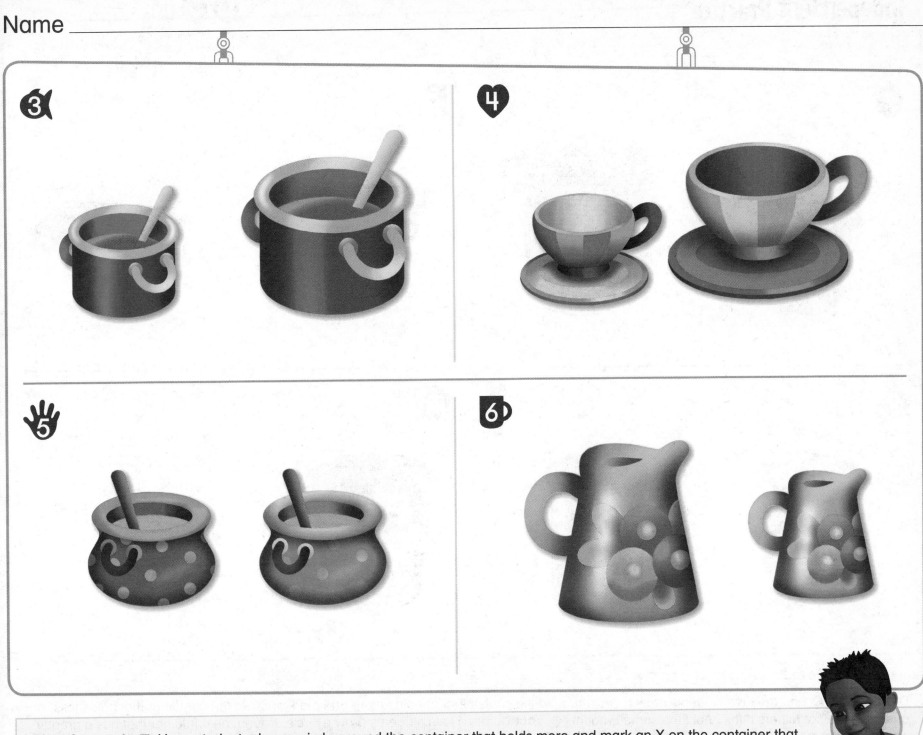

Directions ❸–❻ Have students draw a circle around the container that holds more and mark an X on the container that holds less, or underline the containers if they hold the same amount.

 7

 **8**

 9

10

Directions **7** and **8** Have students draw a circle around the container that holds more and mark an X on the container that holds less, or underline the containers if they hold the same amount. **9** **Vocabulary** Have students draw a circle around the container that has a greater **capacity** and mark an X on the container that has a smaller **capacity**, or underline the containers if they have the same **capacity**, and then explain how they know. **10** **Higher Order Thinking** Have students draw a container that holds less than the container shown.

Name _____

Another Look!

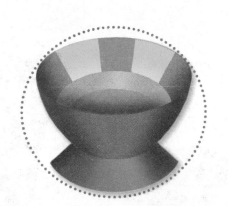

HOME ACTIVITY Set 2 pots that can hold different capacities on the table. Ask your child which one holds more and which one holds less. Check the answer by filling each with water. You can repeat using different containers.

Directions Say: *Which bowl holds more? How do you know? Draw a circle around it. Then mark an X on the bowl that holds less.* ⭐ Have students draw a circle around each container that holds more and mark an X on each container that holds less, or underline the containers if they hold the same amount.

Topic 14 | Lesson 2   Digital Resources at PearsonRealize.com   eight hundred fifteen **815**

2

3

4

5

Directions Have students: **2** draw a circle around the container that holds more and mark an X on the container that holds less, or underline the containers if they hold the same amount; **3** draw a container that holds less than the basket. **4 Higher Order Thinking** Have students draw a bowl, and then draw another bowl that holds more. **5 Higher Order Thinking** Have students draw a cup, draw another cup that holds more, and then draw another cup that holds less.

© Pearson Education, Inc. K

Topic 14 | Lesson 2

Directions Say: *Marta has a pencil and a book. She wants to put the lighter object in her backpack. How can she figure out which object is lighter? Draw the objects where they belong on the balance scale.*

I can ...
compare objects by weight.

© **Content Standards**
K.MD.A.2
Mathematical Practices
MP.2, MP.3, MP.4, MP.8

☆ Guided Practice

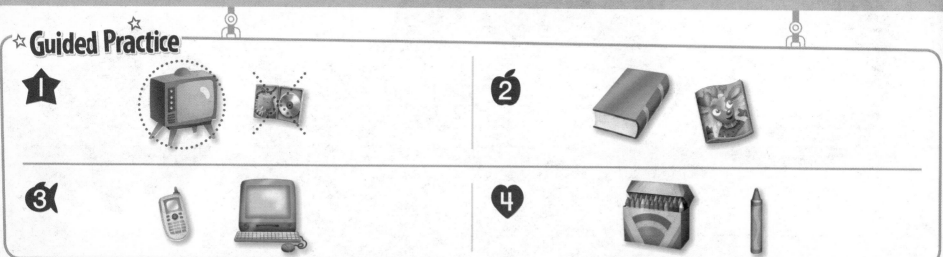

1

2

3

4

Directions ☆—**4** Have students draw a circle around the heavier object and mark an X on the lighter object, or underline the objects if they are the same weight.

5

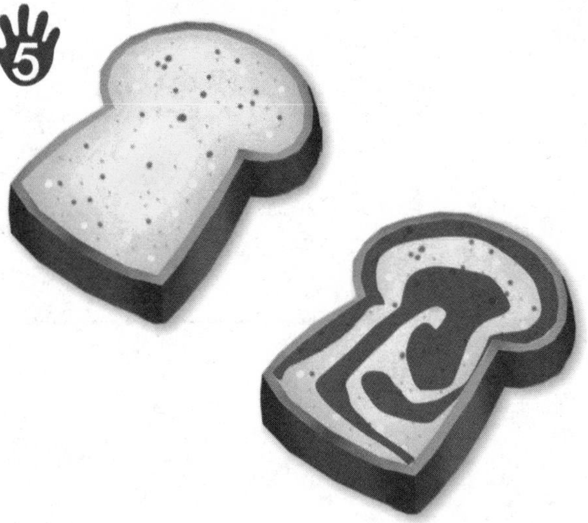

6

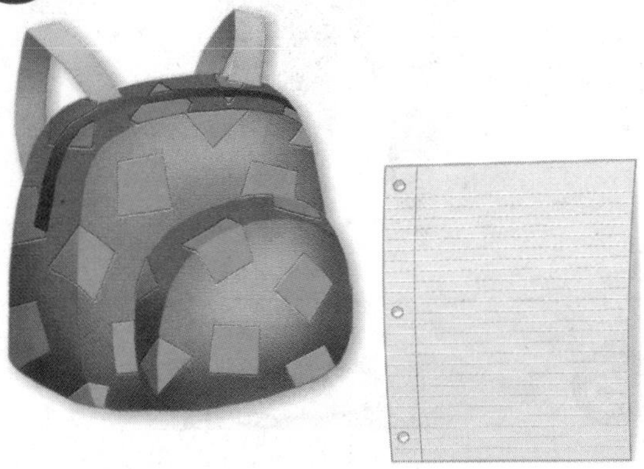

7

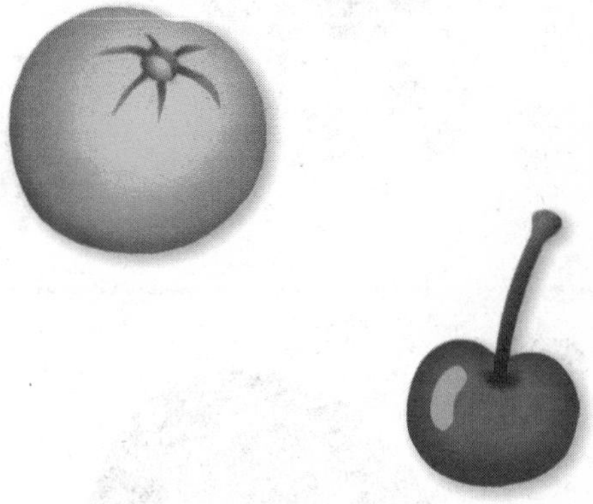

8

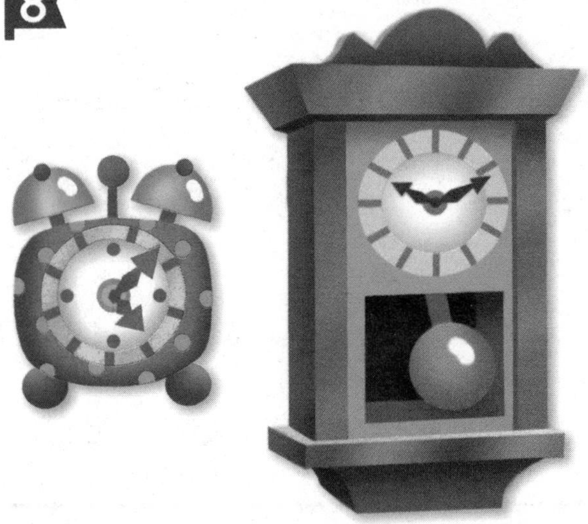

9

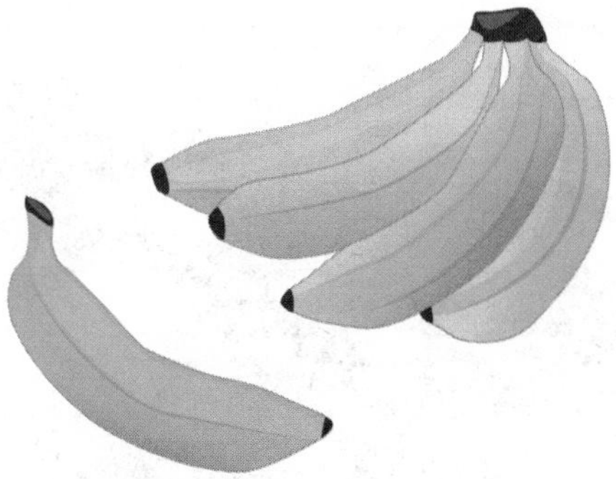

10

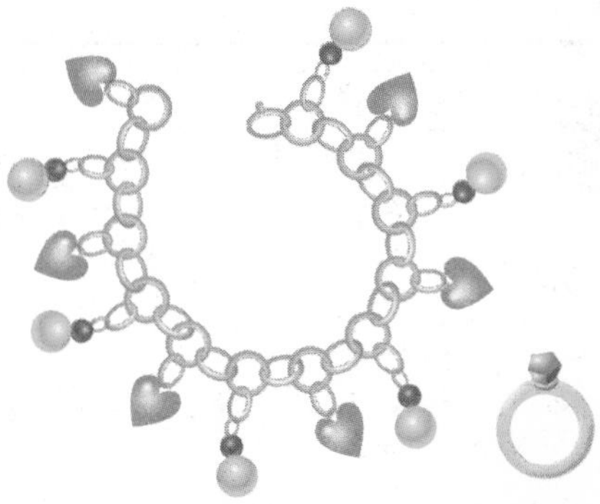

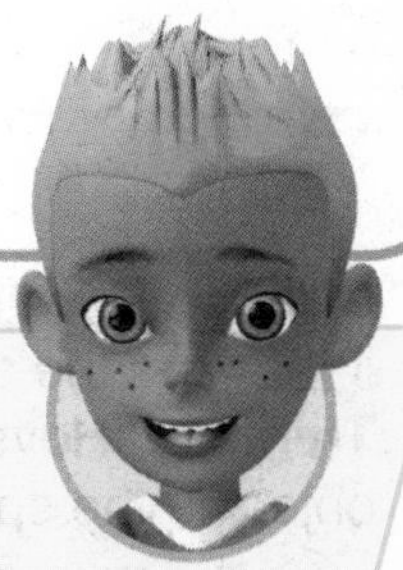

Directions 5–10 Have students draw a circle around the heavier object and mark an X on the lighter object, or underline the objects if they are the same weight.

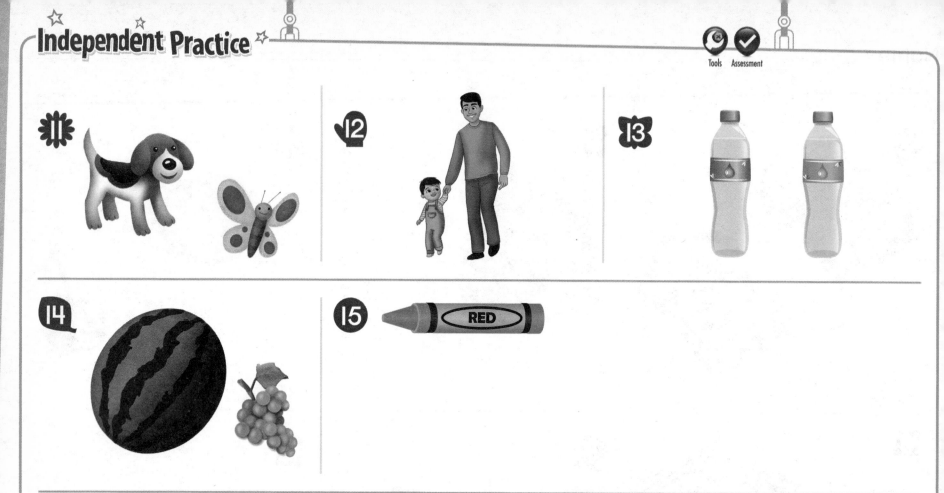

Directions ✿–🌷 Have students draw a circle around the heavier object and mark an X on the lighter object, or underline the objects if they are the same weight. ⓕ **Vocabulary** Have students draw an object that is the same **weight** as the crayon. 🎁 **Higher Order Thinking** Have students draw 2 objects. Have them draw the heavier object in the space next to the lower side of the scale and the lighter object in the space next to the higher side of the scale.

Name _____

Another Look!

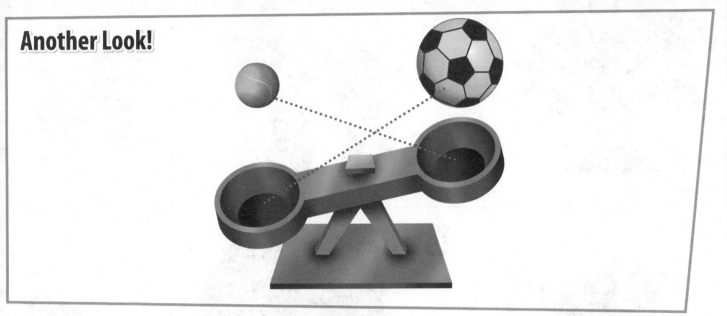

HOME ACTIVITY Ask your child to hold a slice of bread. Then ask your child to find something in your kitchen that is heavier than the slice of bread and then something that is lighter than the slice of bread.

1

2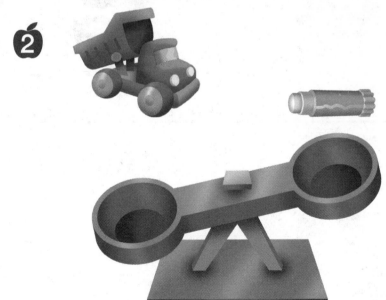

Directions Say: *Compare the objects. Which ball is heavier? Draw a line from the heavier ball to the lower side of the scale and a line from the lighter ball to the higher side of the scale.* **1** and **2** Have students compare the objects, and then match the heavier object to the lower side of the scale and the lighter object to the higher side of the scale.

Directions ❸ **Math & Science** Have students tell which provides more shade, and then have them discuss what man-made objects protect them from the sun. ❹–❻ Have students draw a circle around the heavier object and mark an X on the lighter object. ❼ **Higher Order Thinking** Have students draw one object that is light and one object that is heavy. ❽ **Higher Order Thinking** Have students draw 2 objects that are the same weight.

Name _____

Directions Say: *These are 2 tools for measuring. What can you measure with the cup? What can you measure with the cube train? Draw an object you can measure with each tool.*

I can ...
use attributes to describe different objects.

© **Content Standards**
K.MD.A.1
Mathematical Practices
MP.1, MP.2, MP.5, MP.6

☆ Guided Practice

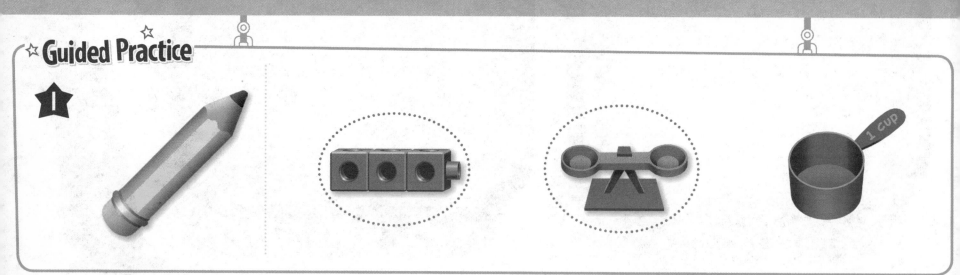

⭐1

Directions ⭐ Have students look at the object on the left, identify the attributes that can be measured, and then draw a circle around the tools that could be used to tell about those attributes.

Name _____

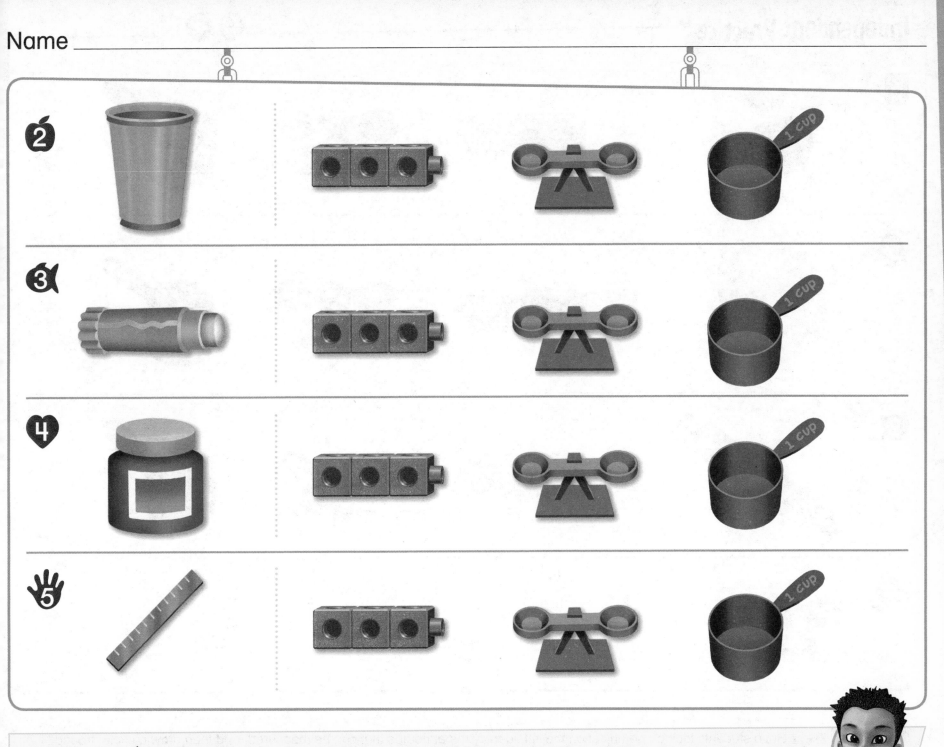

Directions ❷–❺ Have students look at the object on the left, identify the attributes that can be measured, and then draw a circle around the tools that could be used to tell about those attributes.

Topic 14 | Lesson 4

eight hundred twenty-five **825**

Independent Practice

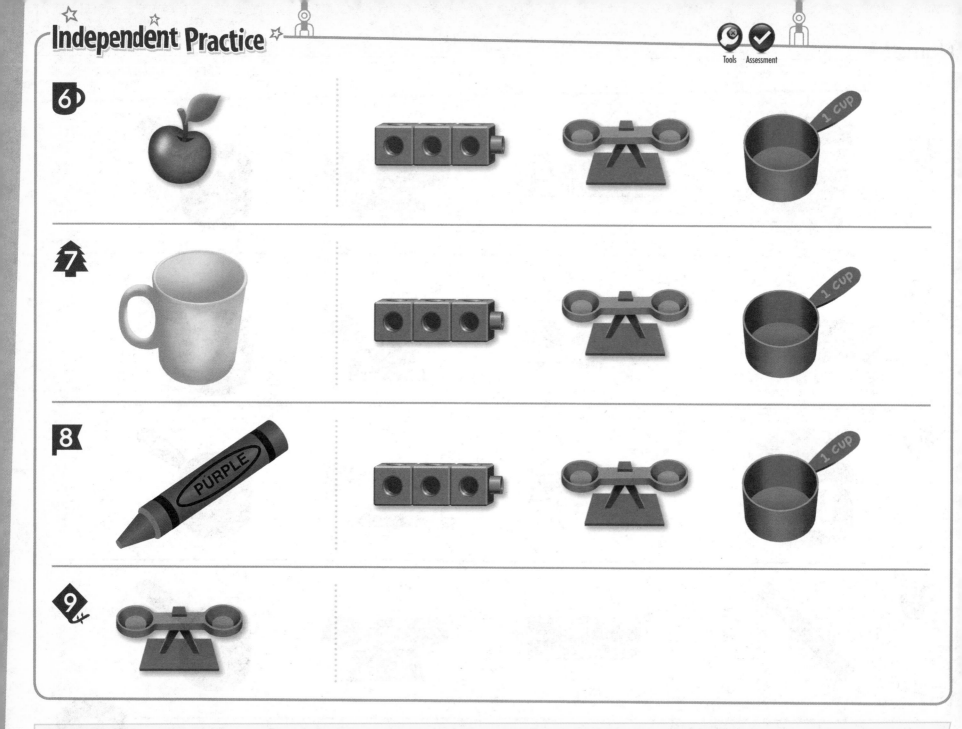

6

7

8

9

Directions **6–8** Have students look at the object on the left, identify the attributes that can be measured, and then draw a circle around the tools that could be used to tell about those attributes. **9 Higher Order Thinking** Have students identify the attribute that can be measured using the tool on the left, and then draw 2 objects that could be measured using that tool.

Name _____

Another Look!

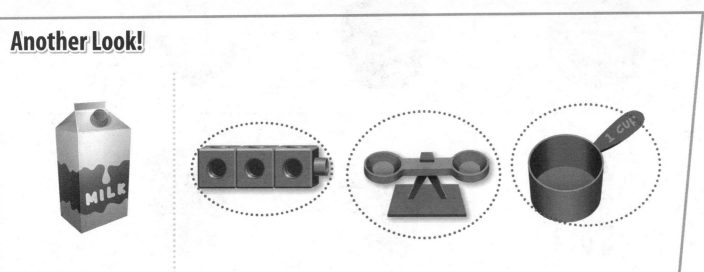

HOME ACTIVITY Choose a few small objects, such as a cup, a book, and a spoon. Ask your child to describe each object, and then name tools that could be used to tell about different attributes of the object (e.g., balance scale, cube trains, measuring cup).

 1

 2

Directions Say: *Attributes, like how long something is, how heavy something is, or how much something holds, can be measured using tools. What attributes does a carton of milk have? Draw a circle around the tools that could be used to tell about these attributes.* **1** and **2** Have students look at the object on the left, identify the attributes that can be measured, and then draw a circle around the tools that could be used to tell about those attributes.

Directions **③** and **④** Have students identify what attribute the tool on the left can measure, and then draw a circle around the object or objects that could be measured with that tool. **⑤ Higher Order Thinking** Have students identify the attribute that can be measured using the tool on the left, and then draw 2 objects that could be measured using that tool. **⑥ Higher Order Thinking** Have students draw an object that could be measured by the attributes of length, weight, and capacity.

© Pearson Education, Inc. K

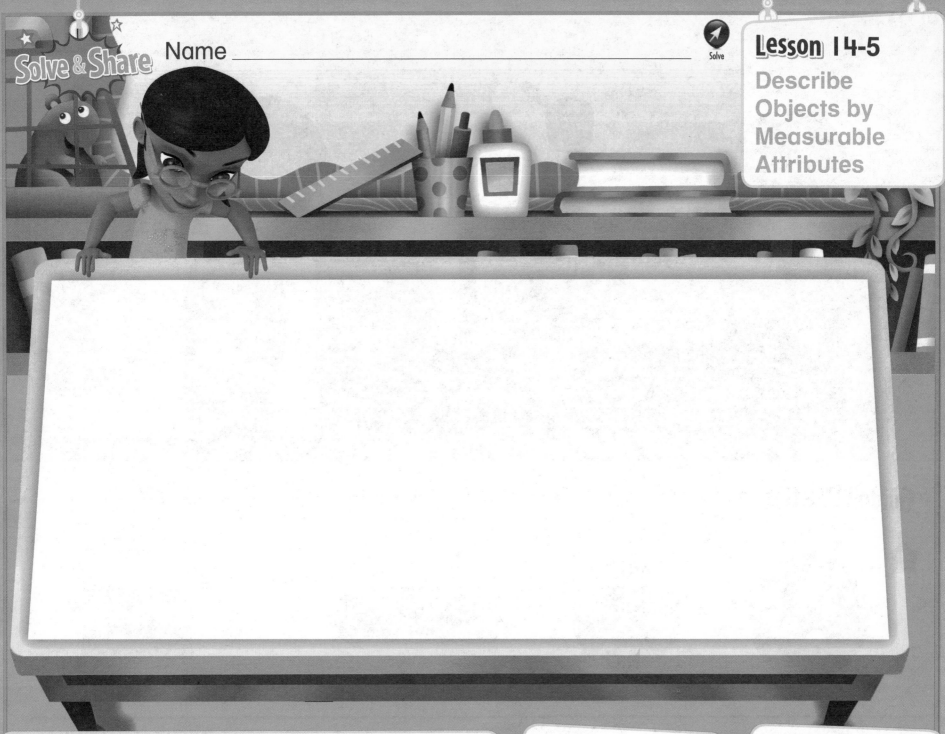

Directions Say: *Choose an object in your classroom to draw. Describe all the ways you could measure it. Then draw the tools you could use to measure the object.*

I can ...
use my words to describe how an object can be measured.

© **Content Standards**
K.MD.A.1
Mathematical Practices
MP.4, MP.5, MP.6, MP.7

☆ **Guided Practice**

1

 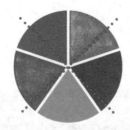  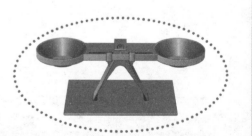

Directions ⭐ Have students look at the object on the left and identify the attributes that can be measured. Then have students draw a circle around the tool(s) that could be used to tell about those attributes and mark an X on the tool(s) that could not.

© Pearson Education, Inc. K   **Topic 14 | Lesson 5**

Name _____

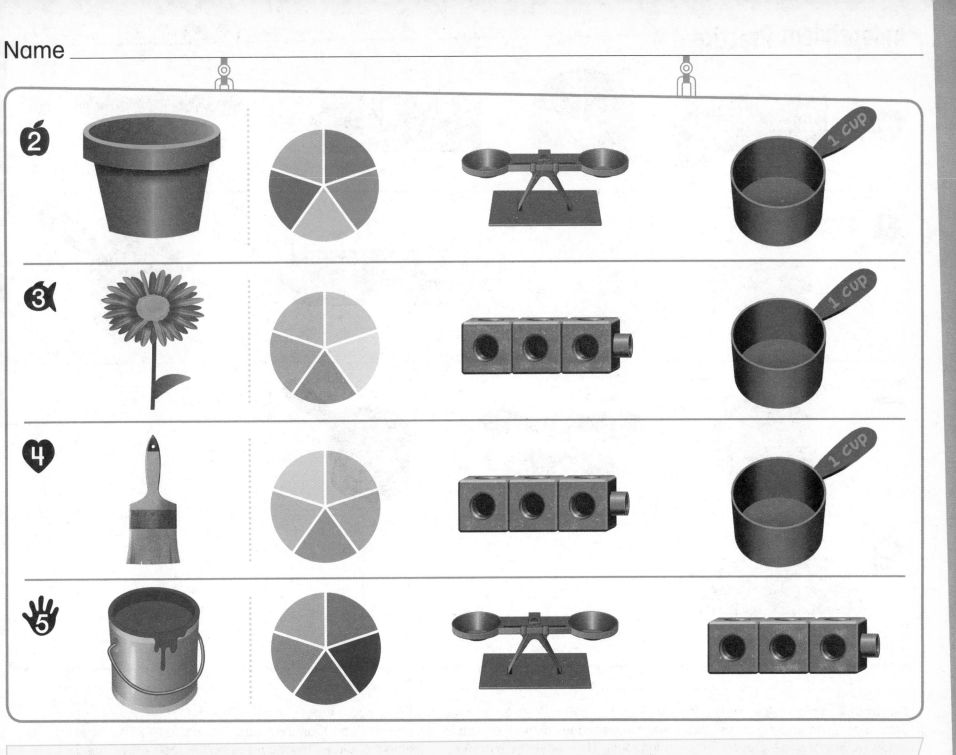

Directions ❷–✋ Have students look at the object on the left and identify the attributes that can be measured. Then have students draw a circle around the tool(s) that could be used to tell about those attributes and mark an X on the tool(s) that could NOT.

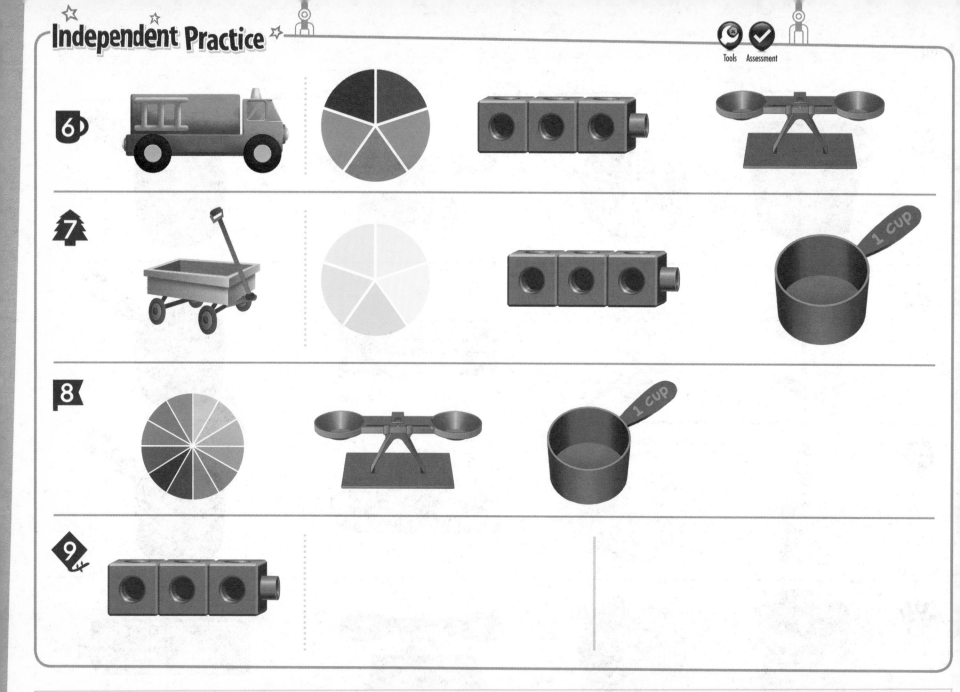

6

7

8

9

Directions **6** and **7** Have students look at the object on the left and identify the attributes that can be measured. Then have students draw a circle around the tool(s) that could be used to tell about those attributes and mark an X on the tool(s) that could NOT. **8** Have students draw a circle around 2 measuring tools. Then have them draw an object that could be measured using the tools they circled. **9 Higher Order Thinking** On the left, have students draw an object that can be measured using the tool shown. On the right, have them draw an object that CANNOT be measured using the tool shown.

832 eight hundred thirty-two   © Pearson Education, Inc. K   **Topic 14** | Lesson 5

Name _____

Another Look!

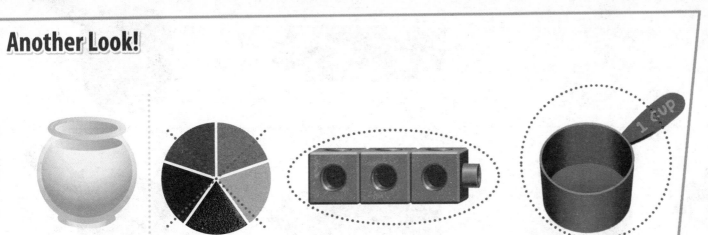

HOME ACTIVITY Show your child several household objects, such as a plate or a mug. Have him or her describe each object, and then name the tool(s) that could be used to tell about the different attributes. Then have him or her name an attribute that could NOT be measured by one of the tools.

 1

2

Directions Say: *Attributes, like how tall something is, how heavy something is, or how much something holds, can be measured using tools. What attributes does a bowl have? Draw a circle around the tool(s) that could be used to tell about these attributes. Then mark an X on the tool(s) that could NOT.* ★ *and* ② *Have students look at the object on the left and identify the attributes that can be measured. Then have students draw a circle around the tool(s) that could be used to tell about those attributes and mark an X on the tool(s) that could NOT.*

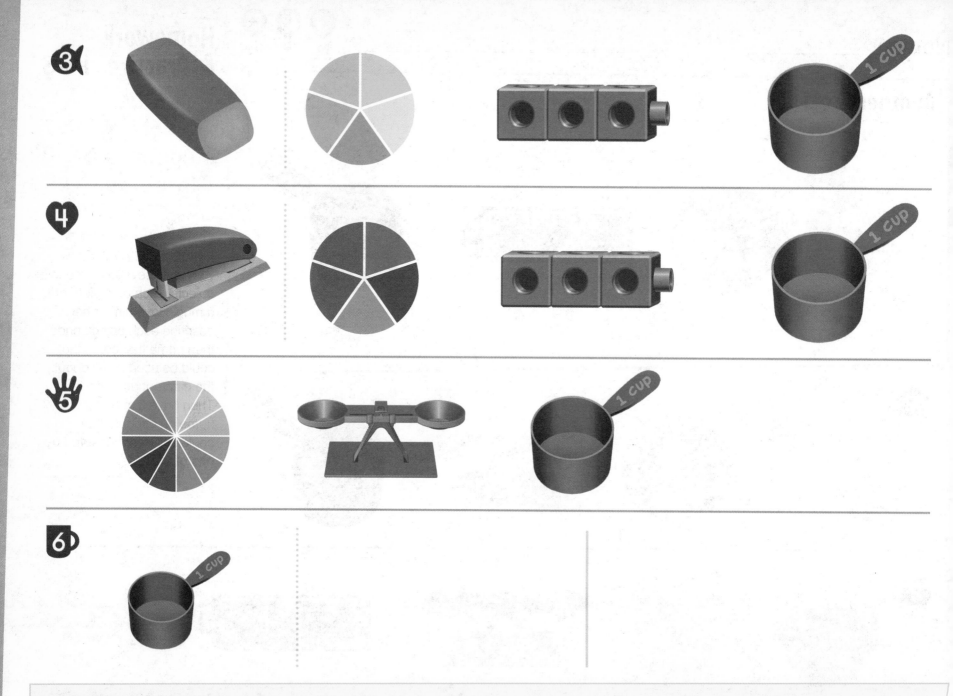

Directions ❸ and ❹ Have students look at the object on the left and identify the attributes that can be measured. Then have students draw a circle around the tool(s) that could be used to tell about those attributes and mark an X on the tool(s) that could NOT. ❺ **Higher Order Thinking** Have students draw a circle around 2 measuring tools. Then have them draw an object that could be measured using those tools. ❻ **Higher Order Thinking** On the left, have students draw an object that can be measured using the tool shown. On the right, have them draw an object that CANNOT be measured using the tool shown.

Name _____

Think.

3

I can ...
solve math problems about objects with measurable attributes by using precision.

© **Mathematical Practices**
MP.6 Also MP.3, MP.4, MP.5
Content Standards
K.MD.A.2

Directions Say: *Marta wants to compare the length of a ribbon to the length of a cube train so she can draw a circle around the object that is shorter. How can she do this? Explain where you place the cube train on the page and why.*

☆ Guided Practice

1

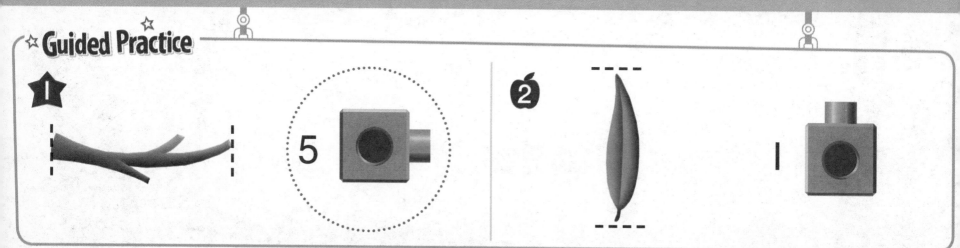

Directions Have students: **1** make a cube train with the number of cubes shown, compare the length of the cube train to the object, and then draw a circle around the one that is longer; **2** make a cube tower with the number of cubes shown, compare the height of the cube tower to the object, and then draw a circle around the one that is taller.

© Pearson Education, Inc. K

Independent Practice

3 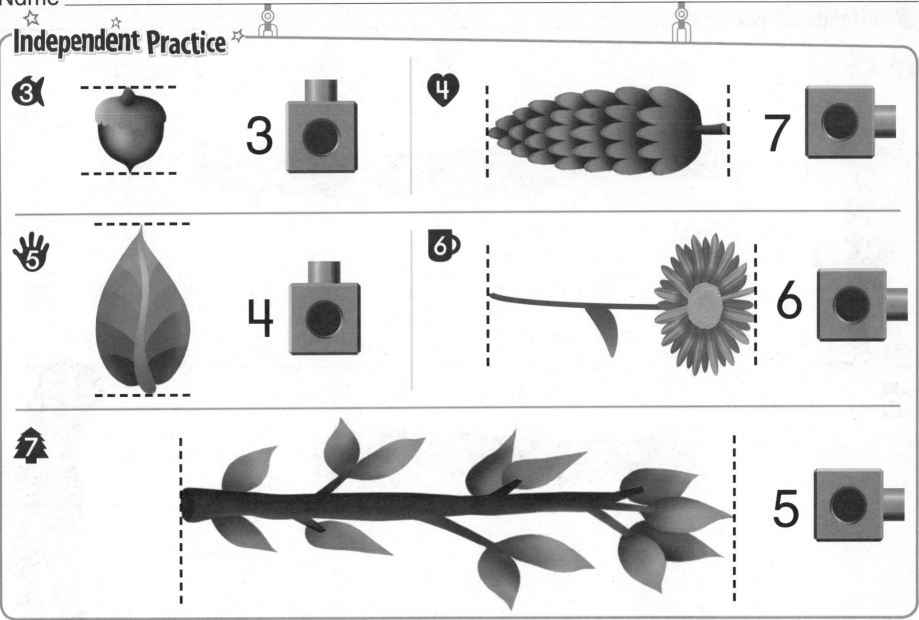 3

4 7

5 4

6 6

7 5

Directions Have students make a cube train or cube tower with the number of cubes shown. Then have them: **3** compare the height of the cube tower to the acorn, and then draw a circle around the one that is taller; **4** compare the length of the pinecone to the cube train and mark an X on the one that is shorter; **5** compare the height of the cube tower to the leaf, and then draw a circle around the one that is taller; **6** compare the length of the flower to the cube train and mark an X on the one that is shorter; **7** compare the length of the cube train to the twig, and then draw a circle around the one that is longer.

Math Practices and Problem Solving

© **Performance Assessment**

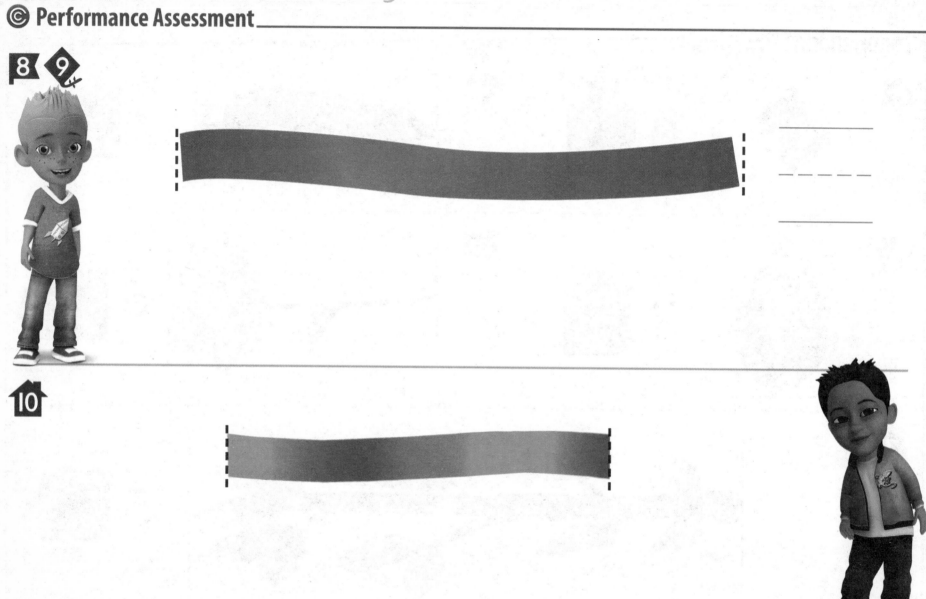

Directions Read the problem aloud. Then have students use multiple math practices to solve the problem. Say: *Alex has a piece of ribbon. He wants to make a cube train longer than the ribbon. How many cubes long will the cube train be?* **8 MP.5 Use Tools** *What tool can you use to help solve the problem? Make a cube train that is longer than the piece of purple ribbon, and then write the number of cubes in the train. Explain your answer.* **9 MP.6 Be Precise** *Why is it important to count the cubes?* **10 MP.3 Explain** *Carlos says that he made a cube train that is 3 cubes long and that it is longer than the length of the orange ribbon. Is he right or wrong? How do you know?*

Name _____

Another Look!

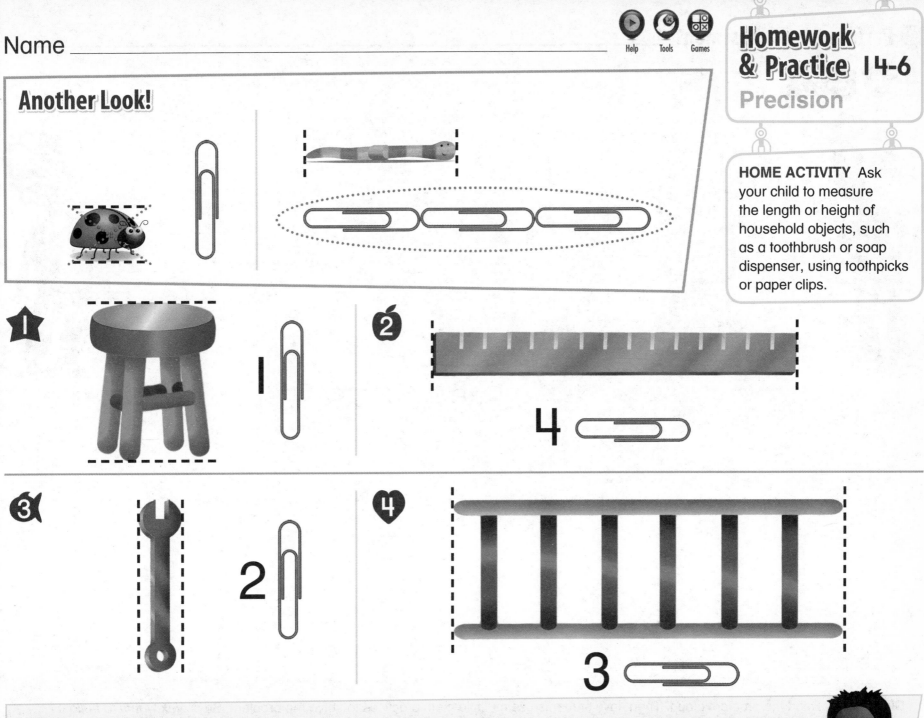

HOME ACTIVITY Ask your child to measure the length or height of household objects, such as a toothbrush or soap dispenser, using toothpicks or paper clips.

⭐ 1

2

★ 3   2

♥ 4   3

Directions Say: *Compare the ladybug to the paper clip. Which is shorter? Mark an X on the ladybug to show that it is shorter. Make a chain of 3 paper clips. Compare the chain to the worm. Which is longer? Draw a circle around the paper clip chain to show it is longer.* Have students: ⭐—♥ make a chain of paper clips with the number of paper clips shown, compare the length of the chain to each object, and then draw a circle around the one that is longer or taller.

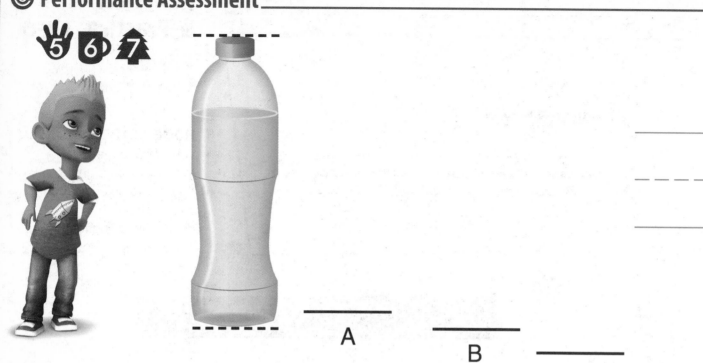

A

B

C

Directions Read the problem aloud. Then have students use multiple math practices to solve the problem. Say: *Alex wants to build a cube tower that is taller than his water bottle. How does he know where to place the cube tower to compare the height?* 👋 **MP.6 Be Precise** *Pick a starting line. Which line do you use to compare your cube tower to the water bottle? Explain your answer.* ☕ **MP.4 Model** *How tall is the cube tower you built? Draw a picture of the cube tower that you built, and then write the number of cubes in the tower.* 🌲 **MP.3 Explain** *Carlos picks Line A to compare. Is he right or wrong? Explain how you know.*

1

5 − 1	2 + 3	1 + 2	1 + 1	4 − 4
5 − 5	1 + 4	0 + 1	0 + 3	2 + 1
2 − 1	5 + 0	5 − 3	1 + 3	3 − 0
4 + 0	3 + 2	5 − 2	5 − 4	2 + 0
1 − 1	0 + 5	2 + 3	4 + 1	5 − 0

2

_____

_ _ _ _ _

_____

I can ...
add and subtract fluently within 5.

© Content Standard K.OA.A.5

Directions Have students: **1** color each box that has a sum or difference that is equal to 5; **2** write the letter that they see.

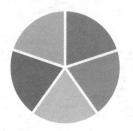

Directions **Understand Vocabulary** Have students: ⭐ draw a circle around the tool that measures **length**; 🍎 draw a circle around the **longer** object; ⭐ mark an X on the pitcher that has a smaller **capacity**; ❹ draw an object that is the same **height** as the cubes; ✋ draw a circle around the group of animals that can be the same **weight**.

© Pearson Education, Inc. K

Name ______________________________

Set A

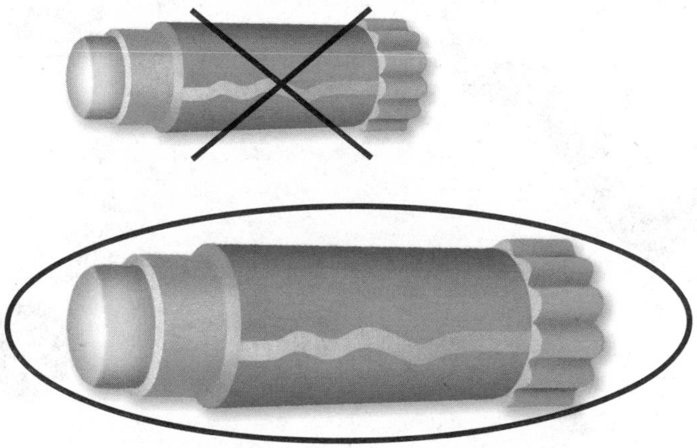

1

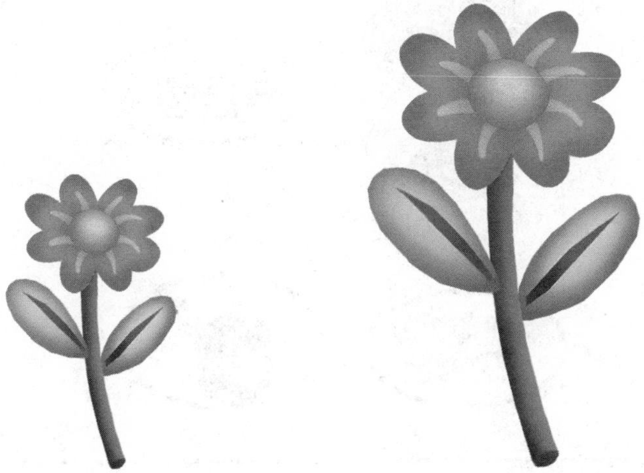

Set B

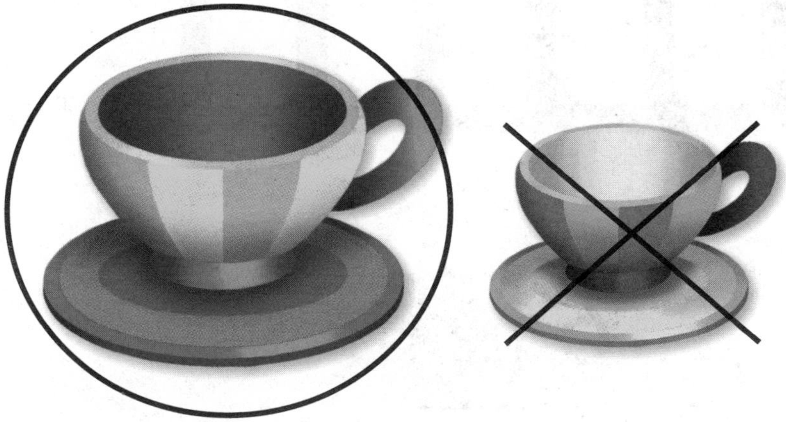

2

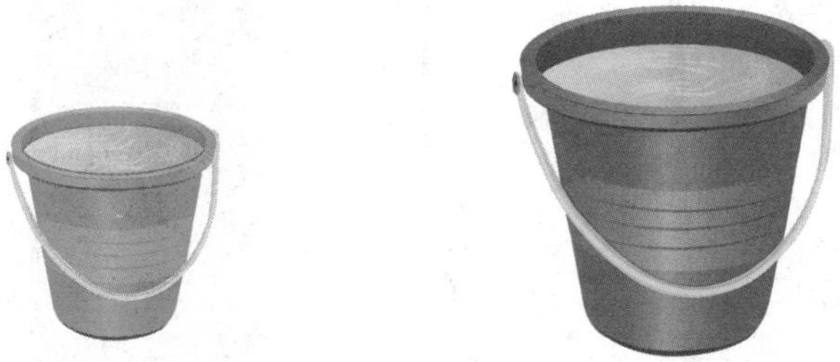

Directions Have students: 1 draw a circle around the taller flower and mark an X on the shorter flower; 2 draw a circle around the bucket that contains more water, and then mark an X on the bucket that contains less water.

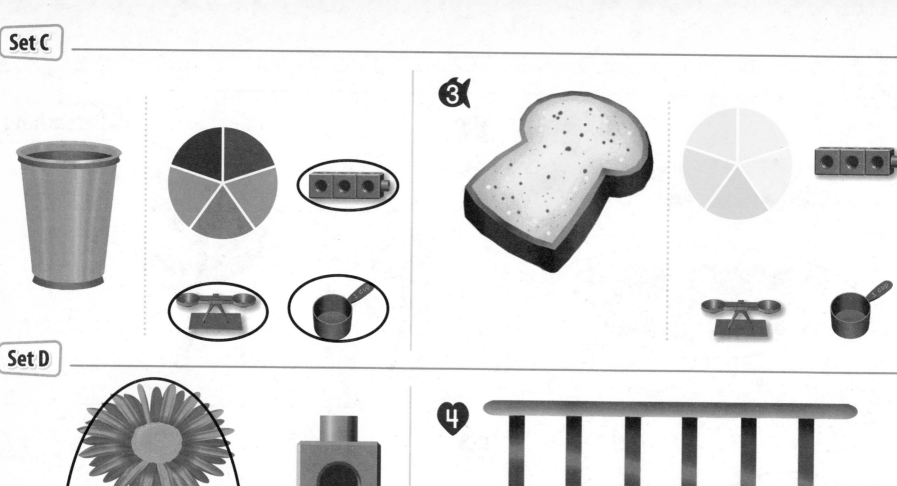

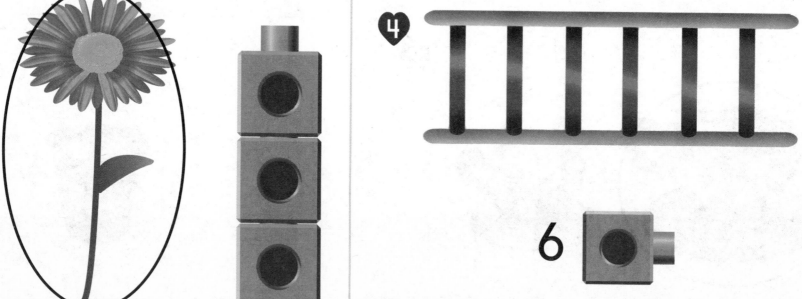

Directions Have students: ❸ look at the object on the left and identify the attributes that can be measured. Then have students draw a circle around the tool(s) that could be used to tell about those attributes; ❹ make a cube train with the number of cubes shown, compare the length of the cube train to the object, and then draw a circle around the one that is longer.

© Pearson Education, Inc. K

Name _____

© Assessment

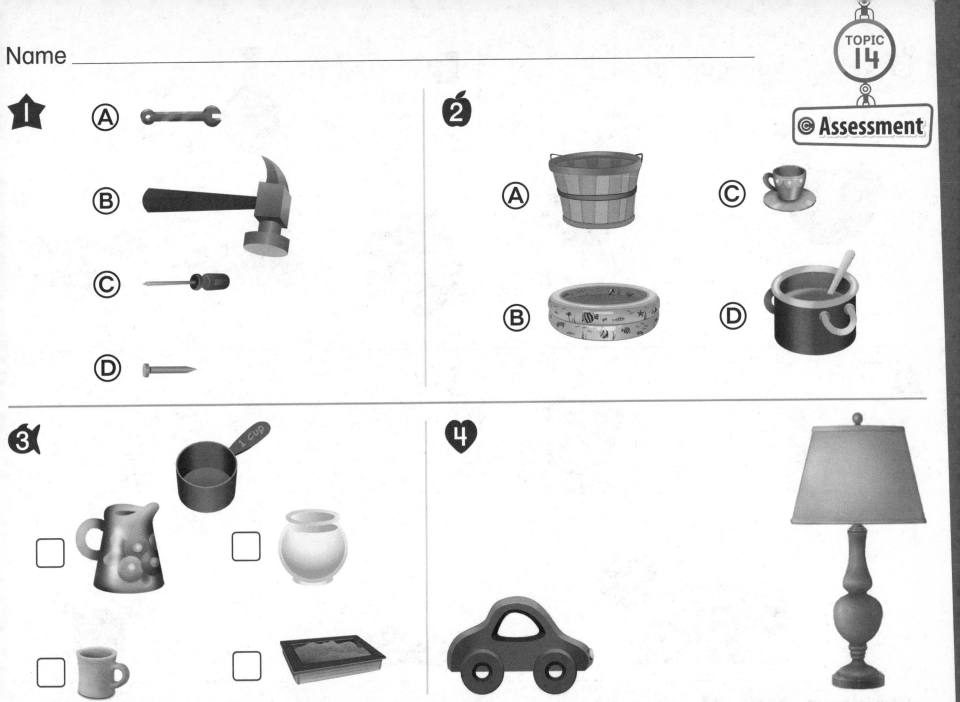

⭐ Ⓐ Ⓑ Ⓒ Ⓓ

🍎 Ⓐ Ⓒ Ⓑ Ⓓ

⭐3

❤4

1 CUP

Directions Have students mark the best answer. ⭐ Which object is longer than the other objects? 🍎 Which object holds less than the other objects? ⭐3 Mark all the objects that can be measured with the tool shown. ❤ Have students draw an object that is taller than a toy car, but shorter than a lamp.

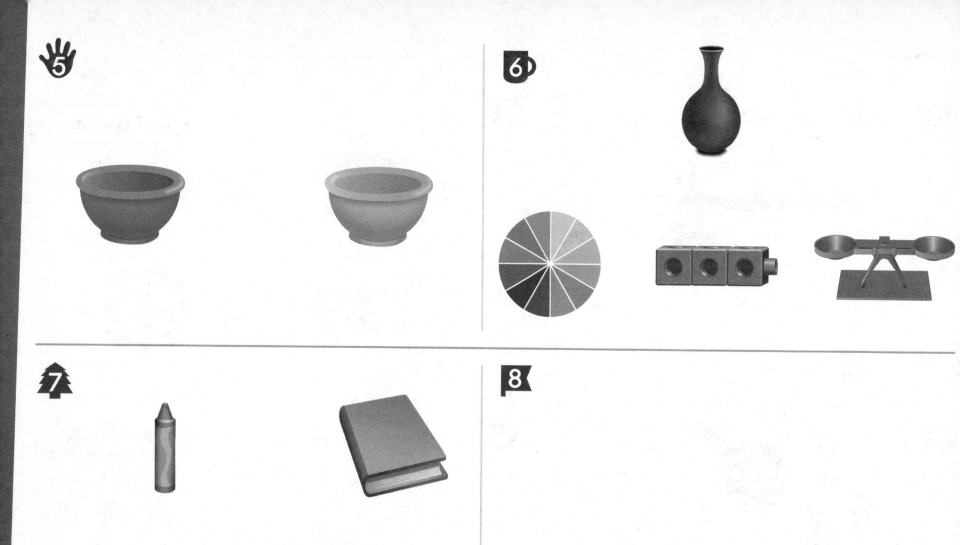

Directions Have students: ✋ draw a circle around the container that holds more, or underline the containers if they hold the same amount; 6️⃣ look at the object and identify the attributes that can be measured. Then have them draw a circle around the tool(s) that could be used to tell about those attributes and mark an X on the tool(s) that could NOT; 7️⃣ compare the objects, and then match the heavier object to the lower side of the scale and the lighter object to the higher side of the scale; 8️⃣ draw an object that can be measured using both of the tools shown.

© Pearson Education, Inc. K

Name _____

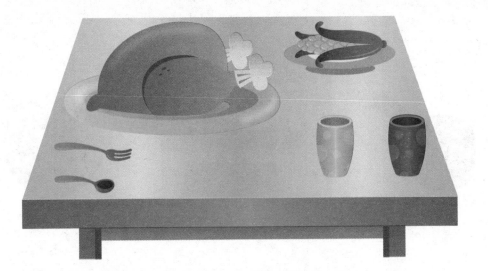

Directions **Time for Dinner!** Say: *Teddy helps his father make dinner. They use different things in the kitchen.* Have students: look at the fork and the spoon, and then draw a circle around the longer object and mark an X on the shorter object; ❷ look at the yellow cup and the red cup, and then mark an X on the cup that holds less or underline the cups if they hold the same amount. Then draw a container that would hold more than the red cup; ❸ look at the turkey and the corn, and then draw a circle around the heavier object or underline the objects if they have the same weight. Then draw an object that would weigh less than the corn.

4

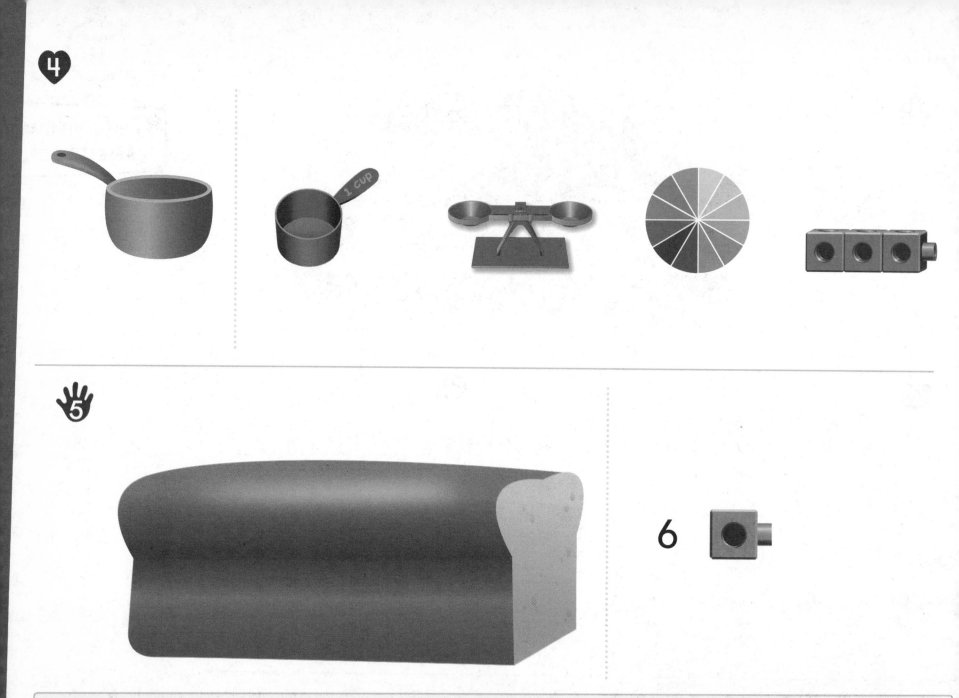

5

6

Directions ♥ Say: *Teddy and his father will use this pan. What attributes could you measure with the pan?* Have students draw a circle around the tool(s) that could be used to tell about those attributes and mark an X on the tool(s) that could NOT. ✋ Say: *Teddy and his father will eat this bread for dinner.* Have students make a cube train with the number of cubes shown and draw the cube train. Have them compare the length of the cube train to the bread, and then draw a circle around the object that is longer.

Topic 14 | Performance Assessment

Here's a preview of next year. These lessons help you step up to Grade 1.

STEP UP to Grade 1

STEP UP Lessons

Name _____

Solve & Share

Your bag has 2 different colors of connecting cubes. Take out a handful of cubes. Make sure to get some cubes of each color.

How can you use numbers to show how many cubes you picked in all? Show how.

I can ...
write equations to show the parts and the whole.

© Content Standard 1.OA.C.6
Mathematical Practices MP.2, MP.4

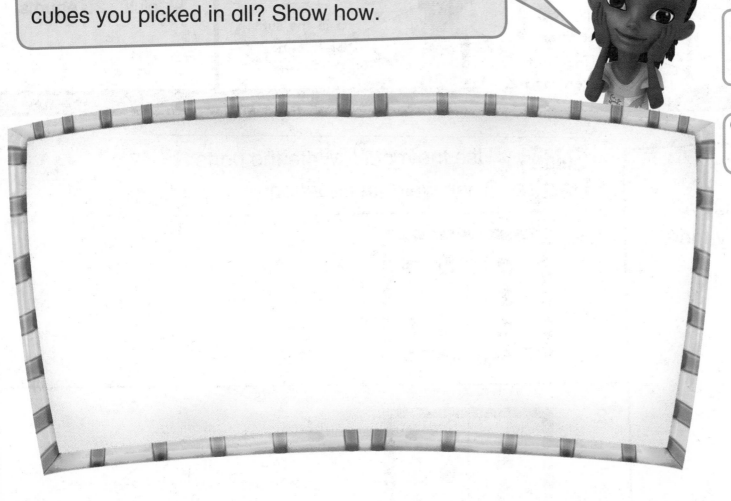

Step Up | Lesson 1
Digital Resources at PearsonRealize.com
eight hundred fifty-one **851**

Kenny picked 4 red cubes. Then he picked 2 blue cubes.

You can describe the parts as 4 and 2 and write $\underline{4} + \underline{2}$.

plus

The parts are 4 and 2.

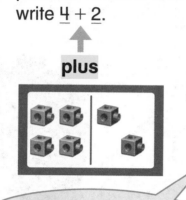

You can **add** the parts to find the **sum**. 4 and 2 is 6 in all.

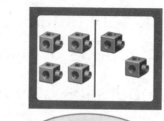

6 is the sum of 4 and 2.

You can write an **equation** to show the parts and the whole.

$$\underline{4} + \underline{2} = \underline{6}$$

4   plus   2   **equals** 6.

Do You Understand?

Show Me! What can you do to find how many there are in all?

☆Guided☆ Practice

Use the model. Write the parts. Then write an equation.

1.

$$\underline{3} + \underline{4}$$

$$\underline{3} + \underline{4} = \underline{7}$$

2.

$$\underline{} + \underline{}$$

$$\underline{} = \underline{} + \underline{}$$

Name _____

Independent Practice ⭐ Use the model. Write the parts. Then write an equation.

3.

___ + ___

___ + ___ = ___

4.

___ + ___

___ + ___ = ___

5.

___ + ___

___ = ___ + ___

6. **Higher Order Thinking** Jim picked up 9 rocks. He picked up 4 of them on his way to school. He picked up the rest on his way home. How many rocks did Jim pick up on his way home?

Draw a picture to solve. Then write an equation.

___ + ___ = ___

7. © MP.2 Reasoning Ben found

4 orange leaves.

Then he found 3 yellow leaves.

How many leaves did Ben find in all?

Draw a picture to show the story.

Then write an equation.

_____ + _____ = _____

8. Higher Order Thinking Draw a picture to show an addition story about red worms and brown worms. Write an equation to tell how many worms there are in all.

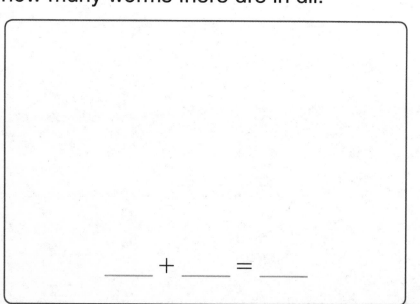

_____ + _____ = _____

9. © Assessment Ava drew 9 apples. 3 of them are green. The others are red. How many red apples did she draw?

Which equation matches this story?

Ⓐ $9 + 3 = 12$

Ⓑ $4 + 5 = 9$

Ⓒ $3 + 6 = 9$

Ⓓ $3 + 3 = 6$

Solve

Lesson 2
Facts with 5 on a Ten-Frame

Solve & Share

Put some counters on the bottom row of the ten-frame. What addition equation can you write to match the counters?

I can ...
use a ten-frame to help solve addition facts with 5 and 10.

© **Content Standard** 1.OA.C.6
Mathematical Practices MP.3, MP.4, MP.7

____ + ____ = ____

You can use a ten-frame to show an addition fact with 5.

$5 + 3 = ?$

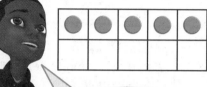

Start with 5. Then add 3 more.

5 and 3 more is 8.

There are 8 counters in the ten-frame.

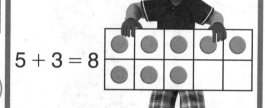

$5 + 3 = 8$

The ten-frame shows another addition fact. You have 8. Make 10.

2 boxes are empty. Add 2.

8 plus 2 more is 10.

$8 + 2 = 10$

Do You Understand?

Show Me! How does a ten-frame help you add $5 + 4$?

☆ Guided Practice ☆

Look at the ten-frames. Write an addition fact with 5. Then write an addition fact for 10.

1.

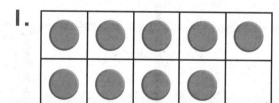

$5 + \underline{4} = 9$

$9 + \underline{1} = 10$

2.

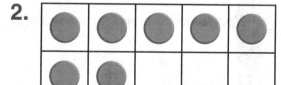

$5 + \underline{} = \underline{}$

$\underline{} + \underline{} = 10$

Name _____

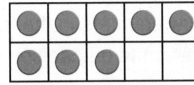
Independent Practice   Look at the ten-frames. Write an addition fact with 5. Then write an addition fact for 10.

3.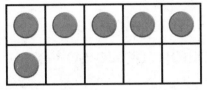

5 + ____ = ____

____ + ____ = 10

4.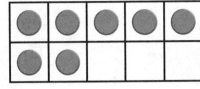

5 + ____ = ____

____ + ____ = 10

5.

5 + ____ = ____

____ + ____ = 10

6. **Higher Order Thinking** Using 2 colors, draw counters in the ten-frames to match the addition equations. Then write the missing numbers.

7 + ____ = 10

9 + ____ = 10

Which number will make 10?

7. © **MP.4 Model** A team has 5 softballs. The coach brings 3 more. How many softballs does the team have now?

Draw counters in the ten-frame. Then write an addition fact to solve.

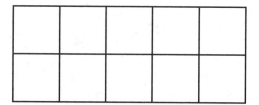

_____ + _____ = _____ _____ softballs

8. © **MP.4 Model** Marcia reads 5 books. Tanya reads 2 books. How many books did the girls read in all?

Draw counters in the ten-frame. Then write an addition fact to solve.

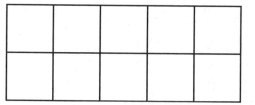

_____ + _____ = _____ _____ books

9. **Higher Order Thinking** Write a new story about adding to 10 in the ten-frame in Item 7. Then write an equation for your story.

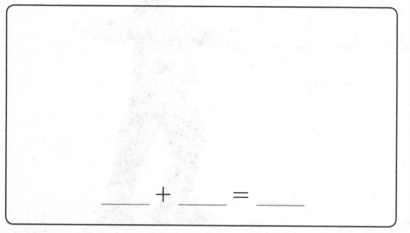

_____ + _____ = _____

10. © **Assessment** Scott's team has 5 footballs. Scott's coach brings some more. Scott's team now has 10 footballs.

Which addition fact shows how many footballs Scott's coach brought?

Ⓐ 5 + 5 = 10

Ⓑ 10 + 5 = 15

Ⓒ 7 + 3 = 10

Ⓓ 10 + 7 = 17

© Pearson Education, Inc. K

Name _____

Step Up to Grade 1

Lesson 3

Add in Any Order

Solve & Share

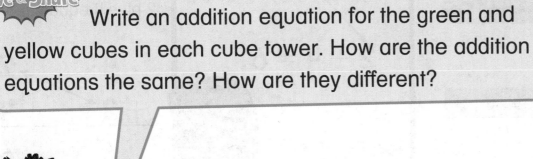

Write an addition equation for the green and yellow cubes in each cube tower. How are the addition equations the same? How are they different?

I can ...
use the same addends to write two different equations with the same sum.

© **Content Standard** 1.OA.B.3
Mathematical Practices MP.2, MP.3, MP.4, MP.7

____ + ____ = ____   ____ + ____ = ____

4 and 2 is 6.

2 and 4 is 6.

$$4 + 2 = 6$$

$$2 + 4 = 6$$

4 plus 2 equals 6.

2 plus 4 equals 6.

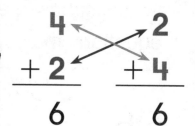

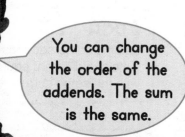

You can change the order of the addends. The sum is the same.

You can write 2 addition equations.

Do You Understand?

Show Me! How can you use cubes to show that 5 + 3 is the same as 3 + 5?

☆ **Guided Practice** ☆ Color to change the order of the addends. Then write the addition equations.

1.

$$\underline{3} + \underline{2} = \underline{5}$$

___ + ___ = ___

2.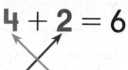

___ + ___ = ___

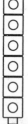

___ + ___ = ___

© Pearson Education, Inc. K

Step Up | Lesson 3

Name _____

Independent Practice Write the sum. Then change the order of the addends. Write the new addition equation.

3. 2 + 6 = ____

____ + ____ = ____

4. 3 + 6 = ____

____ + ____ = ____

5. ____ = 1 + 7

____ = ____ + ____

6. 4 + 3 = ____

____ + ____ = ____

7. 4 + 5 = ____

____ + ____ = ____

8. 4 + 2 = ____

____ + ____ = ____

Number Sense Use the numbers on the cards to write 2 addition equations.

9.

____ + ____ = ____

____ + ____ = ____

10.

____ = ____ + ____

____ = ____ + ____

11. © **MP.4 Model** Rico and Nate collect 3 cans on Monday. On Tuesday, they collect 7 more. How many cans did they collect in all?

Draw a picture. Then write 2 different addition equations.

_____ + _____ = _____

_____ + _____ = _____

12. **Higher Order Thinking**

Draw a picture of 4 fish.
Make some blue.
Make the rest red.

Write 2 addition equations
to tell about the picture.

_____ + _____ = _____

_____ + _____ = _____

13. © **Assessment** Look at the 2 addition equations. Which is the missing addend?

$8 = \underline{\ ?\ } + 2$

$8 = 2 + \underline{\ ?\ }$

Ⓐ 6

Ⓑ 7

Ⓒ 8

Ⓓ 9

Both addition equations have a 2 and a 8.

© Pearson Education, Inc. K

Step Up | Lesson 3

Name _____

Solve & Share

Alex has 5 connecting cubes on the table. He hides some cubes. How can you use numbers to show how many cubes are hidden?

Introducing Subtraction Expressions and Equations

I can ...
write equations to find the missing part of a whole.

© **Content Standard** 1.OA.C.6
Mathematical Practices MP.2, MP.4

Alex has 8 cubes.
He hides some cubes.

5 is the part you see. What is the hidden part?

You can describe the whole as 8 and one of the parts as 5. Find the hidden part by writing 8 − 5.

8

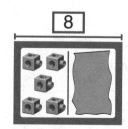

You can **subtract** to find the **difference**. 8 − 5 is 3.

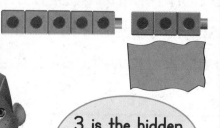

3 is the hidden part. It is the difference.

You can write an equation.

$$8 - 5 = 3$$

8

8 minus 5 equals 3.

Do You Understand?

Show Me! The whole is 9. One of the parts is 3. How can you find the difference?

Guided Practice Complete the model. Write the parts. Then write an equation.

1.

6

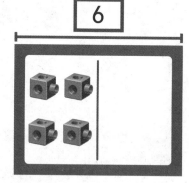

$$\underline{6} - \underline{4}$$

$$\underline{6} - \underline{4} = \underline{2}$$

2.

8

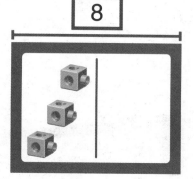

$$\underline{} - \underline{}$$

$$\underline{} = \underline{} - \underline{}$$

© Pearson Education, Inc. K   **Step Up** | Lesson 4

Independent Practice   Complete the model. Write the parts.
Then write a subtraction sentence.

3.

| 7 |

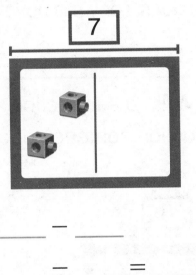

___ ___
___ ___ = ___

4.

| 9 |

___ ___
___ ___ = ___

5.

| 6 |

___ ___
___ ___ = ___ ___

---

6. Higher Order Thinking There are
7 kittens in all. 1 is inside a basket.
The rest are outside. How many
kittens are outside the basket?

Draw a picture to show the story.
Then write the missing part.

$$7 - \underline{} = 1$$

7. © **MP.2 Reasoning** Lena has 8 rocks. She drops 4 of the rocks into a pond. How many rocks does Lena have now?

_____ rocks

8. © **MP.1 Make Sense** Tony picks 7 flowers. He gives 4 flowers to his sister. How many flowers does Tony still have?

_____ flowers

9. **Higher Order Thinking** Rob has 9 marbles. He gave some marbles to a friend. He has 2 marbles left. How many marbles did Rob give to his friend?

Choose the subtraction sentence that matches the story.

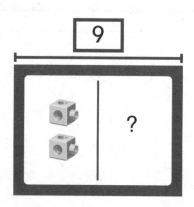

Ⓐ 9 − 3 = 6

Ⓑ 9 − 2 = 7

Ⓒ 7 − 3 = 4

Ⓓ 7 − 2 = 5

10. © **Assessment** Write a subtraction story and a subtraction sentence about the model.

_____ − _____ = _____

Name _____

Solve & Share

Jenna has 6 beach balls. 4 of them blow to the other side of the pool. How many does she have left?

How can you use an addition fact to find the answer to
6 − 4 = ____? Use counters to help you solve the problem.

I can ...
use addition facts I know to help me solve subtraction problems.

 Content Standards 1.OA.B.4, 1.OA.C.6, 1.OA.D.8
Mathematical Practices MP.2, MP.4, MP.5, MP.7

____ + ____ = ____   So, ____ − ____ = ____.

You can use addition to help you subtract.

$7 - 3 = \boxed{?}$

7

$3 + \boxed{?} = 7$

What can I add to 3 to make 7?

7

$3 + \boxed{4} = 7$

The missing part is 4.

7

$3 + 4 = 7$

Think of the addition fact to solve the subtraction equation.

$7 - 3 = \boxed{4}$

Do You Understand?

Show Me! How can an addition fact help you solve $7 - 6$?

✩ Guided ✩ Practice Think addition to help you subtract. Draw the missing part. Then write the numbers.

1.

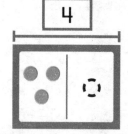

4

$4 - 3 = ?$

$3 + \_\_\_ = 4$

So, $4 - 3 = \_\_\_$.

2.

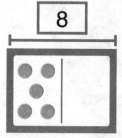

8

$8 - 5 = ?$

$5 + \_\_\_ = 8$

So, $8 - 5 = \_\_\_$.

Name _____

Independent Practice Think addition to help you subtract. Draw the missing part. Then write the numbers.

3. | 9 |

6 + ____ = 9

So, 9 − 6 = ____.

4. | 5 |

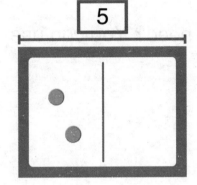

2 + ____ = 5

So, 5 − 2 = ____.

5. | 7 |

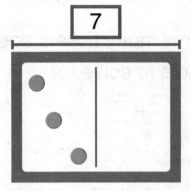

3 + ____ = 7

So, 7 − 3 = ____.

6. Higher Order Thinking Draw the shape to complete the equation.

If △ + ★ = ▮ ,

then ▮ − △ = ____ .

Write an addition and a subtraction equation to solve.

7. © **MP.5 Use Tools** Claire needs 9 tickets to get on a ride. She has 4 tickets. She needs some more tickets.

How many tickets does Claire still need? You can use tools to solve.

Which tool could help you solve this problem?

_____ + _____ = _____

_____ − _____ = _____

_____ tickets

---

8. **Higher Order Thinking** Erin has a box that holds 8 crayons. 2 crayons are inside the box. She uses addition to find how many are missing. Is Erin correct? Explain.

$8 + 2 = 10$

10 crayons are missing.

9. © **Assessment** Which addition facts can help you solve the problem? Choose all that apply.

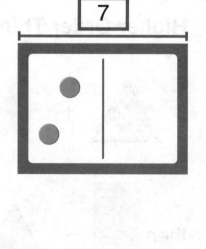

7

$7 - 2 = ?$

☐ $5 + 2 = 7$

☐ $3 + 4 = 7$

☐ $2 + 5 = 7$

☐ $6 + 1 = 7$

© Pearson Education, Inc. K

Name _____

Solve & Share

Carlos made stacks of 6 books, 4 books, and 6 books. How can you use addition to find the number of books in all 3 stacks?

Write 2 different equations to show how many books in all.

I can ...
find different strategies to add three numbers.

© **Content Standards** 1.OA.B.3, 1.OA.A.2
Mathematical Practices MP.2, MP.3, MP.4, MP.7

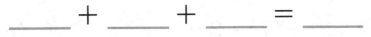

___ + ___ + ___ = ___

___ + ___ + ___ = ___

You can add 3 numbers.

$8 + 6 + 2$

Pick 2 numbers to add first.

You can make 10.

$⑧ + 6 + ② = \underline{16}$

10

$8 + 2 = 10$
$10 + 6 = 16$

You can make a double.

$8 + ⑥ + ② = \underline{16}$

8

$6 + 2 = 8$
$8 + 8 = 16$

You can add any 2 numbers first.

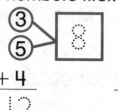

③
⑤   8   3
+ 4   ⑤
12   +④   9
                12

The sums are the same.

Do You Understand?

Show Me! Why can you pick any 2 numbers to add first when you add 3 numbers?

☆ **Guided Practice** ☆ Add the circled numbers first. Write their sum in the box. Then write the sum of all 3 numbers.

1. $② + ⑦ + 3 = \underline{12}$

   9

   $2 + ⑦ + ③ = \underline{12}$

   10

2. $⑥ + ⑤ + 4 = \underline{}$

   ☐

   $6 + ⑤ + ④ = \underline{}$

   ☐

© Pearson Education, Inc. K

Step Up | Lesson 6

Independent Practice

Circle 2 numbers to add first. Write their sum in the box at the right. Then write the sum of all 3 numbers.

3.
```
  6
  5
+ 1
```
□

□

4.
```
  5
  4
+ 8
```
□

□

5.
```
  2
  7
+ 4
```
□

□

6.
```
  7
  2
+ 7
```
□

□

7.
```
  5
  3
+ 7
```
□

□

8.
```
  4
  6
+ 4
```
□

□

9. Number Sense Find the missing numbers.
The numbers on each branch add up to 17.

Each branch has 3 numbers that add up to 17.

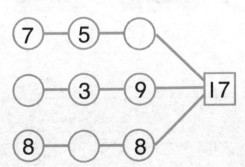

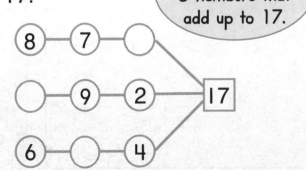

10. © **MP.7 Look for Patterns** Oscar puts 9 books on a shelf and 3 books on another shelf. Then he puts I book on the last shelf. How many books did Oscar put on all three shelves?

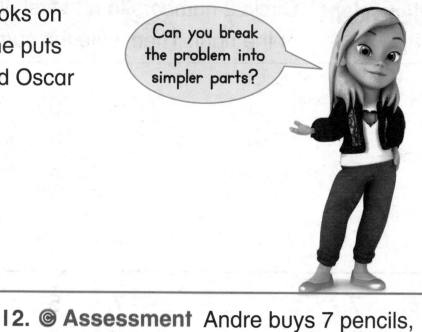

Can you break the problem into simpler parts?

_____ + _____ + _____ = _____

_____ books

11. **Higher Order Thinking** Explain how to add $9 + 6 + 1$. Use pictures, numbers, or words.

12. © **Assessment** Andre buys 7 pencils, 5 markers, and 3 pens. He wants to know how many items he bought in all. He added $7 + 3$ first. What should Andre add next? Explain.

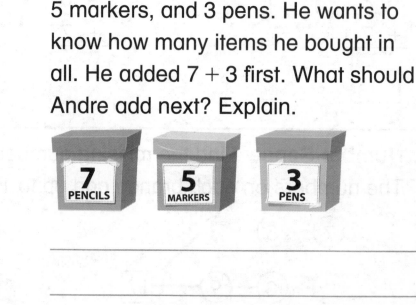

7 PENCILS 5 MARKERS 3 PENS

Name _____

Solve & Share

Marta put counters on some ten-frames. What is an easy way to count how many counters there are in all? Count how many and write the number.

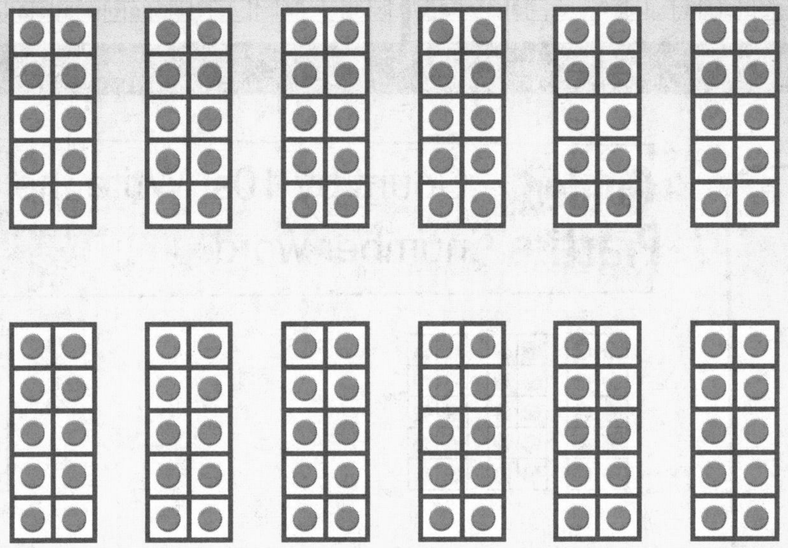

_____ counters in all.

Let's count by 10s.

1 ten	2 tens	3 tens	4 tens	5 tens	6 tens	7 tens	8 tens	9 tens	10 tens
10	20	30	40	50	60	70	80	90	100
ten	twenty	thirty	forty	fifty	sixty	seventy	eighty	ninety	one hundred

11 tens is 110. One hundred ten

12 tens is 120. One hundred twenty

Do You Understand?

Show Me! When might it be better to count by 10s instead of by 1s?

☆ **Guided Practice** ☆ Count by 10s. Write the numbers and the number word.

1. _____3_____ tens

30

thirty

2. _____ tens

_____

_____

© Pearson Education, Inc. K

Step Up | Lesson 7

Name _____

Independent Practice ☆   Count by 10s. Write the numbers and the number word.

3.

_____ tens

_____

_____

4.

_____ tens

_____

_____

5.

_____ tens

_____

_____

Write the missing numbers.

What is Mike's pattern?

6. Higher Order Thinking

Mike writes a pattern.

He forgets to write some numbers.
What numbers did Mike forget to write?

10, 20, 30, _____, _____, 60, 70, _____, 90, _____, 110, 120

7. © MP.2 Reasoning Leah has 4 boxes. 10 books are in each box. How many books does Leah have in all?

_____ tens

_____

_____

8. © MP.1 Make Sense Bo has 6 boxes. There are 10 books in each box. How many books does Bo have in all?

_____ tens

_____

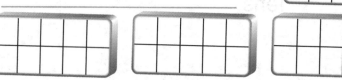

9. Higher Order Thinking Cory counts by 5s to 50. Kobe counts by 10s to 50. Write the numbers Cory says.

5, _____, _____, _____, _____,

_____, _____, _____, _____, 50

Write the numbers Kobe says.

10, _____, _____, _____, 50

What numbers do both boys say?

_____, _____, _____, _____, _____

10. © Assessment Marisol has some books. She puts them in piles of 10. Which number does NOT show how many books Marisol could have?

Ⓐ 30

Ⓑ 40

Ⓒ 45

Ⓓ 50

© Pearson Education, Inc. K

Name _____

Solve & Share

Jada and Alex take turns counting by 1s. Jada counts from 98 up to 100. Now, it's Alex's turn to keep counting. Say the next 3 numbers Alex should count. Tell how you know you're right.

98, 99, 100

____ , ____ , ____

I can ...
count by 1s to 120.

© **Content Standards** 1.NBT.A.1
Mathematical Practices MP.2,
MP.6, MP.7

This block shows 100. You say one hundred for this number.

100

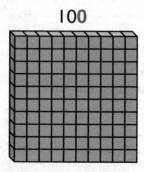

The next number you say is one hundred one because you have 1 hundred and 1 one.

101

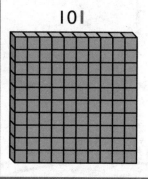

When you count forward, you keep counting by 1s.

101, 102, 103, 104, 105

105 means 1 hundred and 5 ones. You say one hundred five.

When you count higher, you start with the words one hundred.

116, 117, 118, 119, 120

116 is one hundred sixteen.

Do You Understand?

Show Me! How would you say and show 110 when you count? What number comes next?

☆ Guided ☆ Practice

Count forward by 1s. Write the numbers.

1. 98, __99__, 100, __101__, __102__

2. _____, _____, 93, _____, 95

3. 112, _____, _____, 115, _____

880 eight hundred eighty

© Pearson Education, Inc. K

Step Up | Lesson 8

Name _____

Independent Practice ☆ Count forward by 1s. Write the numbers.

4. 97, _____, _____, _____, 101

5. _____, 104, _____, _____, 107

6. _____, 117, _____, 119, _____

7. _____, 101, 102, _____, _____

8. _____, _____, 111, _____, 113

9. 111, _____, _____, 114, _____

Use the clues to find each mystery number.

10. **Number Sense** Clue 1: The number comes after 112. Clue 2: The number comes before 116.

The mystery number might be:

_____, _____, _____

Clue 3: The number has 4 ones.
Circle the mystery number.

11. **Number Sense** Clue 1: The number comes before 120. Clue 2: The number comes after 114.

The mystery number might be:

_____, _____, _____, _____, _____

Clue 3: The number has 7 ones.
Circle the mystery number.

12. **Vocabulary** Marta is counting to 120. She says the number that is one **more** than 117. What number does she say?

13. In this chart, Manuel writes the numbers 105 to 111 in order. Then he spills water on it. Some numbers rub off. Help Manuel fill in the missing numbers.

105		107	108			111

14. © **MP.2 Reasoning** Savannah hikes 1 mile every day. After hiking on Monday, she has hiked 102 miles. After hiking on Friday, how many miles will she have hiked?

_____ miles

Think about the days and the numbers you count on.

15. **Higher Order Thinking** Pick a number greater than 100 and less than 116. Write the number in the box.

Then write the three numbers that come before it and the number that comes after it.

_____, _____, _____, ☐, _____

16. © **Assessment** Which shows the correct order for counting forward by 1s? Choose all that apply.

☐ 100, 101, 103, 102

☐ 115, 116, 117, 118

☐ 104, 105, 106, 107

☐ 115, 116, 119, 120

Name _____

Solve & Share

Guess how many cubes are in your bag. Then empty the bag in the space below. Without counting each cube, guess how many cubes there are. Write each guess. Now count the cubes and write the total number of cubes.

Lesson 9
Tens and Ones

I can ...
count and write numbers by tens and ones.

© **Content Standards** 1.NBT.B.2
Mathematical Practices MP.2, MP.4

Guess 1: _____ cubes

Guess 2: _____ cubes

Actual number:

_____ cubes

35 stands for 3 **tens** and 5 **ones**.

The 3 in 35 is the tens digit.
The 5 in 35 is the ones digit.

35 has 2 digits.

Tens	Ones
3 tens	5 ones

Tens	Ones
3	5

35

You can use a model to show the tens and ones.

The tens digit goes on the left. The ones digit goes on the right.

Do You Understand?

Show Me! How are these numbers alike? How are they different?

46	64

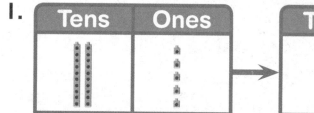
★ **Guided Practice** ★ Count the tens and ones. Then write the numbers.

1.

Tens	Ones

→

Tens	Ones
2	5

25

2.

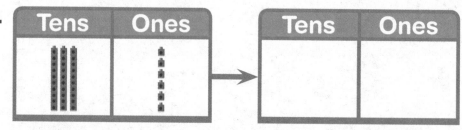

Tens	Ones

→

Tens	Ones

_____

Name _____

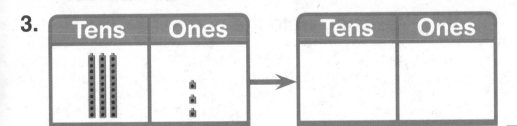

Independent Practice ✧ Count the tens and ones. Then write the numbers.

3.

Tens	Ones

→

Tens	Ones

_____

4.

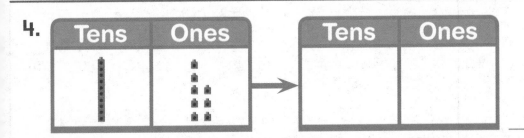

Tens	Ones

→

Tens	Ones

_____

5.

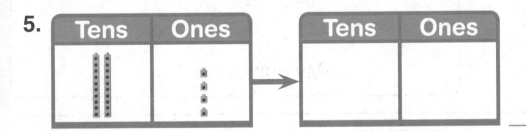

Tens	Ones

→

Tens	Ones

_____

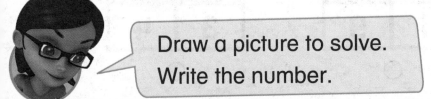

Draw a picture to solve.
Write the number.

6. **Higher Order Thinking** Mary has a number. It has the same number of tens and ones. What could Mary's number be?

7. © **MP.4 Use Tools** Sam has juice boxes at his party.

There are 4 packages of 10 and 8 extra juice boxes.

How many juice boxes are there in all?

Write the number of tens and ones. Then write the total number of juice boxes.

Tens	Ones

_____ juice boxes

8. Higher Order Thinking Draw a picture to show a number greater than 25 and less than 75. Then write the number.

My number is _____.

9. © **Assessment** There are 19 juice cartons. Which model shows the number of juice cartons?

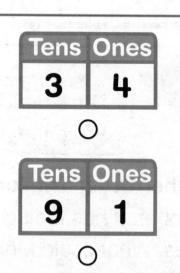

Tens	Ones
1	9

○

Tens	Ones
3	4

○

Tens	Ones
2	9

○

Tens	Ones
9	1

○

© Pearson Education, Inc. K

Name _____

Solve & Share

How can you use place-value blocks to find the number that comes after 12? What about the number that comes before 12? Show your work. Write the numbers.

I can ...
find numbers that are more or less than a given number.

© **Content Standards** 1.NBT.B.3, 1.NBT.C.5
Mathematical Practices MP.2, MP.5, MP.6, MP.8

The number after 12 is _____.

The number before 12 is _____.

Do You Understand?

Show Me! How can you find 10 more than a number?

☆ **Guided Practice** ☆ Complete each sentence. Use place-value blocks if needed.

1. | 34 |

I more than 34 is _35_.

I less than 34 is _33_.

10 more than 34 is _44_.

10 less than 34 is _24_.

2. | 14 |

I more than 14 is _____.

I less than 14 is _____.

10 more than 14 is _____.

10 less than 14 is _____.

© Pearson Education, Inc. K

Name _____

Independent Practice ✮ Complete each sentence. Use place-value blocks if needed.

3. 71

I more than 71 is _____.

I less than 71 is _____.

10 more than 71 is _____.

10 less than 71 is _____.

4. 50

I more than 50 is _____.

I less than 50 is _____.

10 more than 50 is _____.

10 less than 50 is _____.

5. 19

I more than 19 is _____.

I less than 19 is _____.

10 more than 19 is _____.

10 less than 19 is _____.

6. 49

I more than 49 is _____.

I less than 49 is _____.

10 more than 49 is _____.

10 less than 49 is _____.

7. 85

I more than 85 is _____.

I less than 85 is _____.

10 more than 85 is _____.

10 less than 85 is _____.

8. 42

I more than 42 is _____.

I less than 42 is _____.

10 more than 42 is _____.

10 less than 42 is _____.

9. Higher Order Thinking Circle the picture that shows 10 more than 34. Explain how you know.

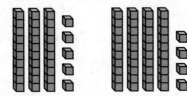

_____

_____

_____

10. © **MP.8 Generalize** Marlon wants to write instructions to tell his friend how to find 10 more than any number. What instructions should Marlon write?

_____

_____

_____

11. Number Sense Fill in the missing numbers. Use place-value blocks to help you.

10 Less

_____

I Less | **84** | I More

_____

10 More

12. Higher Order Thinking Write and solve a riddle for a number greater than 70 and less than 90. Use "I more than" and "I less than" or "10 more than" and "10 less than" as clues.

Clues: _____

_____

_____

My number is _____.

13. © **Assessment** Match each number with its description.

38	10 more than 23
3	I less than 19
18	I more than 37
33	10 less than 13
65	10 more than 55

© Pearson Education, Inc. K

Glossary

A

above

add

$$3 + 2 = 5$$

addition sentence

3 and 5 is 8.

attribute

B

balance scale

behind

below

beside

break apart

$$6 - 3 = 3$$

capacity

category

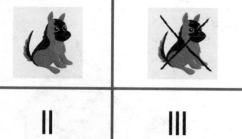

|| |||

chart

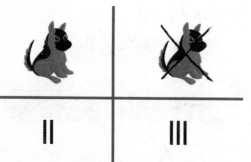

|| |||

circle

classify

column

1	2	3	4	5
11	12	13	14	15
21	22	23	24	25
31	32	33	34	35

compare

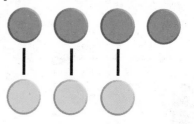

cone

count

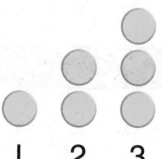

1   2   3

cube

cylinder

D

decade

1	2	3	4	5	6	7	8	9	10
11	12	13	14	15	16	17	18	19	20
21	22	23	24	25	26	27	28	29	30
31	32	33	34	35	36	37	38	39	40
41	42	43	44	45	46	47	48	49	50
51	52	53	54	55	56	57	58	59	60
61	62	63	64	65	66	67	68	69	70
71	72	73	74	75	76	77	78	79	80
81	82	83	84	85	86	87	88	89	90
91	92	93	94	95	96	97	98	99	100

difference

$$8 - 3 = 5$$

E

eight

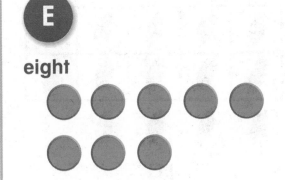

8

eighteen

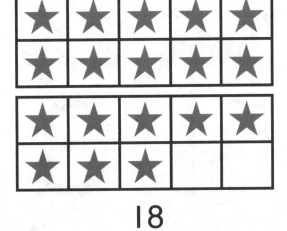

18

eleven

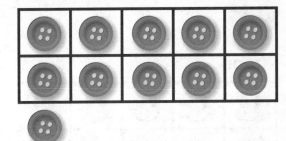

11

equal

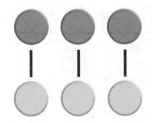

equal sign (=)

$$4 + 3 = 7$$

equation

$$5 + 3 = 8$$

$$8 = 8$$

F

fifteen

15

five

5

flat surface

four

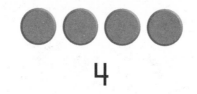

4

fourteen

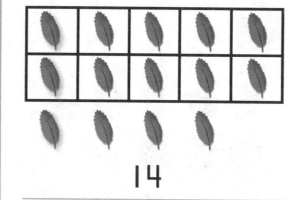

14

G

greater than

group

H

heavier

height

hexagon

How many more?

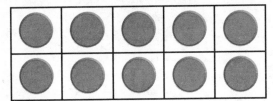

hundred chart

column

row →

1	2	3	4	5	6	7	8	9	10
11	12	13	14	15	16	17	18	19	20
21	22	23	24	25	26	27	28	29	30
31	32	33	34	35	36	37	38	39	40
41	42	43	44	45	46	47	48	49	50
51	52	53	54	55	56	57	58	59	60
61	62	63	64	65	66	67	68	69	70
71	72	73	74	75	76	77	78	79	80
81	82	83	84	85	86	87	88	89	90
91	92	93	94	95	96	97	98	99	100

I

in all

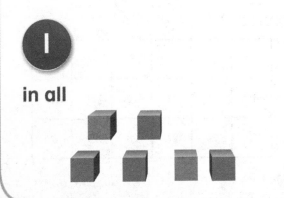

in front of

J

join

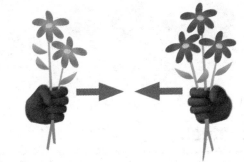

L

left

length

less than

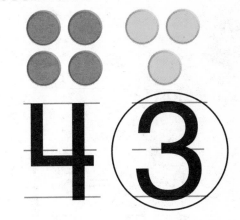

4 ③

lighter

longer

M

minus sign (−)

$$8 - 3 = 5$$

model

N

next to

nine

9

nineteen

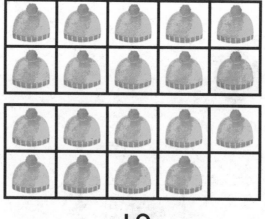

19

none

0

number

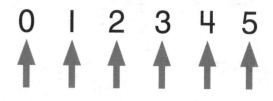

O

one

1

ones

5	6	7	8	9	10
15	16	17	18	19	20
25	26	27	28	29	30

operation

$4 \oplus 2 = 6$

$4 \ominus 2 = 2$

order

$0 \rightarrow 1 \rightarrow 2 \rightarrow 3 \rightarrow 4 \rightarrow 5$

part

pattern

10   20   30   40   50

plus sign (+)

$3 + 1 = 4$

rectangle

roll

row

1	2	3	4	5
11	12	13	14	15
21	22	23	24	25
31	32	33	34	35

same number as

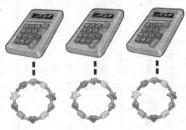

separate

seven

7

seventeen

17

shorter

side

six

6

sixteen

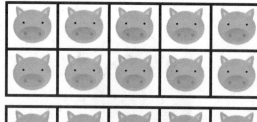

16

slide

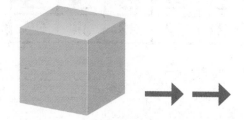

sort

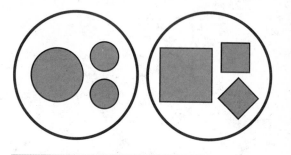

sphere

square

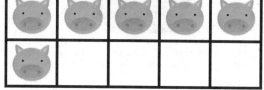

stack

subtract

$$3 - 1 = 2$$

subtraction sentence

4 take away 3 is 1.

sum

$$2 + 3 = 5$$
↑

take away

taller

↑

tally mark

|| |||

ten

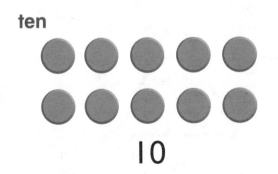

10

tens

5	6	7	8	9	10
15	16	17	18	19	20
25	26	27	28	29	30

thirteen

13

three

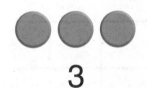

3

three-dimensional shape

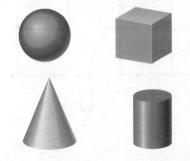

triangle

twelve

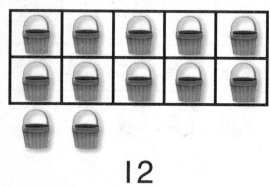

12

twenty

20

two

2

two-dimensional shape

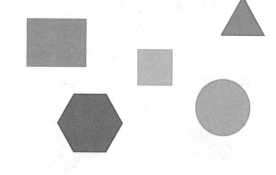

V

vertex/vertices

W

weighs

weight

whole

Z

zero

0

Photographs

Every effort has been made to secure permission and provide appropriate credit for photographic material. The publisher deeply regrets any omission and pledges to correct errors called to its attention in subsequent editions.

Unless otherwise acknowledged, all photographs are the property of Pearson Education, Inc.

Photo locators denoted as follows: Top (T), Center (C), Bottom (B), Left (L), Right (R), Background (Bkgd)